Prai...

'Searingly funny and fierce...

'An important and beautiful story told with tremendous heart.'
– Mia Freedman

'In a book that breathes wisdom, the words *"Ascension* is the magic that happens when women dare to be fearless and release the goddess power within" captivate. As we follow Sasha's compelling and moving personal story, we learn about truth, injustice and empowerment in a way that challenges and inspires. The seeds of reflection that she plants throughout the book will give you the opportunity to grow and flourish in a garden where your uniqueness is celebrated.' – Paul Callaghan

'Sasha writes with purpose and power. You'll wish your younger self read this book, and you'll thank Sasha for writing it. *Gigorou* is a gift.' – Alley Pascoe

'Packed with grace, nostalgia and so much style. Not just one woman's story, but a blueprint for how to step gloriously into your rightful space.' – Justine Cullen

'*Gigorou* is a brilliant representation of the way we walk in two worlds from a young age, asking ourselves how we fit into Western society when they don't accept us and we don't see ourselves reflected.' – Elaine George

Sasha Kutabah Sarago is a Wadjanbarra Yidinji, Jirrbal and African-American woman. Sasha's TEDx talk 'The (De)colonising of Beauty' was selected as TED.com 2021 Editor's Choice and has fuelled her passion for redefining femininity and womanhood from a First Nations perspective. Sasha has appeared on NITV's *Awaken: Black Is Beautiful*, SBS's *Insight: Growing Up Mixed Race* and the ABC's *The School that Tried to End Racism*. She has also directed documentaries *Too Pretty to Be Aboriginal* and *InsideOUT*, and written articles published in *The Guardian*, *SBS Voices*, *Fashion Journal* and *Frankie* magazines.

gigorou

It's time to reclaim beauty. First Nations wisdom and womanhood.

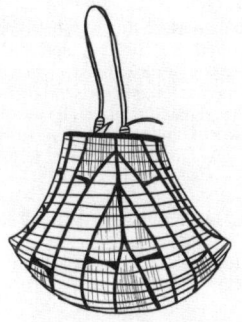

SASHA KUTABAH SARAGO

PANTERA
PRESS

PANTERA PRESS

The information in this book is published in good faith and for general information purposes only. Although the author and publisher believe at the time of going to press that the information is correct, they do not assume and hereby disclaim any liability to any party for any loss, damage or disruption caused by errors or omissions, whether they result from negligence, accident or any other cause.

Some passages in this book include knowledge and cultural expressions of Aboriginal and Torres Strait Islander peoples. This knowledge comes from Country and its people, and has been handed down through the generations. It is Indigenous Cultural and Intellectual Property (ICIP) that belongs communally to First Peoples, who continue to practise culture. First Peoples have cultural protocols about how their ICIP can be shared and used, and the unauthorised use, adaptation and publication of ICIP without the prior free informed consent of First Peoples is a breach of ICIP protocols.

First published in 2023 by Pantera Press Pty Limited
www.PanteraPress.com

Text copyright © Sasha Sarago, 2023
Sasha Sarago has asserted her moral rights to be identified as the author of this work.

Design and typography copyright © Pantera Press Pty Limited, 2023
® Pantera Press, three-slashes colophon device, and *sparking imagination, conversation & change* are registered trademarks of Pantera Press Pty Limited. Lost the Plot is a trademark of Pantera Press Pty Limited.

This book is copyright, and all rights are reserved.
We welcome your support of the author's rights, so please only buy authorised editions.

Without the publisher's prior written permission, and without limiting the rights reserved under copyright, none of this book may be scanned, reproduced, stored in, uploaded to or introduced into a retrieval or distribution system, including the internet, or transmitted, copied or made available in any form or by any means (including digital, electronic, mechanical, photocopying, sound or audio recording, and text-to-voice). This book is sold subject to the condition that it shall not, by way of trade or otherwise, be lent, re-sold, hired out, or otherwise circulated in any form of binding or cover other than that in which it is published and without a similar condition being imposed on the subsequent recipient.

Please send all permission queries to:
Pantera Press, P.O. Box 1989, Neutral Bay, NSW, Australia 2089 or info@PanteraPress.com

A Cataloguing-in-Publication entry for this book is available from the National Library of Australia.
ISBN 978-0-6454767-3-6 (Paperback)
ISBN 978-0-6454129-5-6 (eBook)

Cover Design: Amy Daoud
Art Direction: Sasha Sarago
Publisher: Lex Hirst
Editor: Tom Langshaw
Project Editor: Anne Reilly
Copyeditor: Jasmin McGaughey
Proofreader: Bronwyn Sweeney
Typesetting: Kirby Jones
Author Photo: Caroline McCredie
Printed and bound in Australia by McPherson's Printing Group

Pantera Press policy is to use papers that are natural, renewable and recyclable products made from wood grown in sustainable forests. The logging and manufacturing processes are expected to conform to the environmental regulations of the country of origin.

The paper this book is printed on is certified against the Forest Stewardship Council® Standards. McPherson's Printing Group holds FSC® chain of custody certification SA-COC-005379. FSC® promotes environmentally responsible, socially beneficial and economically viable management of the world's forests.

For Black women trying to find their way back banaga (home).

Contents

Acknowledgements ix
Foreword by Chelsea Watego xiii

Introduction 1
1   Indigeneity 7
2   Pretty Woman 22
3   Murri Kid 26
4   Soraya 36
5   Too Pretty to Be Aboriginal 47
6   Majal Gigorou 55
7   Dear Black Men 77
8   Napranum 86
9   Jinnali 92
10 *Cosmopolitan* 106
11 *The Matrix* 114
12 Perils of a Black Model 120
13 Cattle Call 135
14 Yarrabah 151

15	Shame Factor	162
16	Gin Jockey	173
17	Archetypes	178
18	Louis vs Jawun	202
19	*Ascension*	210
20	Seat at the Table	228
21	Murray	246
22	Mundu	258
23	First Nations Fashion Is the New Blak	264
24	Blak Goddess	273
25	God Is a Black Woman	282
26	Blak Femininity	289
27	Dear Niecey	296

Playlist   302

Acknowledgements

Country

I pay my respects to the Wadjanbarra Yidinji and Jirrbal (the Wadjan Bama) and Gadigal people of the Eora Nation, in which *Gigorou* was inspired and written.

I give thanks to our Elders, past and present, who continue to nourish us culturally and spiritually. Always was always will be Aboriginal land. Sovereignty never ceded.

Firstly, I want to acknowledge the Brackenridge (Braikenridge), Sarago and Kendrick mob, who raised, protected and guided me to be the woman I am today.

To my matriarchs, Aunty Ruthie, Aunty Bella, Aunty Debbie and Aunty Kym, your stories give me the confidence to rewrite my own.

Uncle Darren, thank you for our family history and the belly laughs. You brought joy to my childhood which I treasure to this day.

Dearest Pheeney, you always said I was a late bloomer, but I've blossomed divinely as God intended. From moppy to Kutabah.

Thank you for being a straight shooter and teaching me how to embrace my gigorou.

Thank you, Dad, for your wisdom and belief in me when I couldn't see my worth. Our long talks and road trips keep me grounded. That's why I have the audacity to wear crushed velvet.

Ray Ray, you are my anchor in rough seas. The hard part is over. May we live the Soft Life now that we know how.

Rebecca Phillips, thank you for being the sista I've always prayed for – a pure lens in which to see myself and examine my cultural integrity and sovereignty.

Marvellous Darling, Kumbi Mukaro, every conversation we have inspires me to be a better person. Your spiritual counsel encourages me to let every light shine in my house.

Mark Nannup, my brotha, thank you for challenging my poverty mindset, bringing new experiences and Blak art into my world.

Edem Badu and Charmaine Hunzwi, thank you for holding space for my vulnerability and finding yourselves in my words.

Cultural and Community Consultation

Thank you Margaret Freeman (Wabubadda Aboriginal Corporation), Sonya Takau (Girringun Aboriginal Corporation), Virginia Robinson (Dharriwaa Elders Group), Harold French (Moree Local Aboriginal Land Council), Professor Jakelin Troy (The University of Sydney) and Jacinta Tobin for your time, direction and blessings.

Thank you Uncle Ernie Grant, Uncle Abe Muriata, Aunty Rhonda Brim, Aunty Annie Wonga, Murrumu of Walubara,

Acknowledgements

Gudju Gudju Fourmile and Uncle Chad Stone for passing on the creation stories, language, weaving and culture, so it remains with us forever.

Nana Doreen and Jr, thank you for being with me in mundu (spirit). You already know I still have many more chapters to write. And it's only the beginning.

Lastly, a special thank you to Pantera Press for all your support in bringing *Gigorou* to life.

Foreword
by Chelsea Watego

While it is most true that the most disrespected and unprotected person is the Black woman, I have never known them to be powerless, ever.

I know of Black women who would talk openly about the curation of their own funerals well before their time was to come, from picking their favourite song, to the 'guest list' for said event. Some might think it a morbid thing, but it is not. More than claiming some sense of agency upon one's death, it is about being the ultimate arbiter of one's life story.

Over the years, I've encountered Black women who in moments of supposed powerlessness would muse about their forthcoming memoir. Here we would laugh about the chapters that would be reserved in that imagined book that no-one had asked us to write; chapters reserved for those people who had tried their very best to reduce us to nothing.

It is in the telling of our stories, on our terms, that we are recast as narrator rather than the passive subject they presume us to be.

My own memoir would find its way into the world, complete with those chapters finally manifested into existence. Here, I would insist upon narrating not just my story, but too the happy endings we fought for, and which we deserved. The spirit and style of the book was influenced by the writing of Dr/Aunty Jackie Huggins' *Sister Girl*, which depicted not just the pain felt by Black women in the colony, but captured our beauty, power, wisdom and fire.

The Black woman's memoir, or rather manifesto, is a genre most neglected but one that is most necessary – to all of us as Black women, in how we see ourselves in a social world that despises us.

Sarago's *Gigorou* makes an exciting entry into this genre with all of those chapters that we have all dreamed of – 27 to be precise.

It was the opening chapter of *Gigorou* that captured so spectacularly the Black woman's clapback. Here she would tell the story of the first time she had a racial slur directed her way, from a boy who lived around the corner, no less. Sarago's reflections on navigating the terrain of race are instructive, yet it was the simple but concise description of that boy, as 'an asshole of a kid [who] didn't have any friends', that truly gave me life.

But the Black woman's memoir isn't the burn book you might think.

Each of these chapters of *Gigorou* takes us through varying moments in Sarago's life, from the mountaintop highs of industry recognition to the everyday mundane interactions around the house. On each of these occasions, Sarago is met with moments that were meant to confuse and confound, but it is via her narration that we are reminded that what happens to us typically has little to do with who the fuck we are, and instead cautions us about the world we must walk in.

It is clear that the Black woman's manifesto comes from a place of care – for Black women.

Indeed, as I read this book, I was walking through any number of battles personally and professionally. I would carry the manuscript around with me to work, to weekend writers' festivals, seeking out solitary moments to escape with it, and in it. It sat on random cafe tables and on my own bedside table. No matter where I read the text, what place I was in geographically or emotionally, I always felt like I was at home within it.

You see, there is a real joy in the stories we tell of ourselves, and a comfort in those accounts that refuse to perform within the parameters of the role that we've been cast, a designation that was never of our choosing.

And I cannot describe the joy I felt when I came to learn that my own 'manifesto' had found a home on Sarago's bedside table. I was reminded of the importance of the Black woman's manifesto, in what it does for ourselves and each other as Black women. As Sarago herself states, 'Can't nobody uplift a Blak sista like another Blak sista.'

There is an intimacy to Sarago's book that feels like what I imagine the experience her mum sought to provide women who graced the Majal Beauty Salon in the Cairns CBD. And while her book chronicles the journey of navigating the industry ideals of Western beauty standards, so much of her wisdom reminds us that reclaiming our beauty is really an 'inside job'.

Sarago's manifesto, in following in the tradition of the genre, is a book of love letters that speaks to the souls of Black women, of being the wrong kind of Black, to being too pretty, but not pretty enough, of being exploited, betrayed and let down, and yet too of being loved.

Sarago shows a generosity and genius in inviting us into those moments and sharing her learnings about life and love, and loss.

I will never forget her reflection upon the loss of her brother and 'soulmate'. When she said, 'I pray a man would love me close to how my brother did,' I heard her.

Black women know too well how unevenly love is distributed in this place. We know too intimately the heartache of a love that is not reciprocated, and of a love that is all but refused us.

It is her final chapter, Chapter 27, which represents the most critical of all in the Black woman's manifesto, a chapter that not all of us have been able to readily conjure up.

And that is the love letter that Sarago writes to her younger self. Sarago reminds us of the most important love of all, not of the selfless love that we so generously afford others, but the love we grant ourselves.

This is the chapter that every Black woman must be the author of in their own lives; for this love of self is precisely where our power lies.

Introduction

When I look in the mirror, I'm staring at a brand new person. Who she'll be 18 months from now is anyone's guess. But I can't wait to meet her. This type of self-love wasn't easily forthcoming for me. It's tough, and it's certainly not pretty, peeling yourself up from ground zero. But, phew! Mama, I made it! And I'm just getting started.

Self-loathing and contorting myself into what society wants me to be is a shit show behind the scenes, compared to the highlight reel I, and others, post on Instagram. When you are more than a monolith, your journey is challenging. There's no handbook given to young girls on navigating a world that refuses to see them.

By now, you're probably wondering what gigorou (jig-goo-roo) is. Gigorou means beauty or beautiful in Jirrbal, my grandmother's language. Since I can remember, I didn't feel gigorou; in fact, the complete opposite. I did what most young women do. I went in search of my beauty in all the wrong places. I read *Cleo*, *Cosmopolitan* and *FHM* magazines for tips on becoming thinner, desirable and more attractive. I watched the Miss Universe pageants and the video vixens from hip hop and R&B videos. I even turned to Steve Harvey's *Act Like a Lady, Think Like a Man* to figure out what femininity was, and where I was going wrong.

I have always been fascinated by beauty. My mother was a beautician and owned Majal Beauty Salon in Cairns. As Mum's assistant, I had the behind-the-scenes scoop on all things beauty. But it was Beverly Johnson, Louise Vyent and Iman's 1989 'The most unforgettable women in the world wear Revlon' campaign that planted the seed in my mind – the vision of becoming a Black supermodel. So, for me, there was no escaping the industries that can leave people vulnerable – questioning their worth. As a Black model, I've spent years knocking on fashion's door. Mimicking Western beauty standards: trying to convince the gatekeepers I was the one for the job. But they didn't tell me about the fine print. I would never be enough, not by their rules. I watched my mother make other women look and feel beautiful, and I wondered what the secret was to cure my insecurities.

As young girls and women, we are up against the battle of the beast: patriarchy, capitalism and privilege. We didn't have the language to pinpoint what we were experiencing in my day. Now I know it as colourism, internalised racism, sexism and misogynoir. Growing up, I was dedicated to persuading people to see me as Sasha instead of a fraction: half, quarter or mixed. Discovering my Blackness – understanding it, proving it, rejecting it only to reclaim it again – was one hell of a rollercoaster ride.

Introduction

Part of my healing journey to reconcile my childhood and ancestral wounds was launching *Ascension* – Australia's first digital lifestyle platform for women of colour – to celebrate our sistas – by reinserting us into the conversation of fashion and beauty in this country. I also stepped onto the famous red dot and redefined beauty in my TEDx talk, 'The (De)colonising of Beauty'. Setting the record straight, I get to reclaim my femininity – authentically – on my terms.

Writing *Gigorou* was hard, but it encouraged me to confront a dark past I'd hidden away. And hang up the masks I put on to anaesthetise the pain and to deceive others. What forced me to purge was writing off the tail-end of a COVID-19 lockdown. That and the tragic death of George Floyd, and the Black Lives Matter uprisings – what I call the day the world chose to see Black people's humanity. Although the process of baring my soul during social unrest was emotionally and psychologically draining, magically, it was validating: not only does my Black life matter, but also my trauma and joy. It gave me the strength to delve into the core of my story. Going back to where it all began 60,000 years ago.

Historically, First Nations women have been excluded from Australia's national consciousness. I didn't grow up reading many books about phenomenal Blak women: their legacies, womanhood and beauty. Along with other Blak girls, I had to create a space for myself when there was none.

With copious cups of tea and yarns that stretched into the early mornings, learning the stories of my matriarchs gave me the authority to rewrite, reimagine and reclaim Blak Femininity through our eyes, voices and footsteps. It is because of the Blak Matriarchy I exist.

Gigorou is a love letter to Black women – my nieces and younger self. Bub, you're going to be just fine. The world ain't ready for you.

We live in a world that denies us the liberty to sit in silence with our wisdom and the confidence to trust ourselves. Nearly every day, we are bombarded with advertising, publications, social media and commentary on how to look, think and feel. Our uterus, sexuality, relationship status and motherhood are under attack – ironically – by establishments and persons that don't represent us. I believe we're all going through a rite of passage in some way, saying goodbye to one stage of life to embrace another. Leaving behind people, mindsets, careers and places that no longer serve us. And some may be on a layover, contemplating what their future will be. And that's okay. Please go at your own pace.

Written with a whole lot of spirit and sass from a First Nations and African-American woman's perspective, *Gigorou* takes you back to the old ways – to restore the cultural and spiritual knowledge my Ancestors have passed on to my Elders. Sadly, a lot was left unspoken and has been lost due to colonisation.

As I come into my Big Aunty Energy – just around the corner from Eldership – I must preserve what I can salvage for the next generation. *Gigorou* is a reclamation of language and lends a modern-day interpretation of the jujaba (creation) stories gifted to me and the contrasts between Western, ancient, traditional and contemporary.

If you've ever felt awkward, hated your body, struggled to find your voice or to stand in your power, dimmed your light to hide in other people's shadows, ignored red flags, suppressed

Introduction

your anger, suffered from imposter syndrome and made poor choices – then this book is for you.

Heads up: I'm an '80s baby. This book is a crash course in intersectionality via my obsession for beauty, fashion, pop culture and rooting for everyone Black.

But it also aims to shift societal paradigms, which involves truth-telling and exposing a disturbing colonial history woven into my and, unfortunately, many other First Nations women's stories. I implore you to sit with these truths to understand how the past affects the present.

Take your time. There is no rush. This is a journey I hope we can walk together as I guide you through three parts of the book. First, my memoir, second, political discourse and lastly, the creation stories and intimate conversations about Blak Matriarchs – which hold the key to the answers I've been searching for.

I want to share one final thing before you read this fire book. I promise no spoiler alerts, just a taste of what's to come.

Shortly after I was selected to participate in Australia's first Indigenous women's calendar, my grandfather gave me my skin name, Kutabah, which means 'little fish' in the Yidinji language. My totem is the black bream. In Aboriginal culture, our skin names help us determine who we can and cannot marry – are they the right skin? Totems are blessed to us, and we are given the honour to protect the plant or animal assigned to us. They are our kin. To ensure its survival and eliminate overconsumption, we do not eat our totem. That way, there is enough nourishment for everyone.

When my grandfather gave me my totem, the black bream, embarrassingly, I was disappointed. I wanted something grander, like a crocodile, hawk or kangaroo.

I didn't appreciate the gift as I was still young, finding my way. I never used my skin name until recently. I had to go through my rite of passage to understand the meaning of it. When I did embrace Kutabah, spirit finally spoke to me. She said, 'You are sustenance.' I hope this book provides you with food for thought.

I did not experience traditional initiation – ceremony and the process of scarification on the skin to signify the stages of womanhood – I still have clean skin, which means traditionally, I cannot take part in ceremonies or women's business.

However, my Ancestors have reassured me I have gigorou guga (beautiful skin). My scarification are the trials and tribulations I have endured in life – what I've gone through in order to embrace my gigorou.

Are you ready to embrace yours?

1

Indigeneity

Indigeneity is your birthright, always here, always waiting for your return.

Sasha Kutabah Sarago

My mother is a Wadjanbarra Yidinji and Jirrbal woman. We are the Wabubadda, 'the little people' of the rainforest in the Jirrbal language. Our traditional countries span from the Atherton Tablelands, Daintree, right down to Tully in Far North Queensland. Through the bloodlines of my great-grandfathers, George Brackenridge and Hassim Massem, I am also of Mauritian and Javanese descent.

On the other side of the coin, my father is African-American: we are survivors of the transatlantic slave trade. Ancestry.com traces our lineage back to West Africa: Ghana, Côte d'Ivoire, Mali, Benin and Togo. The motherland calls for me; we have unfinished business. One day we will meet, and then the missing pieces of my story will be revealed.

On a night out in Perth, Western Australia, 1983, my 24-year-old mother, Delphine, met her soon-to-be husband, James, a 22-year-old US Marine. As the story goes, my father had swapped his R&R day with another Marine on the ship. And during Dad's night out, he spotted my mother in the nightclub and asked her what she 'did'.

Unimpressed, she said, 'a mother' – trying to avert his friendly advance.

My father couldn't hear her over the loud music and thought she said, 'a model'.

Dad wouldn't be mistaken. My mother is stunning. Eventually, Dad's charm won Mum's heart. After a 10-month long-distance romance, they were married in Innisfail, Queensland. She and I became Kendricks. Crazy, huh. Talk about fate: the right place at the right time.

Not everyone was impressed by the new lovebirds. Mum and her baby sister, Aunty Debbie, were thick as thieves. Understandably, Aunty Debbie was pissed off at Dad for whisking us away to the other side of the world.

Given the huge culture shift, my father requested we be stationed in California, USA, rather than Okinawa, Japan. He thought living in an English-speaking country would make our transition easier.

Camp Pendleton Military Base, located in North San Diego County, California, became our new home. We were now living with other military families within a sea of quadrants. I enjoyed the air of prestige when rolling up to the security checkpoint after an outing. My parents flashed their military badges, the soldier scanned and handed them back with a sharp nod of respect. Leading me to believe my parents were of importance, which swelled my pint-sized ego.

My parents ran a tight ship. Waking up at the crack of dawn to carpe diem was normal. Beds were made each morning – not military-style, where a quarter could be bounced off diving-board-stiff sheets, but close to it. Toys and clothes had homes, and it wasn't the floor.

Through sleepovers, I found out not every family shared the Kendrick principles, which came as a shock. Watching my friend's mum pick up after her was mind-bending. Mrs Kendrick would never, I thought, as I embraced the sleepover with no rules – a Black child's hall pass. I tried to apply that same exemption at preacher Michael's home and got my ass whooped for jumping on his king-size bed. Little Montell, the preacher's son, said it was okay. I should have listened to my intuition.

My siblings and I were also taught to live by the Save and Conserve rule – because money didn't grow on trees. In our house, lights and fans were turned off when you left a room because, 'Do you have electricity money? No? That's what I thought.'

As an adult, one time when I was visiting my friend, she asked why her house was dark when she came home. She'd assumed I was out or asleep. I explained it was a childhood courtesy not to run up other people's light bill. And that's when we had an impromptu therapy session. The outcome: I am no longer a child with no money to pay the bills. I am grown and have permission to flood my life and rooms with light. Dad taught us how to reduce greenhouse gas emissions way before Mr Thompson, my science teacher, did.

They say a girl's first love is her father. And to this day, no man has managed to take my father's place. Dad set the bar incredibly high. It started with raising a child who is not biologically his. I am his daughter and he is my father. I've always wanted him to know that I don't take lightly his love or choice to be my father when another man chose to abandon me.

I remember my sister Soraya and I watching Dad shine his black Marine boots with polish and a shining rag until the boot tip reflected a Marine's pride and honour. Soraya reached for an item from his military footlocker and was scolded: 'Don't touch.' But Dad soon felt sorry for us. He was leaving his babies behind for deployment and, to appease us, handed over a green glow stick, which he taught us to activate by clicking. I had no idea it was combat and survival operations lighting for troops. Sissy and I turned the lights off in our room and had a rave party with them. Dad also gave us some of the military ration packs that his platoon ate out in the field. They were a treat to us, even if they tasted bland. Because it was from Dad, it was special.

It was all fun and games until one day, Dad dressed up in full Marine gear, including his dreaded gas mask, hid behind a door and jumped out at us. Thinking he was Predator, Soraya and I ran screaming, losing a piece of our soul that day. Mum wasn't happy at all.

Everything my father did was analysed under a microscope. Dad was suspicious by nature and answered questions with questions, overturning every rock checking for clues until he was satisfied things were legit. TSA security checkpoints had nothing on Mr Kendrick. This heavy scrutiny served me well when it came to my own attention to detail.

Indigeneity

My father trained me to question authority, as long as it wasn't his. If things didn't make sense, it was my duty to enquire until the math added up. And if that math didn't add up, I had only myself to blame. '*You* did it!' Dad would say, with his famous 'I tried to tell you' expression. Regardless of his rank in the military, Dad didn't take nobody's shit, sidestepping court martials like a quarterback about to be sacked. He told us to focus on being individuals and not worry about what others thought of us. That's all good and fine, I thought, but not when you have us out here looking crazy in corduroy outfits.

To this day, FOMO isn't a thing to me. I suffered the unthinkable when I came home from my friend's house one day and wondered why my brother and sister had giant lollipops and Donald Duck and Minnie Mouse plush toys.

'Where did you get that?' I asked.

'Disneyland!'

Mum had tried to warn Dad it wasn't a good idea just taking Soraya and Jr to Disneyland. 'Wait until Sasha gets back.' But that was Dad: spontaneous; he lived in the moment. Why delay fun when you can have it now?

My father's favourite words were, 'May the force be with you' and, like Yoda, Dad prepared us for galactic war – the one in life and the one within ourselves.

Dad's wisdom still finds its way into my birthday cards with a message of enlightenment – and a wad of cash. My father's love language is gifting. I love pinching the envelope to feel how thick it is. It backfired one birthday when I opened the card and found nothing. My heart sank. Dad couldn't contain his laughter at my reaction. Then he told me to check the pouch of the teddy bear he'd bought me. Of course, I lit up like Times Square when the green bills spilt out.

When Dad was on long deployments in another country, the church was our second family. I remember the hot bus rides to church a couple of counties away. The church was where I cracked out my baby tambourine to praise the Lord as the choir sang and clapped their hands like they meant business.

Although the preacher's sermon elevated our spirit and nourished our soul, he was also the guest who overstayed his welcome. Always one last thing to say which extended the service well beyond the program.

Really, Pastor?

I would be thinking about Sunday lunch going cold in the banquet room.

On cue, just before the preacher wrapped up, I'd pretend to fall asleep before Ms Parker, our Sunday-school teacher, could pick me to close the morning worship with a prayer. But one Sunday, when Ms Parker was sick, one of the Elders took over her class and she got one of the other children to rustle me from sleep and get my behind up there. She saw right through my trick. Petrified, I fumbled the prayer as my knees knocked together. From that day on, I cursed that old raisin under my breath whenever I saw her at church.

Praise and worship didn't have an expiry date. When the sun rose, we thanked the Lord for a brand new day, our food, shelter, and making it safely to our pillow at night. I thank my mother for all the hours we sat with her in Bible study. There's not a day I don't feel the conviction of spirit to do what is right. I am confident that regardless of being a church girl, I'd be a good person, but something about being raised a God-fearing Christian and trusting in a higher power solidifies your faith.

I didn't understand why Dad was exempt from coming to church with us. Mum tried to get him to attend, and he did several times, but I could tell he didn't enjoy it. And I wished he was there for my baptism. All the kids in the church knew you were saved when you got dunked in the ocean. Not droplets on the forehead like the plot of season five, episode three of *Insecure*: Lawrence's mama wasn't having it for her grandchild. 'I'm gonna take him to Pastor Clarke for a full dip,' she said.

I agree. Baby Elijah Mustafa Walker's soul ain't saved until he's been submerged like a submarine.

It's not that my father didn't believe in a higher power; he was more spiritual. He had his conflict with the Lord. On my mother's end of the spectrum, it was made crystal clear nothing was worthier than God's grace. As a child, it's hard to live by this when your eighth birthday is at Chuck E. Cheese, and Salt-N-Pepa's 'Push It' comes on, and all your friends proceed to, 'ahhh, push it,' but you can't because it's the devil's music.

But I was a sinner and prayed what I did in the dark didn't come to light. I'd sneak over to Cookie's house, the cool mama on base, and join her Soul Train parties eating barbecue. My heart skipped a beat whenever I heard the doorbell ring – was that my mama? Thank God I never got caught.

Something I respected about my mother was that she never sugar-coated life. She lost her mother at an early age and had to learn through trial and error. So she doused us with the facts of life as raw and uncomfortable as it was presented to her.

Mum kept our home holy. 'Shondala, shondala, shondala,' echoed down the hall, oil crosses marked our doorways, and scriptures hung on the walls. In my and Soraya's room, we had Ephesians 6:1, 'Children, obey your parents in the Lord, for this is right.' Combined with Dad's lectures, which were as long as the preacher's sermons, the Kendrick kids didn't stray far from the flock.

Residing on the military base wasn't all about memorising Bible passages and becoming a Jedi Knight. Our complex housed four families, including us. We lived on the second floor. Adjacent to us was Melina, one of my best friends. She was Mexican. Ramona and Veronica, my other partners in crime, resided downstairs – they were both Native American. Melina's mother babysat my sister and me when my parents had to work. Lunchtime at Melina's was everythang. We ate tamales, enchiladas, tacos, rice and beans; you name it, it was on the menu. When we weren't at Melina's house, you could smell Ms Lopes's cooking from our front door: pots clanging, muffled Spanish as boiled spices permeated the upper wing.

As much as I loved Ms Lopes's cooking, between my mother's baking and Dad's soul food, they held it down in unit four. If you've watched *High on the Hog: How African-American Cuisine Transformed America* on Netflix – in our house, it was like that. When our Ancestors were stripped of their traditional foods, our magic was reinvention – taking the scraps we were given, we turned them into the delicacies they are today. That's why we call it Soul Food: you can taste the love, care and pride we pour into our cooking. Holidays, Sunday dinners, after church services or when Daddy was in the mood: ribs, fried chicken, black-eyed peas, collard greens, cornbread, macaroni and cheese, potato salad, sweet potato and peach cobbler pies were served. Hmmph … don't nobody make potato salad like my Daddy! My sister is the only one to master his potato salad recipe – of course, with her own signature twist. You know you can cook when there's a showdown among family members for seconds. Fights have broken out over Daddy's cooking.

Many of my mother's curries had hints of the Malay flavours passed down from her grandmother, Nana Minnie Joseph. Belachan, a concentrated prawn paste, was used: it smelt awful but tasted so good. A curry wasn't complete unless the jar of chillies and Tabasco sauce came out. Our household relished in bully beef and rice, coconut curry chicken, chicken vermicelli, damper and Johnny cakes. These are the dishes that bring me down to earth. A spoonful of home, a reminder of who I am and where I come from.

When Melina and I were only eight years old, Ms Lopes was already planning Melina's quinceañera – a Mexican tradition celebrating a young girl turning 15: her coming of age. Melina's cousin was having her quinceañera soon, so her house was filled with family coming together to plan the special occasion. Soraya and I were over Melina's house so much that we thought we were on the planning committee. My sister and I silently approved many dresses and accessories that were on display. I secretly wanted a quinceañera. The amount of joy and love this tradition brought was something I wished for. You can imagine how gutted I was when Ms Lopes told me I couldn't attend their quinceañera: 'I'm sorry, hunny, it's a family gathering.'

I ended up drowning my sorrows in the sandbox with Ramona and her brother Buddy, who weren't going to the quinceañera either. This wasn't the only thing Ramona and I had in common. We were both tomboys. You'd never guess it from the number of church dresses my mother made me wear. Ramona and I challenged the boys to arm wrestling, tag, soccer games and skateboarding with reckless abandon.

Eventually, the reality of being a girl set in.

Between our mothers we were told, 'Stop acting like a boy; sit like a lady and be nice.'

The local boys weren't kind either. They often got jealous of Ramona's fancy footwork and my eagle-eye defence on the soccer pitch. Frustrated, they'd hurl 'stupid girls' and eject us from the game until all was forgiven. It's funny how some things don't change.

But what I treasured the most about our friendship was nights out under the stars in Ramona's backyard. Out came the barrel. Buddy filled it with kindling and Ramona's father sparked it to life. My eyes danced in synch with the flames as they grew taller. It was probably the only time us kids were quiet. Ramona, Veronica, Buddy and I sat around the fire on slow bake. We let the crackling fire tell a tale, prompting Ramona's uncle to share his. Chanting in his native tongue, Uncle's trills arrested me with each rise in inflection – the interminable wails cracked me open in a way that caused me to yearn – for what. I didn't know. All I knew was, whatever this was, it was sacred.

Buddy was still learning and joined in too. Their cries travelled with the smoke up to the heavens, to their Ancestors. As their cries ascended, my mother heard the songs from our kitchen window. She said it comforted her while she was so far away from home.

After four years living on base, my father ended his career in the military, and we moved from California to Wichita, Kansas. We found our bearings in the Midwest, settling into life with tornado sirens, blizzards, snowball attacks and wild racoons in the summer that replaced the wild bushfires, earthquake scares and sandy beaches of our life in California.

My mother had a job at a nursery, and after work, she'd collect us from afterschool care. On our way home, we passed Keeper of the Plains – a Native American man who stood 13 metres high – a steel sculpture created by Kiowa-Comanche artist Blackbear Bosin. This formidable being was the centrepiece between the Arkansas and Little Arkansas rivers, situated on sacred ground. Mimicking the Elder, I too closed my eyes, raised my hands above my head in prayer formation, my face elevated to the roof of the car. I paid my respects every time we passed him. Mum caught me doing it one night in her rear-view mirror, and, embarrassed, I tucked my hands under my bum and stared out the window. She just smiled and carried on driving.

Even as a little girl, I knew to always honour the people and places I frequented. I started to notice my affinity with indigenous cultures. Mum told me I was Aboriginal, but I didn't know what that meant. Living in the US made it hard for Mum to teach us about our culture. But the beauty of indigeneity is that while it may lay dormant, it's always there.

At my new school, College Hill Elementary, I had to work to find my place. When a group of Black girls needed another person to join their dance troupe, I didn't hesitate. Gina, the alpha of the pack, tapped me on the shoulder in the lunchroom one day and asked me if I could dance. 'Yes,' I lied: I really didn't know if I could. Fake it till you make it, I guess.

'All right then, join us in the music room tomorrow at lunch.' Gina wasn't asking; she was telling.

Gina and her girls were popular and pretty much ran things at College Hill. So, as soon as I started hanging out with them, my social status skyrocketed. In any girl group, you soon learn the pecking order. Beebe and I weren't the strongest dancers, so we practised in private to get better. Every lunchtime, 12:30 on the dot, Janet Jackson's 'Escapade' pumped out of the speakers as Gina choreographed our upcoming performance.

One time, we were rehearsing in the gymnasium: that day I had on an old pair of undies. Between the vigorous thrusts of the running man, Roger Rabbit, switch up to the cabbage patch to Kid 'n Play's scissor legs, I started to feel my undies slipping down. Gina was a drill sergeant. So, there was no way I was messing up this routine. I don't know how I dodged social suicide, but I put the 'I' in improvise. Thank God I was positioned in the back row. I managed to discreetly pull up my undies as we transitioned into the tootsie roll. Hands-on-my-hips shimmy shimmy and *yank*. I couldn't wait for practice to end. I immediately went to the bathroom and tied up my raggedy old undies with a rubber band.

Yes! I threw those goddamn panties away. That's why your mother tells you to wear clean underwear in case of an accident – especially new ones, to avoid the drama.

Gina and the girls were never my besties, but we were Black girls bonding. And that was enough for me.

In California, I was labelled 'mixed'. With what? Your guess is as good as mine. Kids in the neighbourhood assumed my mother was Mexican or Filipino. I'd correct them: 'No, she's Aboriginal.' No matter how hard I argued I was BLACK, my plea was ignored. Back then, nobody knew about Australia or Aboriginal people. Hell, I didn't either. But I still defended it. My mother and I were Aboriginal; therefore, we were Black – PERIODT.

Against my volition, I was branded light-skinned with the good hair: colourism had indeed followed us from the plantation. Being around Gina and the girls gave me a sense of comfort. For once, my Blackness wasn't a point of contention. Fleeting as the friendship was, I delighted in being a part of the Black sistahood. And like the seasons, it changed the day we all tried out for the choir. They got in; I didn't. I cried all the way to the car and let our union dissolve like my tears.

College Hill became training wheels as I learnt to ride the rough terrain we call race. It was also where I got called my first racial slur. Walking home from school with my new friends, Regin and Maria, a younger boy who lived around the corner started teasing us. He was an asshole of a kid and didn't have any friends. After endless roast sessions back and forth, I think we got the better of him.

Then came, 'Anyways you're just a N**ger.'

Nigga had been reclaimed and was expressed affectionately and as a form of discipline in my family. But never this way. This was the KKK N-I-G-G-E-R version. They say DNA holds trauma. I believe this. Even now, the N-word, cotton, hanging rope, the American and Australian flags send stress signals inside me; to me, they are symbols of genocide.

Regin and Maria tried to console me until I barked back, '*Cracker!*' In my opinion, it doesn't hit the same, but I felt vindicated nonetheless.

I told my Aunty Rochelle about the incident, and although she respected my decision to defend myself, she encouraged me to do like the Obamas: when they go low, we go high. But the Libran in me sought justice by any means necessary.

With all the pressures that came with race relations, I delighted in celebrating the First Nations peoples who were made to feel invisible in their own country like First Nations Australians.

So, when the traditional custodians of the Kaw Nation, the Kanza (Kansa) people – meaning 'People of the South Wind' – hosted College Hill's Native American Heritage Month, I came to life again as I did back in California in Ramona's backyard. Over a week, our school participated in various cultural activities. The Kanza women taught us beadwork. We ate dumpling stew, blue corn mush, squash and fry bread. The Kanza men transformed the oval: traditional tipis stood tall like skyscrapers. Standing inside a tipi was mind-blowing. Inside we drummed, our little hands holding the beat while the Elders sang and the young ones danced. This felt familiar. I wanted them to stay forever. But as they say, all good things must come to an end.

Saying goodbye to Indigenous History Month was a hard pill to swallow. Everything about it filled me with renewed vitality in parts of my being I didn't know existed. Weeks after the gathering, I chose to envision the sports field as the Sovereign

Nation of the Kaw. I couldn't understand how my classmates carried on; business as usual. Did they not feel the emptiness I felt? Places hold stories – stories you might not know. Nonetheless they remain, whether you can feel them or not.

In 1922, Chief Lucy Tayiah Eads, Cha-me 'Little Deer', became the first female chief of the Kaw Nation. After her father, Chief Wah-Shun-Gah (Washungah), a principal chief, passed away, there was no-one to fulfil his role for some time. At 34 years old, the mother of seven, a land and business owner, Eads was elected by her tribe to manage negotiations with the US Government regarding land claims, treaty provisions, oil and gas rights, and other business dealings. She also fought for recognition of the Kaw people – their culture and identity.

Chief Lucy wasn't the only woman of influence of the Kaw Nation. According to a *Wichita Eagle* article published on 13 June 1926, John Barnum, a Civil War veteran, confessed how enamoured he was by Opi Ela, meaning Elk's Tooth, the daughter of a Wichita chief. So much so, he wanted to name the area after her. In the end, the leaders chose to name the community after her tribe, the Wichitas.

In class, I never learnt the state of Kansas was named after the Kanza people. Or about the first female Kaw chief, Lucy Tayiah Eads, and the ethereal Opi Ela.

These days, I often question how things came to be and what I might find when I scratch the surface. And as novelist Chimamanda Ngozi Adichie eloquently reminds me, there is a danger in a single story.

2

Pretty Woman

From birth I was a shy and placid kid. Mum once told me a story about how she forgot to strap me in my car seat. She slammed on the brakes and heard a thud in the back. Mortified, Mum opened the back door and found me face down, kissing the floor.

'You didn't cry or make a sound,' she said. 'I just locked you back in and drove off.'

Mum loved having a little girl to dress up. When I was two years old, she styled my curls in a threaded hairstyle, dressed me in white, and made me point my toes. I was her little African princess.

I loved going through Mum's old polaroids of me, Mum and Aunty Debbie posing in our new outfits. Mum wanted to be a model, but she was 5'2" (1.58 m). So, when I turned nine, she enrolled me in a beginner's modelling course at M&I talent agency in America. This way, she could hit two birds with one stone: build my confidence and live her modelling dream vicariously through me.

I took to modelling like a duck to water. Ms V., the agency's director, introduced the class to high fashion. Ms V. was a spitting image of Krystle Carrington from *Dynasty*. Shoulder pads large enough to land an aeroplane on, pearls and Sally Hansen red nails. Ms V. was your quintessential southern belle. Her charm enraptured us. I wanted her to adore me as much as I did her, so I worked extremely hard. I made sure I mastered every half-turn and top of the T crossover. Thirty years on, I still know how to perform a full-circle turn mid-runway, thanks to Ms V. It's a skill you never know when you'll need, kind of like algebra.

Our course was a chance for new talent to be signed by New York's top modelling agencies: Elite Model Management, IMG, Ford and Page Parkes, who were all invited to our fashion showcase. *Pretty Woman*, the blockbuster movie of the year, had women dying to swap places with Julia Roberts; they wanted to snag themselves a Richard Gere. So, the creative team decided to base the graduation theme around the box office hit.

Rehearsing to Christopher Otcasek's 'Real Wild Child' and Natalie Cole's 'Wild Women Do' unleashed my inner femme fatale way before puberty hit. I had my eyes on the prize. I was just one show, one contract away from being a Black supermodel.

My obsession for fashion began when I saw Naomi Campbell, Tyra Banks, Veronica Webb and Iman dominate the catwalk – #BlackGirlMagic before it was a hashtag. These Black women claimed their space in an industry that glorified Eurocentric beauty standards. The very act itself was rebellious. Seeing them on magazine covers, in music videos and launching fashion weeks inspired this nine-year-old to live lavishly. Flying to London, Paris, Milan and New York, gliding down runways with no fucks given, drinking champagne with designers and eating caviar with the filthy rich. Yes, please, this was the life for me. Naomi Campbell tore runways up like a chiffon scarf falling on a samurai sword. And with my undeveloped hips, I made them sashay, shante to Naomi's rhythm.

Mum, in all her glory, was there to help her baby girl become a star. While prepping for my graduation showcase, our living room became a makeshift catwalk. We didn't have an umbrella, though my routine required one, so out came the sink plunger. Each night, Mum critiqued me to perfection. Even Ms V. complimented my fierce strut. I prayed fashion's finest would notice me on the big night.

Roy Orbison's 'Oh, Pretty Woman' serenaded the auditorium as models from all over Kansas came out to impress. Beyoncé says she channels her alter ego Sasha Fierce before a performance. She's not the only one. My daddy-long-legs shook before taking the first few steps; after that, it was game on. Head up, back straight. I swayed my hips as Naomi Campbell taught me, flashing my Colgate smile. The last model coming down the runway veered too close for comfort. Glaring at her, my Bambi eyes screamed *move over*. Of course, she didn't hear me. I pulled a rabbit out of my hat and slid past Space Invader on what little catwalk I had left. Hitting my last full-circle turn with supreme grace. *Bam!* How do you like them apples?

Waiting patiently for the show to end, I didn't want to talk to anyone. Did I win or not? The MC called my category on stage. We all lined up, and out came the artificial smiles. After incessant ramblings, thanking the entire township of Wichita, I heard SASHA KENDRICK echo in the stadium. I froze! That's me, that's my name! I had just won Best Female Performance Under 12s.

Because Mum and I were Miss Universe pageant junkies, I knew exactly what to do: bewilderment, sudden gasps and – wait for it – a trickle of fake tears. Don't get me wrong, I was genuinely excited, but ooouu chile I was so *extra*.

And there she was, Ms V.'s arms open wide to give me the validation I longed for. Agency reps from Elite and IMG came over to congratulate me and let Ms V. know they'd be in touch. I was on their radar. Floating on cloud nine, I placed my thigh-high trophy on the living-room mantel.

The adulation of a room full of strangers left me wanting more. Unfortunately, the pursuit of fame doesn't heal the awkward Black girl syndrome – that, my friend, is an inside job.

3

Murri Kid

'We're moving back to Australia.'

Mum's breaking news didn't faze me as I hoed into a bowl of Cocoa Puffs. Sitting across from me, Mum searched my face for a reaction, but the fear of soggy cereal had my focus instead.

Besides, I had an inkling my parents' marriage was on the rocks. The red flags were everywhere: we no longer went to church; Mum's friends group had changed. The rigid regimen we once adhered to had vanished. I could wear nail polish, street clothes and play secular music – once a cardinal sin. Dad was distant, hardly at home, mostly playing basketball with his mates.

I had no clue the real reason we'd moved to Kansas from California was Dad's attempt to save his marriage. Dad's military career was taking its toll on my mother. His continual deployments, leaving Mum to raise us three kids on her own, insecurities and infidelity broke the camel's back. Two people who loved each other were no longer on the same page. It seemed 'all you need is love' just wasn't enough.

So, Mum decided to put the past behind us with a one-way ticket headed for Down Under. To soften the blow of separation, Mum bought me a pair of Jellies. And I learnt how to compartmentalise to distract me from getting on a plane without my father. Children really are resilient. Kudos to Mum for flying internationally with three kids under 10.

Corny as it sounds, when Australia came to mind, I pictured kangaroos jumping around town, pet koalas and Crocodile Dundee's catchcry, 'G'day mate', before he slipped an extra shrimp on the barbie. Can you blame me? Have you seen the Tourism Australia archives?

The other reference I had was that Pippi Longstocking said all Australians slept upside down in bed. Even though she was a character in a Swedish kids' book, everyone I knew loved Pippi, so I figured it must be true.

Flying in to Gimuy and travelling by car to Innisfail, the humidity nearly killed me. Fields of sugar cane chased us as we headed towards the lush green rainforest as far as the eye could see. Pulling up to my Aunty Coralie's driveway, I was disappointed a pitcher of ice-cold lemonade wasn't there to greet us. Did I mention how uncomfortably hot I was?

'Dellie!' Aunty Coralie shouted, swooping Mum up in her arms; their embrace seemed like it would never end. Mum gestured for us to join her.

Aunty Coralie and Mum were first cousins, and they hadn't seen each other since Mum moved to the US. My sister and I soon had our faces pressed up against my aunty's bosom, our nostrils flooded with the fragrance all middle-aged women seem to wear; then came the generous smacks of kisses. The awkwardness subsided when she released us. Then Aunty Coralie led us to the living room and left us to plonk ourselves on the couch, jetlagged.

Before we could settle in, Aunty was back to collect us, ushering us through the beaded curtains of the back door to deliver us to our kin. Instantly, we were overwhelmed by beaming faces. Aunty Coralie sensed our nervousness and grabbed our hands. Soraya and I were passed around on a sushi train of big smiles, hugs and kisses.

And just like that, we made it back banaga (home), back to the mob.

Meeting the adults was a piece of cake. The real test was meeting our cousins; sizing each other up could go either way.

The first thing I noticed was my cousins didn't wear shoes – something I couldn't fathom. I came from a culture of clean, bright sneakers and bleached white socks. When Giancarlo Esposito bugged out after a Larry Bird fan scuffed his white Air Jordans in Spike Lee's *Do the Right Thing*, his outrage was universal – a matter of life and death. A sneakerhead raised me. Our pride were our kicks.

We'd lived in reasonably safe neighbourhoods in the US; what about broken glass, needles and trash lying around? I soon realised these concerns weren't necessary; we were now living in a small town. Apprehensive, I watched as my long-lost cousins played tiggy. Their shrieks of laughter were too much to resist. My father would have died if he'd seen what I was about to do … I bent down and began to untie my laces, releasing my feet from their armour; off came my purple socks. The blades of grass caressed my bare feet as they sank into the earth. A luxury I'd rarely enjoyed, living in the concrete jungle. I left my inhibition beside my shoes and ran off to join my cousins.

Then came the rude awakening. My cousins upped the ante: with their Teflon feet they walked barefoot everywhere. From 33°C scalding bitumen, bindi-infested lawns, to creek beds. Who did this? Struggling to keep up, I hobbled along, trying to avoid anything that could puncture my virgin feet. Watching me try to deal with this impossible challenge, they laughed. None of this was funny to me. Nor was my cousin handing me a green ant's bum to eat; now they were just taking the piss.

These outdoor shenanigans were less of a bother to me than being hassled over my heavy American accent. After my cousin innocently asked my aunty, 'Why does she talk like that?', I started observing my cousins talking lingo and tried to teach myself, so I'd be able to speak it too. I desperately wanted to sound Murri. No matter how hard I tried to loosen my speech, the American twang held my tongue hostage. My enunciation of words such as 'water' tickled my cousins with amusement. A male cousin a little older than me mocked me every chance he could. 'Can I have some waattter,' he'd say, glancing over at me to peep my reaction.

Self-conscious, I chose a vow of silence.

Now, this is where I, along with my cousins, learnt the principle of One Mob and the beloved Nigerian Igbo proverb, 'Oran a azu nwa' – it takes a village to raise a child. Noticing the change in my demeanour, my aunty gathered us kids together in the living room. She explained our mob didn't tolerate singling each other out.

'You are all the same,' she said. 'I don't care if you speak this way or that or if you're big or tall. If I catch you pulling each other down, you better watch out.'

From that day on the teasing ceased.

Oh, don't you worry, there were many more sit downs, especially when it came to our shades of deadly. When one of the kids started chucking off, 'No, you're not Black, you're white,' Aunt shut it down real quick.

She said our mobs were deadly because we were made up of the lightest to darkest shades, from straight, curly, Afro to sun-bleached hair. Blue, grey, green to dark brown eyes.

From these conversations, we learnt being Murri wasn't governed by the colour of our skin or an accent. It was rooted in our bloodline, culture and the community that claimed us.

Years on, my Aunty Ruthie told me a story about our gumbu (great-grandmother). Our gumbu's yabu (mother) was an Aboriginal woman and her father was migaloo (white), his identity unknown. Because my gumbu was born with light skin, members of her tribe didn't want her, presumably from shame and her visible point of difference. Tragically, my gumbu was thrown into the river. Thankfully, Gumbu's aunty jumped in and saved her niece. Consequently, my great-aunt's actions instilled the principle we live by today: We are One Mob; no matter what, no-one gets left behind.

We didn't have 'Oran a azu nwa' before Mum brought us back home. Our familial talks covered off stranger danger, protecting your valuables and what to do if you're called the N-word. Dad's family was not close-knit or within proximity if things popped off. So, we had no choice but to look out for ourselves. This is the reason Mum returned to Gimuy when her marriage began to crumble. Mum told me later on, when I was older, that she knew she couldn't raise her kids by herself in a strange country with no support system.

It was the best decision Mum made. As kids, the mantra of sticking together rang in our minds. And we did just that. These talks laid the foundation for the unbreakable bonds many Blak cousins share. In a world that constantly tries to divide our identity into fractions, the only thing we could count on was each other. When all was said and done, Aunt would tell us to pull the mattresses out into the living room so we could all watch a movie and eat custard together.

As kids, the best thing about living on Country meant year-long summers and endless playtime. Our adventures had us climbing coconut trees. The agile cousins scurried to the top and threw down coconut missiles from the sky. We crafted mango catchers from pole vault pieces of bamboo and a silver coat hanger, grateful for the juicy ones we discovered on the ground. Jackpot! One of us ran into the house to retrieve a plastic plate, vinegar, soy sauce and salt to dip our mangoes into the brew, making lemon faces until our palette could handle the tang. Sifting through fallen tamarind seeds was like searching for Easter eggs. What we didn't get from nature's door, we got at the corner store – a place where Mum would book up groceries on credit until payday. And home to our cherished salty plums. Salty plums to Murri kids are what beefy jerky and gobstoppers were to others. Blak gold, the currency used to get out of chores and bribe our siblings' silence.

If we were doing a TikTok 'Tell Me You're a Murri Kid Without Telling Me' challenge, all we'd need to do was flash our tangerine-stained tongues, lips and fingertips. And by the pitch of Mum's cursing, you knew she'd stood on a salty plum seed we accidentally left on the floor. Stepping on a salty plum seed is equivalent to stepping on a Lego.

When it was stinking hot, off to the freshwater swimming hole we'd go. Because there were more kids than car space, the little ones had to sit on the passenger floor or lay flat at the back of the station wagon. It was the eldest kids' job to yell out if they saw bully-man (police). But there's always that one big-eye mook mook who had to pop their head up. And when they did, everyone erupted in unison, 'GET DOWN', followed by a swift smack to the head.

I hated the fact I couldn't swim. I often waded in the water close to the big people where it was safe. I'll never forget my cousin egging me on. With the help of a chorus of cousins geeing me up, I mustered the courage to do a cannonball off the boulder. I hit the water and nearly drowned. My uncle had to rescue me. My doggy paddle wasn't quite strong enough. After that, I stayed my non-swimming ass on the creek bank where it belonged.

Another cherished pastime was fishing. If only we knew how crocodile-infested some of the spots were. I don't know how my uncles swam across Innisfail's Johnstone River in their heyday – home to four-metre crocs; no thank you. But Blakfellas were always hungry to chuck a line in regardless of the location. Fishing adventures always ended in one of us getting growled for tangling up someone's prized fishing lines. Or playing mediator when we fought over whose turn it was to cast a net or pull in a crab pot.

You'd think I'd learnt from nearly drowning months before. Nope, not me. I chose to try my luck again.

Standing on the beach with my cousin, I watched my uncles load up their dinghy. I could hear them boasting between them about who would snag the biggest catch. When my uncle finished loading the boat, he asked if we wanted to come. The invitation was too epic to pass up. Before I knew it, we'd drifted so far away that the shoreline became small as an ant.

Uncle explained the dark blue patches of the sea were the deepest parts. I felt the icy chill as we glided over them. Staring down, I wondered what lurked beneath. My chest tightened when I noticed there were no life vests onboard, just us in the middle of the ocean. All geared up, my uncles jumped overboard, and we passed them their spear guns. Only to watch them disappear into the abyss.

Some time had passed and I began to panic. What if they don't come back? I looked at my cousin to see if she was concerned. Hardly. She was too busy sunbaking. At least I had enough common sense to elevate the other spear gun away from us to stop it from piercing the rubber vessel.

I prayed for my uncles' safe return, and when two sea monsters emerged, scaring the shit out of us with a handful of yigara (crayfish), I knew I had lived to see another day. Wonders never cease.

Digging for pipis on the beach was a much safer option, but the stretch of sand had its dangers – pufferfish and jelly fish. The

Old People told us to look out for dirty old gujagay (crocodile). 'Don't swim or fish at the same spot,' they'd say. 'Gujagay be lurking.'

Our Elders taught us about the wadjan (rainforest), baygal (wait-a-while vine), danali (stinging bush plant) and our totem, the gunduy (cassowary): 'Don't mess with her; she'll rip you to pieces.'

Kup maris and hungis brought biggest mobs together for feasts of dugong, bungurru (turtle), gundal (barramundi), yigara, dugur (yams) and damper. Our little bellies swelled three times their size after a mad feed. Biggest mob feast means biggest mob dishes. And being a girl in the family sucked. After one such kup mari, my Uncle Darren told my sister several times to clean out the big pot with leftover bungurru. Coming into the kitchen, he noticed my sister hadn't scraped out the pot; frustrated, he grabbed it and moved towards her. Frightened, she screamed blue murder. Soraya jumped back like the pot was the boogieman.

There's a backstory here. Soraya had a pet turtle back in the US when *Teenage Mutant Ninja Turtles* was all the rage. So, cleaning the pot full of turtle represented her dead pet.

To this day, we still laugh about the turtle story. Yet she and I have never tried eating turtle. My sister killed it for me that night – no pun intended.

When the dishes were done and the night eased into a quiet stir, the first few strums and the guitar's tuning signalled the evening matinee under the stars was now in session. I loved it when Uncle Peter broke out his guitar, and the other uncles whipped out theirs. Reggae and soul were their specialties.

UB40's 'Red Red Wine', 'Kingston Town', 'Cherry Oh Baby' eased into Bob Marley and the Wailers' 'Stir It Up', 'I Shot the Sheriff' and 'No Woman, No Cry'.

Thinking about these garrimal (summer) nights, along with the music festivals my uncles played at the Kuranda Amphitheatre, suspends me in nostalgia. All the troubles our Elders carried were suddenly no more. Us kids would run and play for hours. Little Murri kids, rolling down the hill into the dead of night.

4

Soraya

Derived from the word 'thurayya', Arabic for the Pleiades, a group of seven stars in the constellation of Taurus.

My mother named Soraya after a rare heirloom rose. That's Soraya all right: soft petals guarded by thorns. Ray Ray, as she's affectionately known to me, is my ride or die. The little sister who'd rock her cot up against the wall to get our attention. Rat us out as kids. Embarrass us with grand displays of theatrics and generally make life difficult for me.

At school, she begged to hang out with my friends and me.

'No!' I'd hiss. 'Go hang out with your own friends.'

'They won't play with me.'

Ughhh! I wonder why.

Ray Ray had a penchant for burning bridges. She was combative and impatient, and rubbed others the wrong way with her inquisitiveness. Feeling sorry for her, I let her tag along with me, constantly reminding her when it was an A to B conversation, 'Shhhh, it's none of your business.' That didn't stop her from adding her two cents.

Speaking of cents, my crew always pulled up to the tuckshop to buy frozzies. Nothing like frozen cordial to cool us down and hype us up. Red ones were my jam. We'd pop out our frozzie from the white plastic cup and flip it upside down to eat it base first. This day, as per usual, Ray Ray was tagging along. We waited for her to buy her treats. My crew was ready to bounce, but she was still at the counter. I looked over to see what the hold-up was. I could see Pam, the tuckshop lady, talking to Ray Ray, who was standing on her tippy toes because she couldn't quite reach the counter. Ughhh, now what. I went over to investigate.

'Ray Ray, what's wrong?'

'The lady won't give me my money,' Ray Ray moaned in distress.

I looked at Pam for answers, and she broke it down for Ray Ray, probably for the hundredth time. She explained Ray Ray's items cost $2, which was exactly what Ray Ray gave Pam. But Ray Ray thought every time you give someone money, you get some back. Pam was trying to tell Ray Ray there was no change to give.

But that was Ray Ray. When she got something in her head, she'd argue it until she was black and blue. She did this best with our baby brother, Jr; they were two years apart. Given the five-year age gap between Ray Ray and me, I got some reprieve. I never liked arguing. I am a lover, not a fighter, and preferred to live up to the Russian meaning of my name: the helper and defender of mankind.

Ray Ray wasn't all that bad. She did find a $100 bill in the chip rack at the servo. She was eye level and saw it straight away as I was buying milk and bread. I felt her tugging at me, her cute little chipmunk face waving it in the air. I didn't want the clerk to know she found it, so I shushed her, grabbed it and put it in my pocket. Ray Ray might not have understood the fundamentals of change, but she knew money when she saw it. Let's just say that Christmas, instead of being the broke kids with the whack ass presents, we got to flex with the rest of the neighbourhood. New skates, who dis? I believe an angel left that $100 note for us. The way it was sitting there perfectly, as Ray Ray described it years later, it had to be.

She may have saved Christmas that year, but she was still hard-headed. Rain, hail or shine, her tomfoolery never let up. On our way to school one morning, I told her to stay close to me. Of course, she bypassed what I said, climbed a pile of wet dirt and began to sink into it like quicksand. All I could hear was a muffled scream: no Ray Ray in sight. Hysterical, I raced to her with everything I had, praying she hadn't suffocated to death under the caving mud. Coming to her rescue, I pulled her out. She was alive and safe. We didn't make it to school that day.

Oh, it didn't stop there, her bond with mud. Take the day she didn't want to wear her ugly school uniform and ran out the house. Mum told me to go get her. So, I chased her to our aunty's place. Soraya ran straight to the backyard and jumped clean over a patch of mud, which I didn't see. Needless to say, I ended up sliding in it like a batter trying to steal home base. The entire right side of my body was sideswiped in mud and grass; I was fuming.

Mum asked me what happened. All I could do was yell through clenched teeth, 'I hate her!'

Soraya

As we got older Soraya loved to debate our brother Jr, who sometimes came out with outlandish tales, but it was harmless.

'Let him tell his yarn if that's what he believes,' I'd plead with Soraya.

'No, he's lying,' she'd yell back.

'So, what?'

Needing to retire from the sheer stress of it all, I'd head off. And back and forth they'd go until she got the best of our brother. Then he'd try to assert his masculinity by throwing something or storming off. To his credit, he did manage to push her into the garden bed one night. I *died* when Ray Ray told me. God, I wish I'd been there to witness it. 'See what happens when you run your mouth,' I told her.

Jr had to have been powered by pure adrenaline. He was bony: picture Wiz Khalifa vs Serena Williams.

As much as Soraya was ready to rumble, she always fought for what was right, plunging into battles for those she loved.

Those who knew my brother, Jr, knew he loved his kids. All he ever wanted was to be a father. When you take away a father's right to see his children, they are left broken-hearted.

I don't think he meant for things to get out of control. Or for his cry for help to go horribly wrong. He just went too far, and now he's not here. But that was Jr, a young man who seemed to have nine lives but somehow lost count. He was only 25, and he loved 2Pac; they were both Geminis. Crazy as it sounds, they had a lot in common. I'd listen to 2Pac's music, watch his interviews and documentaries so I could feel closer to my brother. I could see why Jr saw himself in 2Pac. Dr Jekyll, Mr Hyde. Jr would give you the shirt off his back one minute and punch you in the face if you weren't keeping it real. The ultimate contradiction.

He put Ray Ray and Mum through hell the last few years before he passed. Banging down doors in a rage, running drunk from police with a knife in his hand, taking Mum's car and crashing it into a streetlight at 110 kilometres an hour on a quiet suburban road, jumping out of the vehicle before it caught alight.

Jr was my soulmate – my evil twin, he'd joke. I prayed a man would love me close to how my brother did. He is my measure of true love. Jr is the father of three beautiful children. A brother, son, nephew and cousin. Our protector here on Earth and beyond. Our bond lives on and he is now in the Dreaming with the Ancestors, who have undoubtedly helped him mend his wounds. He is our teacher sending his knowledge back to us.

How do you prepare to let someone go when you aren't ready? We were on autopilot while organising Jr's funeral. Mum, Dad, me and Soraya numb like zombies. On our way back from the shopping centre I pulled the car over. I couldn't remember how to drive.

I said to Soraya, 'I can't think.'

So, we sat there in silence waiting for the haze to pass. Our baby brother was gone. It was just us. No more three musketeers.

Even though Jr and I were similar, Ray Ray and him were like oil and water. Soraya's love for him ran deep. She picked up the sword he left behind, ready to fight the system for custody of his children.

Soraya

Despite the disruption to her three children's stability, she made things work. As the sole breadwinner, with Mum firmly by her side, taking in two toddlers with complex needs wasn't easy. When she received guardianship, and my brother's kids came into her care, my nephew didn't speak. Now, 12 years old, he argues with Soraya exactly like his father. And like clockwork, I jump in to break up their arguments.

'Why are you arguing with a child?'

'I'm the adult. He listens to me.'

'You know he's just like Jr.' My reasoning brushed aside, as it was back when we were kids.

My brother's spirit lives on through his son and daughters. It's a peace that gives us hope as we continue to battle the system 18 years on and counting.

We lost one child to the system along the way, my brother's eldest daughter. And they say the Stolen Generations is a policy of the past. It's not. It's still happening.

Imagine what it feels like to be a grandmother or an aunty denied the human right to raise your kin. Imagine your nana doing everything in her power to ensure her children weren't taken away, only for it to skip a generation and for her grandchildren to be taken. Imagine what it feels like to be up against a money-making machine where non-Indigenous carers profit off the bodies and labour of Blak children. Dormitories replaced with juvenile detention centres; white picket fence homes riddled with abuse.

High staff turnover means you brief multiple caseworkers, reliving the trauma but hoping *this time* your child comes home with you. Files go missing, emails unanswered. False promises and no solution. Fight the system, they say. How – when Blak families don't have the money or resources to fight the monster stealing and killing our children?

For 18 years, my niece was taught to hate her Blak skin, act white, babysit other children in care, feed and groom horses on a property she'd never belong to, let alone inherit. Only to be tossed out to fend for herself when no longer of use, leaving behind her a vacancy to be filled by another Blak child, primed for a life of abuse and exploitation.

And so, the cycle continues. This is our story. One of many censored and unheard stories stored away for the archives. I hope one day my niece reads this. We fought for you, bub. We never stopped fighting for you. I pray your father guides you to us when the time is right. And you find the closure you're looking for.

This is what the system does to Blak parents, women and families.

And they wonder why we are so angry?

Our anger comes from fighting the system for our children, men and communities. If you ask me, we haven't gotten angry enough. We don't have the privilege to express anger in its raw form, not like we should. Why? Because we have to keep calm and think straight – think of the ramifications our anger incites. What can be lost? In the end, there's too much at stake.

Our anger gets us abused, ignored, gaslit, ostracised and killed.

When white people get angry and we can't, it's an injustice they will never know. When do Blak women gain the freedom to reveal their scars – their broken hearts?

Who's fighting for us?

Soraya

They label us the Angry Blak Woman to insult us. And for a while it did. But not anymore, because our anger is *power*. It is *alchemy*. They know it, and now we do.

So today, tomorrow and the next day, we will be angry until there is change. We will be angry because if we don't, we'll erase what our Ancestors fought for.

We didn't come this far to give up.

Our anger comes from a long line of matriarchs – passed down to them, to us, which we will pass on to the young women who come after us.

I've never admitted to Soraya the guilt I carried for living in the city: choosing to build my career in spite of our brother's death. That's how I cope. I find new feats to conquer. New projects to focus on. It helps me anaesthetise the pain.

Why wasn't I strong enough, like Ray Ray, to be a mother?

The truth is, I didn't have it in me. It hurts to admit it.

But when you listen to the Old People and remember what they told you, you know everything runs its course. That the seasons guide you and everything you require is in due time. Garrimal (summer) is when the mirrayn (black bean) flowers; that's when the storms come, and the jarrugan (scrub hens) and guyiarri (brush turkeys) are laying their eggs. Lore says, take only enough eggs to eat; leave some behind, so there'll be more left when garrimal returns.

And then the story of Majal, Old Man Birrgil and Waareenday comes to mind.

Old Man Birrgil (Winter) did not care for the tropical heat; with much haste, he avoided it whenever possible. Contrary to the heat, when birrgil lingered, it produced a lovely harvest of berries. The cold kept the rain at bay, blessing Old Man Birrgil with fine sunny weather to go hunting. During that time, no-one knew how to make the birrgil stay until Waareenday rested on her journey. Waareenday, a faithful servant of Old Man Birrgil, was responsible for hauling his ice blocks up to the Gambil (Tablelands) to leave on the range.

Waareenday traversed around the Billnguy Creek that trickled down the mountainside. On her route, there was a staircase that rescued Waareenday from the difficult path. One day, weary of her travels, Waareenday stopped to rest on a flat stone. She placed the block of ice beside her. Tired, she closed her gayga (eyes) for a bit of sleep. When she awoke, the ice had melted and grown into majal, a cockyapple tree. Frightened by what had happened, she turned into a stone that still rests beside the Billnguy. To this day, when a good birrgil is needed, you take buni (fire) and blaze the trunk or limb of the majal. The bigger the blaze, the bigger the birrgil.

When you understand the old stories, it eases the pain. Sometimes we are Old Man Birrgil and cannot stand the heat in the moment. Sometimes the burden we carry – like Waareenday's –

is not ours to bear alone. Our pause does not signify failure. In fact, it allows others to make sure majal continues to bear fruit. And when the season is right for our return, we bring along our buni to ensure the harvest remains abundant.

I've always been a mother. I just needed time to hunt down my dreams, like Old Man Birrgil, and acquire my own buni (knowledge) so I can use it to set ablaze the majal (our children) so that they can blossom. And when the time comes, I will pass my buni on to them.

When we let society dictate our role as women and mothers, that's how we lose our power. I know I did. The guilt I carried came from measuring myself against a colonial system instead of lore. Lore is inherent in Blak women and motherhood. If we listen and respect lore, we know there is more than one mother. Aunties are mothers; each has a special gift that the other doesn't. This means one mother is not left to raise a child alone. To know this is to have peace of mind; no child goes without.

Society assigns us with unrealistic expectations that one woman must have, be and do it all. Where does the stress of modern-day motherhood come from? Okay, aside from the kids driving you crazy. Are you operating as a nuclear family? Or from the principles of lore?

Our majal (our children) are individuals; and so is their spirit and journey. Buni (knowledge) does not belong to one person but many. It can be sparked alight at any time, any place, by anyone. So, why do we think only one person has buni?

Gigorou

My sister is not a touchy-feely person. She's like Catherine, her grandmother. She is staunch, swears like a sailor, and the only difference between her and Nana Catherine is she doesn't pack a pistol in her handbag. Her love language is acts of service and buying gifts. She's practical: you are loved if you have a roof over your head, electricity and food. You know where you stand with her. Soraya's steady resolve has taught us to hold strong. I see this in our kids. They have a mind of their own, and very little sways them.

As much as I wrestled with her parenting style, spirit told me, 'There are too many ants telling bees how to make honey. She is Waareenday and you are Old Man Birrgil. Everyone's buni is different. Your buni speaks life into the children through affection and affirmations, raising their self-esteem. And your journey right now is to guide your nieces through their rite of passage into womanhood.'

As I take on this role, I no longer believe I am less of a woman because I did not birth children. I no longer believe I am an old, bitter, barren cat lady who will die alone. I let the biological clock tick away because lore states it's none of my concern.

My sister taught me you are not for everyone. So let them talk. I hope I have taught her a thing or two.

Soraya: you are Gurburu, the Seven Sisters that shine in the sky. The thorn in my side.

5

Too Pretty to Be Aboriginal

Being the eldest, I automatically became the second parent when Mum and Dad separated. Which meant my two siblings were glued to my hip. This is why motherhood freaked me out: it's a full-time job plus overtime. And from what I observed at 11, mothers were grossly unappreciated. To that end, my sole motivation in life was independence.

So, when my best friend Janelle invited me to her 12th birthday party, it was a chance to seize freedom. For that to happen, I had to get my mother's permission. As children, you learn to master the parental ask. It's even more amusing watching it play out as an adult. The trick is to remove all traces of desperation, maintain steady eye contact, a slight smile, and away you go. I entered the kitchen and slowly approached my mother so as not to alarm her. I placed the pearly envelope on the table and slid it over to meet her eyes. When she reached for it, the speech I had thoughtfully prepared came tumbling out. I stood there appearing unfazed but inside I was jittery.

Mum was vigilant when it came to whose house we stayed over; meeting the parents was mandatory. Come to find out, Mum knew Janelle's father, so I got the thumbs up. Until now, Ray Ray and I were Velcro. Everywhere I went, she went. I think my mum knew teen spirit was in the air. She reassured me the umbilical cord between my sister and I was cut.

Yes! I thought, no baby sister tagging along so she could snitch. Now, what to wear?

I rummaged in my closet for the dress. This was no ordinary dress. It was the one I wore when I won Best New Talent back in Kansas. Something about this dress made me feel grown, oh that's right, it was the black off-the-shoulder, slim bodice waist and puffy white ruffles with polka dots – that's what it was. Out came my prized mariachi sandals. Imelda Marcos, you've got nothing on me. My big Diana Ross hair called for an obnoxiously large pink scrunchie and a jean jacket to set it off. I scrutinised my outfit as if I was the late André Leon Talley. My crush, Justin, was going to be at Janelle's party, and I was ready to catch his eye. So, I had to look cute.

Janelle's party was on everybody's lips at school and so was the prospect of Justin asking me out. Birds were chirping, Justin likes Sasha. The anticipation alone made me dizzy. You already know Janelle and I held a think tank on what to do when he popped the question: 'Do you wanna be my girlfriend?'

The day had come. I spent hours in the mirror doing a final check. I stared back at myself: you got this.

Before I hopped out of the car, Mum kissed me and told me to call her if anything went wrong. Pffft, I thought, what could go wrong?

Walking through Janelle's front door, a fuzzy red neon light, disco ball and laser beams created a kaleidoscope on the walls. A handful of our crew from school had already arrived.

Janelle lunged out of nowhere to hug me. 'You're here! What do you think?'

I nodded emphatically with approval over the blasting music. The birthday girl grabbed me a drink of punch before we joined the squad. Carly reached over and fluffed up the ruffles on my dress.

'I love your dress. Where did you get it?' she yelled.

'Thanks. Mum bought it for me in America,' I yelled back. I felt so cool saying that; how international of me.

'Awesome!' Carly was equally impressed.

Fawning over our outfits came to a halt when Janelle nudged the side of my ribs. The sharp pain immediately disappeared when I saw Justin. My heart started beating out of my chest. He was here! Of course, every gesture I made after that was exaggerated, along with my ridiculous laugh to get Justin's attention. Little did I know this wasn't the only attention I'd attract that night.

Three party games in, I stayed close to Justin like white on rice, giving him prime opportunity to ask me out. Not that I had any business having a boyfriend at that age, but it didn't matter; it was all about the rush. *Degrassi Junior High* was my go-to for all things relationships; I had watched the scene when Lucy Fernandez gets her first boyfriend, Paul. I imagined tonight would play out exactly like it did on my favourite teen soap.

Janelle telepathically knew it was girl time. Looping her arm in mine, she escorted me away for a debrief. We were both buzzing off party vibes and sugary punch. Janelle was on her turning 12 high; me, on the precipice of being Justin's girlfriend. In fits of giggles, we hatched out my next move when it came to lover boy.

'Birthday girl. Birthday girl. Where's the birthday girl?'

Janelle's adult sister, Monica, interrupted us. She was an absolute knockout. Monica's little black dress clung to her 36–24–36-inch body, her smoky pantyhose hugging her slender legs. But it was her shifty eyes that told me she was tipsy.

'Who's this?' Monica blurted out.

'This is my best friend, Sasha.'

'Hey, Sasha! Saa-sha or Sash-er?' Monica asked.

'Hey, it's Saa-sha,' I replied meekly.

Our exchange was brief, and I immediately didn't like the vibes Monica was giving off. Her 'I know something you don't know' smirk signalled trouble was brewing.

'Time to open presents!' Ms Roberts announced from the guest room. Saved by the bell.

I sat next to my bestie and watched her in sheer delight. Piles of wrapping paper decorated the floor as she ripped into her presents. Rounds of squeals and hugs abounded. Watching Janelle filled me with promise of what to expect when I reached the big one–two. I wondered what Janelle wished for as she blew out the candles on her birthday cake.

Janelle's mum started to cut up her cake. Patiently, we waited for our slice. Standing in line, I felt that no-good energy behind me. I turned around. Dammit, it was Monica. Her jolly red cup in her hand. Monica leaned down to match my level. She choked out an inaudible question that got lost in the music. After several failed attempts, defeated, Monica moved on.

Until she eventually caught up with me in a quieter spot in the living room. Intent on getting the answer to her question, she asked, 'What's your background?'

I knew what she wanted to know. I'd witnessed my mum constantly being asked this question by strangers. And like any proud Aboriginal child would declare, I said it with my chest, 'I'm Aboriginal!'

'Aboriginal!' Monica screeched it so loud a group of adults nearby matched her disbelief. Given the reaction of the room, being Aboriginal was clearly a dirty word. Monica's incredulous scoff, 'You're too pretty to be Aboriginal!' pierced my ears.

By this time, my blood was boiling, my mouth was dry as I fought back what felt like an ocean of tears. In a frenzied panic, I grabbed my cake and made a beeline to my circle of friends. I thought leaving the scene of the crime would erase the assault that had taken place. Paranoid that my peers had witnessed what happened, I began to fake-laugh at whatever was funny to mask my embarrassment. The rest of the night was a blur. And, at the tender age of 11, my Aboriginality was no longer a source of pride.

In those days, we didn't have the 'You're Too Pretty to Be Aboriginal' TikTok clapback. We internalised our shame and tried to reconcile it as best as we could. Not to say our young ones don't experience this humiliation. I'm just saying we've come a long way empowering this generation to be Strong, Blak & Deadly.

My mother asked me a bunch of questions about the party on the way home; I had one of my own. Why would Monica say that?

A lot of questions went unanswered that evening, including Justin's unspoken, 'Do you wanna be my girlfriend?' Instead, I ended up with a shitty slice of cake and a filthy stain I'd try to get rid of for the next 20 years.

Janelle made a wish that night. I made one too. I wished I wasn't too pretty to be Aboriginal.

Elaine

Now that my Aboriginality was no longer a secret, I decided to put last year's debacle behind me. Janelle and I were no longer friends. Janelle's dad made sure of that. He thought I might be a bad influence on Janelle, seeing I was a Blakfella. Fancy the kettle calling the pot black? He was a Blakfella too. When I told my aunty about the ordeal, she said Janelle's dad was a coconut. It would be years later until I understood what Aunty meant.

So, as the months passed, I kept to myself and remained nose-deep in a book or magazine. On a routine visit to the corner store, I dropped into the newsagency to pick up copies of *Dolly* and *Girlfriend*. As usual, I'd check out the other magazine covers from A–Z until my scan came to a halt. Angelic eyes stared back at me.

Mesmerised, I didn't know where to start. Who was she, and how on earth did she get here? Her sun-kissed brown skin eclipsed the cover. This goddess turned symmetry and symphony into a synonym. Everything about her aligned in total harmony:

bold yet natural; her straight chocolate-coloured hair with golden highlights gently framed the sparkles of jade under her brows. Her voluminous coral pink lips and girl-next-door smile hinted at graciousness. Her porcelain nose chiselled to perfection. In a knee-jerk reaction, I frantically flipped through the pages until I found the cover girl once again. Her name was Elaine George. From top to bottom, left to right, I absorbed every inch of Elaine's editorial. I don't know when I allowed it to sink in that Elaine was, in fact, Aboriginal. I think part of me was in denial. I'd never seen an Aboriginal cover girl before.

Elaine George, you're coming home with me. I grabbed a fresh copy of *Vogue* and handed it to the teller. It was $4.50 and outside of my price range, but leaving Elaine behind wasn't an option.

I dipped into Mum's grocery money to pay for it. Giddy with glee, I nearly forgot to buy the food Mum sent me out to get. Racing home, I balanced the bags of groceries on my handlebars – Elaine, safe in a separate bag. As soon as I arrived home, I carefully presented Elaine to Mum – 'She's Aboriginal' – grinning like the Cheshire cat.

Mum made a cuppa, and we sat down to admire Elaine together. It was unlike the beauty pageants Mum and I religiously watched to root for all the Black contestants. This was different, closer to home. Elaine was one of us – she was Aboriginal. She came from the same bloodline, where beauty began.

In 1993, Elaine George made magazine history: the first Aboriginal woman to grace *Vogue Australia*'s cover. Since then, Dunghutti model Samantha Harris broke a 17-year hiatus. Along with Charlee Fraser, Awabakal model, in 2018 (also snatching

Vogue Turkey, Ukraine and China covers). Yolngu model and actress Magnolia Maminydjama Maymuru and her daughter Djarraran in 2021. For their *Vogue* May 2022 edition, the masthead commemorated Magnolia Maminydjama Maymuru, Charlee Fraser, Elaine George and newcomer Cindy Rostron.

That starstruck 12-year-old who witnessed Blak Herstory ended up modelling alongside her muse in 2003. Elaine George proved to be the most humble and carefree woman – exactly how she appeared to me when I first saw her in the newsagency that day.

Seeing Elaine's beauty beaming from the newsstand removed the sting of Monica's nasty words and restored my pride, robbed from me that night at Janelle's birthday party.

6

Majal Gigorou

Remember when you heard the ice-cream man? Whenever Mr Whippy rolled through our neighbourhood, it was pure excitement every time. I'd break my neck racing home yelling, 'Mama! The ice-cream man', rustling up all the cash me and my siblings could grab. Without fail, we'd track Mr Whippy down – panting and gasping – placing our change on the counter.

Then one day, Mr Whippy stopped coming around. Sure, we asked why and were disappointed when nobody knew. But we moved on, as kids do.

When Dad jumped out of our bedroom closet one afternoon, my siblings and I were in complete shock. Jr and Soraya lunged at Dad like Mr Whippy had come back. I stood still like a stunned mullet. Dad grabbed me, and I hugged him tight. I pressed my fingers into his back while wondering if it was real.

It took some time for me to warm back up to Dad. I felt betrayed there was no announcement of Mum and Dad's reconciliation. Not that my parents' marriage was any of my business, but as second in charge, I felt I had the right to know.

The first few months of Dad's return were the honeymoon phase. I got a kick out of tricking Dad into eating a blob of Vegemite – watching him wince like a cat's bum, then falling to the ground in fits of laughter when Dad wondered why his ice-cordial was unusually sweet.

'Dad, it's concentrated. You have to mix it with water like Kool-Aid.'

Dad was a novelty to others who heard his American accent, and they gravitated towards him like a magnet. Now that Dad was on the scene, we received five-star treatment, far better than we ever had before. Funny that. Nothing like a bit of Americana charm to open fancy doors.

But then the rose-coloured glasses came off. Dad and I butted heads over disciplining the younger kids. As soon as my siblings acted up, I'd jump in to correct their behaviour, and Dad would interject, 'That's my job.'

Oh, really? Fine, please, by all means. Never mind that I've been handling it these past years.

When the mini power struggle dissipated, I went back to being a pre-teen focused on trading 'Sweet Valley High' and 'The Baby-Sitters Club' books.

Dad swapped the American dream for an Aussie one and encouraged Mum to delve into her artwork and embrace the commercial returns that could help set the family up for the future.

I was extremely fortunate to have a mother who lived and breathed beauty. I asked Mum where her love for art and beauty came from, and she told me, from the bush. As a child, Mum would visit Nana Bracken and spend hours playing among the huge raintrees and tall guinea grass. Her adoration for colours came from the splendid fruits and tropical plants she stumbled across. Mum would break off fungus from the dead tree stumps and logs, paint them with the juice of inedible red berries, and colour the fungus green with the sap of the leaves.

Mum's eye for beauty grew; at 15, she studied the textures of people's skin. And a desire to work on a new canvas inspired her to attend beauty school.

As an adult, she received the support of a small business grant and, along with Dad's entrepreneurial mind, Mum took her beauty degree and put it into action, opening Majal Beauty Salon.

Majal was situated in the heart of the Cairns CBD. Our clientele were mainly international travellers searching for, as my mum would say, a bit of a pamper. My mother preached self-care way before its modern-day hype. I learnt firsthand the power of touch – how to make women feel gigorou, inside and out. From the soft circular sweeps of a facial, firm depression into the muscular tissue, our fingertips found hidden pressure points to release pain and stress from the body. Steam enabled pores to open, and like Dr Pimple Popper, we'd perform skin extractions.

But with any apprenticeship, it usually starts out like *The Karate Kid*. Please tell me you had a crush on Daniel LaRusso! If you've seen the movie, you'll remember Daniel wanted to kick into action immediately – but Mr Miyagi was like: Hold up. Baby steps. It was the same at Majal. And like Daniel-san, I questioned why things had to be done a particular way – left to wax on, wax off.

We were in the beauty business; our customers came to us to indulge in a slice of heaven, and it was our job to deliver. And it started with the fabric softener we used on the towels for clientele. We might not have had Egyptian cotton, but we came close. Have you ever dried your face with a scratchy towel? Exactly!

I know you've sat in reception in establishments and looked around while you waited. If you're like me, I inspect everything. Note to all beauty salons, especially the ones delivering injectables: hunny, nobody wants to get needled with foreign substances when the bins are full. The floors ain't seen Pine O Cleen or a mop. And the technician looks greasy. Sweet baby Jesus! What are we running here, a chop shop? So, when I could make every surface in Majal shine like the Palazzo Versace Spa, I was allowed to pass Go and collect $200.

My initiation into beauty started with rule number one: not every face is the same. I watched Mum conduct skin analyses with her clients. When I was confident enough, Mum handed me the reins. I'd take a client's skincare report to our mini lab, aka the kitchen at the back, and whip up their products to go.

Since every skin is unique, there is no one-size-fits-all approach. This means each person's skin tells a different story, a beautiful, sometimes complex one. As beauticians, we had to understand that story to figure out how to make their skin glow. Treating skin is akin to finding out what makes us beyond compare. It may take time and patience, but it's a principle I've relied upon later in life to discover my je ne sais quoi and how to appreciate it in others.

Of course, I would also learn skin can be unpredictable. I found this out by doing a mini facial on a client, and after applying a clay mask, the client asked if the tingling was normal.

'Yes, just a little,' I lied. I didn't have a clue.

The client seemed okay until her alabaster skin morphed into a beetroot. I flicked on the steamer to counteract the burning: it's steam, Sasha; you're making it worse.

I scurried into the other room where Mum worked on another client and motioned for her to come quick. Mum came in, wiped off the mask before it got worse, and told me to mix up another mask to calm the burning. We found out the client was allergic to one of the ingredients. I made sure to document that on the client's profile in *red*.

After that eventful episode, I didn't want to touch another face again. I had horror scenes of clients' faces combusting and frothing at the mouth. But as they say, you got to get back on the horse. Plus, Mum couldn't handle our client roster by herself. Part of being a shrewd entrepreneur is understanding what works and doesn't for a client and finding solutions.

Being honest and overdelivering is what customers value; it keeps them coming back. Even when it's hard to turn away business, the worst thing you can do is lie or under-deliver, which I did on a few occasions. I realised this after Mum had to clean up my messes after I promised the sun, moon and the stars. My lack of assertiveness and ability to manage expectations was the problem. I felt terrible when Mum came out of pocket – offering a free treatment or credit to customers to remedy my mishaps. Honesty is the best policy, and Mum's never wavered. I watched her communicate directly — what she could and couldn't do — which was a strength, not a weakness. If only this policy were universal maybe some of us wouldn't have a garage full of dud informercials products.

When I wasn't playing flamethrower to someone's skin or fumbling services, I was at reception handling the phones, booking Mum's appointments, and dealing with petty cash. You know why they call it petty cash? Because it's petty. It's a breeze to manage once you master keeping receipts as good as you do on your horrible co-workers.

One day, my friend asked me if I got a wage for working at the salon. I didn't, so I asked my parents why, and got a lecture on the ways Black people failed to prosper — because they don't stick together! It wasn't the answer I wanted to hear. A simple, 'We're in the first year of business and we can't afford it' would have sufficed. My friend concluded I should get paid what I was worth. That's why you don't be sharing all your business with your little friends, as my parents warned me.

Resentment kicked in as I added up all the hours I'd poured into the family business and my loss of a social life. That's when I decided to cook the books. Nothing major: just a $10, $20 note here and there. I'd collect all the non-descriptive receipts I could find and classify them as a legitimate sundry until Mum's accountant scrutinised the records, and the jig was up. Mum didn't catch on to what I did exactly, but it became another hangnail she had to nab and clip. But once I got caught, I realised that how I moved affected others, especially those I loved.

One day, I had an hour to myself before I was due back

to help close at the salon, so I decided to hang out with my boyfriend. You know that phenomenon of forgetting what you went into the store for, but as soon as you leave, you remember? Same thing happened when my tongue was halfway down my bae's throat.

'Oh shit, what's the time?'

Racing back to the salon, sure enough, the shop's lights were off, and Mum was gone.

Guilt overcame me as my boyfriend and I rode home. I thought about the laundry Mum had to lug to the car by herself – her tired hands, feet and back from doing appointments all day. And here I was, too busy pashing my boyfriend's face off in the park. Nothing guts you like your parents' disappointment: when they can't even look you in the eye.

My parents gave me the silent treatment and it was the driver for me to get my act together: Operation Straighten Up and Fly Right. I became the best damn receptionist and assistant I could be. I booked enough time for Mum to reset between appointments and made sure she had something to eat. The laundry, kitchen and salon rooms were spic and span, and I kept the fraternising with peers to a minimum. I desperately needed to get my mother's respect back.

Some people envision karma being delivered immediately – the way O-Ren Ishii (Lucy Liu) does in *Kill Bill*: her tiny feet shuttling down the board room table as she goes to slice Boss Tanaka's head off. Take that! How dare you question my cultural heritage. That's extreme.

For me, my karma for poor behaviour was doing facials on clients with bad breath and awful body hygiene. A swift death any day like Boss Tanaka, over a slow death of dragon breath and Rotorua funk.

When I became a team player, I carried myself with a lot more grace. It was then I was able to embrace rule number two: acts of service build healthy communities. Working at Majal instilled a strong sense of giving back, particularly when it came to our mob. Mum was renowned for conducting beauty and wellbeing workshops with local Indigenous girls, women and organisations. My claim to notoriety in high school wasn't for rocking the latest Cross Colours hoodies, baggy jeans or fresh twists. It was sistagals showing off their deadly new eyebrows my mother had shaped for them.

Mum and I would giggle with seasoned waxers who brought in their friends for their first wax. The newbies asked Mum, 'Does it hurt?'

'It stings,' Mum would say.

The comfort of warm wax gliding across their skin before it's ripped off unexpectedly duped them every time. In utter disbelief, bodies elevated while sombre moans had us all laughing. Waxing disarms even the hardest sistas.

Majal represented a safe haven where clients could cast their worries aside and gain a new lease on life. My mother and I saw women stride out the salon, head held high, because they were reminded of their worth. For the record, back then, nobody was checking for Blak women, specifically when it came to our beauty. I come from generations of staunch Blak Matriarchs who fought untold battles to be where they are today. All they were asking for was just a little bit of R-E-S-P-E-C-T. Don't worry we got you, Queen. When you came to Majal, we rolled out the red carpet and gave you your flowers. We made you feel like a natural woman. Can't nobody uplift a Blak sista like another Blak sista.

Mum's salon became an afterschool hang-out for our teen clientele. As the receptionist, I got all the gossip. I felt partly inclined to serve biscuits in order to soak up all the tea being spilt in our waiting room.

Majal's success soared, and Mum's mission to bring beauty to all peoples was apparent. But our service meant so much more to the mob who couldn't travel to town, felt too shame or were unwelcomed by the white beauty establishments. Plus, many of those businesses weren't proficient in Blak skincare and make-up. At Majal, we prided ourselves on sourcing products from other Black companies – we stocked Koori, Barumba, Black Opal and Fashion Fair Cosmetics. Along with Black beauty advertisements plastered throughout the salon. We were already about that Buy Black and Black Is Beautiful life.

Mum believed every woman had a right to look and feel beautiful. Even on a budget. We educated young girls on how to access affordable skincare. In our workshops, we had a selection of avocado, strawberries, cucumber, oatmeal, lemon, honey, cold-pressed and essential oils to show them how to make natural masks, toners and exfoliants. A lot of our tiddas couldn't afford Estée Lauder, Jurlique and Pond's. Milk, bread and the light bill took precedence. Anyways, going au naturel meant you could eat the ingredients. Who said skincare couldn't be fun and delicious?

Majal had us booked, busy and highly favoured. Together Mum and I did formals, debutante balls, wedding parties, girls' nights out and photoshoots. There was not a skin tone, blemish or scar my mum could not disguise or match. Many of the tears I shed came from Mum's transformations on women who harboured violent or troubling scars. I remember a young sista came into the salon for a makeover. She had a knife slash across the side of her face. In little over an hour, Mum concealed the scar. Raising the handheld mirror, it reflected her new face – her past erased. To me, this signified the meaning of purpose: the ability to take away one's burden long enough for one to see their light. A gift my mother didn't squander. She taught me the most significant impact you can make is where you are invested. Not financially, but where your time, energy and heart are present.

And with that, Majal was on the move. Commissioned by the Home and Community Care program, this deadly duo dropped in to show love to the Elders and our mob with disabilities who suffered from arthritis, stiffness, back pain and loneliness. Sadly, many of the residents didn't have family and friends to visit or yarn to them. So, we'd bring out our range of oil blends. 'That smells good,' they'd say.

We'd start by bathing their hands in our potion to eliminate the dryness and bring back suppleness, kneading into the spots where it hurt the most. When one chapter of their story ended, we'd move on to another ailment and let belly laughs eliminate the stale residue from their body. Three deep breaths in, and three deep breaths out. No need to hold on to that anymore, Aunt.

Now, sitting upright with a sparkle in their eyes. Sometimes you need a bit of flint to spark a flame. And a reminder, as long as you have breath in your body – you are still here.

Svet

Majal was a hidden gem you stumbled across; tucked away in the cinema arcade, many pedestrians stopped outside the shopfront wondering who we were. Some ducked in out of curiosity. I often flashed a courteous smile to a passer-by staring into the salon.

Our neighbours were a movie memorabilia shop, cafe and clothing boutique – where I bought my 14th birthday present: overall black shorts with a pin-on skort. That little outfit was so damn cute!

Every day after school, I'd ride my bike to the shop to assist Mum with her evening clients. Sliding the glass door open, aromatherapy greeted me in the most glorious fashion: melting away all the troubles of the day. Mum would either be with a client or at the back.

'Is that you, Sash?' she'd call.

Mum's own artwork hung on the feature wall at reception like a mini exhibition. Not only was Mum a beautician and artist, she added interior decorator to her resume. She jazzed up the salon with a wicker lounge, pink clay walls, splashes of Mediterranean blues and Chinese antique vases. Trust me, sensory overload guaranteed. Bella lipsticks of rouge, sienna, crème d'nude lined our walls. Eye shadows: sands of the Sahara Desert to dust storms of the Outback. Skincare, candy-coloured nail polishes and acrylic nail art custom-designed by Mum. Also on display was an assortment of magazines: *Women's Weekly*, *New Idea* and *Ebony*.

Regardless of the dramas going on at home and school, Majal was my refuge. When business was slow, we would pamper each other with facials, massages and manicures. As much as I hated how I looked, quality time with Mum overrode the insecurities that plagued me. Majal is where I could be beautiful even if the outside world thought otherwise.

To Mum, presentation was vital: as the brand ambassador, how I carried myself reflected on the business. Sit up straight, no slouching and greet customers with a smile. Yes, Mum, I know. When Mum first put me on as the receptionist I was petrified. It's the last thing a shy kid wants to do. But after a while it grew on me. No day was the same; nor were any of our clients.

If it weren't for Majal I wouldn't have met Svet – the Nordic beauty from Sweden. A kind soul, Svet stumbled on her English. I didn't mind being her dictionary and thesaurus. Mid-sentence, she'd pause – searching for the right word. Like any patient tutor, I'd give her a chance to figure it out on her own before she gave me the cue for a lifeline.

I remember when Svet first waltzed into the shop; 6'4" (1.93 m) and slender, with broad shoulders, kitted out in activewear. And the longest vanilla blonde hair I'd ever seen. Svet immediately gravitated to Mum's artwork hanging behind me. 'What is this?' I liked how Svet got straight to the point.

'It's called Brolga; in our language, we call it Guru.' I picked up the storybook for Mum's paintings. 'Would you like to read the story?'

'Please, can you read it?' Svet asked, convinced it would sound better if I read it.

I obliged.

Brolga was a beautiful young girl who loved to dance. It was taboo for women to dance in the old days because only men had this special honour. Brolga did not mean to break the rules, but her desire to dance overcame her body and Brolga did the unthinkable. When the men started dancing she joined them, making her people very angry.

Brolga's grace when she danced was so remarkable, she eventually won the hearts of her people. Word spread fast of Brolga's talent, and many travelled far and wide to see her dance. Brolga's beauty also attracted the affections of many men who wanted to marry her. But Brolga wasn't interested in marriage, for dancing was her one true love. Her obsession for dance compelled her to practise every day – creating new moves to perform. Many men respected her passion for dance except one selfish man who pursued her relentlessly.

Concerned for Brolga's safety, her people told her to stay close by so they could protect her from harm. Brolga obeyed her people, but while practising, she strayed too far from camp and the evil man captured her.

The evil man demanded Brolga marry him. No matter how hard he pressured her, Brolga refused, which infuriated him; if he couldn't have her, no-one would. Using his magic, he put Brolga to sleep. When Brolga awoke, she was no longer a girl. Looking down at her body, she no longer had hands. Instead, she had wings – her legs that of a bird. Although Brolga was sad and thought she wouldn't dance again, it didn't crush her spirit. Because Brolga's love for dance was undeniable, she mustered up the courage to at least try. Joy overwhelmed her when Brolga discovered she could still dance.

For days her people searched for her until one day Brolga spotted them across the plains. Excited, Brolga raced towards them. But she was now a bird, and her people didn't recognise her. Desperate to get their attention Brolga began to dance elegantly as only she could. It was only then her people knew the bird dancing before them was Brolga. From that day on, her people vowed to guard her against evil.

And that is how Brolga, the beautiful young girl, became a bird.

Svet smiled as I finished the story. 'Ahhh, lovely. Your culture is so beautiful ... Is this a salon?'

'Yes, it is.' I handed the Nordic beauty a pamphlet.

Svet sat on the white wicker lounge sifting through the menu. 'Is it okay if I take this?'

'Yes, of course,' I said.

I watched Svet get up, her French braid cascading down her back. She paused at the Bella eyeshadows, testing a shade on her wrist, before moving on to Mum's homemade crème, blending a dab of it into the bronzer she had applied. Sniffing her hand, she inhaled the frangipani and ylang ylang-scented pomade, letting the aroma work its magic.

Calmly, Svet announced, 'I'll be back.' Before she turned to leave, Svet pointed to another painting. 'Can you tell me that story when I come back?'

I turned to see which one she was referring to. 'Ahhh, Majal. Yes, I will.'

As promised, Svet returned one week later. Her smile poured down on me like sun rays. Svet cut to the chase. 'Remember the story?'

'Oh, yes. The story of Majal.' I grabbed Mum's storybook.

Then it dawned on me that I should show Svet what Majal, bush medicine, was. I motioned for her to follow me outside, where we could look closely at the Majal logo Mum had designed.

'Majal means cockyapple,' I explained, pointing to the white flower with brushlike bristles spraying from its red fruit. Svet admired the artwork then shifted her gaze to the sign overhanging our front door, where the letters of Majal were made with boomerangs. Uncle Ernie had given Mum the Jirrbal language to name her shop.

Back inside, we seated ourselves comfortably and I continued.

Majal is mirrijin (medicine) for our people. The leaves and bark are boiled to treat headaches and skin disorders. We use the leaves to leech out venom from a snake or spider bite. Majal has its own poison, which we use to catch fish. We do this by crushing the bark and placing it in the waterhole. Majal's poison draws the oxygen from the water, stunning the fish to the water's surface. Majal is also our calendar. When she blossoms, she's letting us know we can fish for gundal (barramundi), and that the bungurru (turtle) is ready to eat.

Svet simmered on the story before hitting me with a question I couldn't answer: 'Why Australians don't like the Aboriginals?' She wasn't the only one who wanted to know.

A lot had been going on in the previous few years. The 1992 Mabo decision had abolished the lie of terra nullius and reasserted the truth: Indigenous peoples had never ceded sovereignty. Eddie

Koiki Mabo, Reverend David Passi, Sam Passi, James Rice and Celuia Mapo Salee and their lawyers sought the recognition of their traditional rights to Country in the High Court of Australia and won land rights, which we now know as Native Title.

Soon after, though only 14, I'd felt the ripple effects of fear induced by the government; it didn't bode well for us. The Australian public was left asking: What does this mean? Anger swept across the nation, and the attitude of many pastoralists was: I'm not giving my land back to the Blaks. Even local white folks who grew up with us started to change for the worse.

And then controversy broke out on the athletics track when Cathy Freeman carried both the Aboriginal and Australian flags during her victory laps when she won gold for the 200- and 400-metre sprints at the 1994 Commonwealth Games. Her crime: Blak Girl Joy demonstrated on an international stage.

Weird as it sounds, it was nice to have a human interaction with the whitest person I'd encountered, Svet. For once, not paranoid she might judge my people or me. If anything, she had more compassion than many of the locals had for us before the Mabo case left a bitter taste in their mouths.

And that's why I appreciated Majal being situated in the city. Our establishment was often a tourist's first encounter with Aboriginal people – no misconceptions, middle-man, exploitation or appropriation. We weren't the local art galleries selling mob's art – staffed and owned by people who didn't look like us. Or an Aboriginal tour you could jet off to experience for the day – now that was a contentious issue in the community. Some mob were wild: you make us shame dancing up for them whitefellas. Others saw the educational and economic advantages tourism brought to our communities – a positive step forward in bringing us together regardless of who you were.

Mum stayed neutral when it came to Blakfella politics. As a teenager, I still hadn't formed my own opinion. So, I looked to Mum for guidance. Her politics were simple – treat people how you want to be treated. And none of that shame business. She wasn't raising no shrinking violets. Something Grandad passed down to her.

Mum told me she appointed me as receptionist to give me life skills: dealing with people. Struggling with my identity, Majal grounded me in unencumbered conversations and perspectives outside a small town.

And it gave our clients like Svet a chance to rebuild her network as she made Australia her home. A retired volleyball player – she was escaping a gruelling sports career. I sensed Svet wanted to take control over her life in a way she couldn't before. Funny how a person can tell you their story without you even asking.

Svet reached for her credit card to pay her bill on that second visit, and a photo she had tucked away fell out. When I picked it up and handed it to her, she smiled at me weakly.

'My ex-husband,' she whispered sombrely.

Whether we admit it or not, beauty is often a decoy. Some of us really just want to connect.

Jade

Majal brought women from all walks of life through our door. Beauty came in all shapes, nationalities, faiths and personalities.

After a few years, I'd become good at identifying accents. When internationals enquired about our services, I'd try to guess their native tongue. It was cool going through the guestbook seeing where our clients hailed from. We had British, Norwegian and French backpackers, Susan from City Council, Hilda from the Aboriginal Co-op, Delilah whose outfits pledged spontaneity. And ethereal Jade.

Mum handled the high-profile clients – they preferred consultations with someone experienced – while I worked with younger women, which was more fun and authentic for me. My clients suffered from common ailments like acne or dry to oily skin. I knew the skincare routines firsthand and relayed the techniques I found helpful, offering a service our customers could trust.

I guess you can say Jade was the first girl at the salon I found heavenly. I adored Svet, but she was a woman. I could never match her Scandinavian charm, whereas Jade was close to my age. And we were close on the colour spectrum. Jade had bundles of long jet-black hair that fell to her waist. When she moved, it was as if she glided on air. Nothing about her was abrasive, just gentle.

Jade's look consisted of golf shorts teamed with variations of a double-knit sand top; it laid beautifully on her olive skin. How she pulled that fabric off in the FNQ heat, I will never know. She had a thin gold necklace with a teardrop pearl which she wore religiously. Along with natural French-tip nails.

Jade's mother would always come to collect her. She was a tiny Filipina woman who carried a Rose Royce 'Love Don't Live Here Anymore' pang in her heart. I hoped Jade wouldn't suffer that type of affliction.

As a little girl, unconsciously, I'd started to mood-board my definition of femininity. Hands down, Mum was at the centre, but Jade had made it on my board. Every few weeks, Jade would pop into our nail station. I would watch her inconspicuously as she perused the nail polishes. I tried to pick which one she'd choose: Hmmm, today feels like Almond Delight. I'd observed Jade enough to know she stuck to natural tones – she was probably an earth sign, like Virgo or Taurus.

This day, Jade hovered over a fire engine red that Ms G. would sport on her Flo Jo acrylics.

Ms G. was one of Mum's clients — think Sandra Clark from *227*. You could rely on her to come into the salon drippin swagu. I liked Ms G.: she said what she wanted to say – however she wanted to say it. Often, she had me blushing; I can tell you that. But she meant well: not a malicious bone in her body – just a love of life and anyone around her. Sometimes her boisterous nature echoed to the back of the salon. Once, when I was doing a client's facial, I became incredibly embarrassed because the relaxing wooden flutes couldn't drown out Ms G. Luckily, whatever Ms G. was preaching that day tickled my client so much she giggled to herself, which eased my tension. I carried on exfoliating while my client and I listened to Ms G.'s testimony.

Just as I'd predicted, Jade passed me Almond Delight. Next, I got her to soak her hands in the warm water sprinkled with chamomile flowers and rosemary oil. Then I dried them off to massage Jurlique rose hand cream into them. Jade's hands were soft, like they were protected by princess gloves – the ones you take off before high tea. I surmised she didn't have chores. If she did, it was probably loading the dishwasher. Not pulling up bindi weeds and guinea grass like I did.

I grabbed the white buffing block and began grooming Jade's nails. There was something cathartic about sanding away the built-up muck ready to embrace a new coat of arms. Nails are considered prime real estate to show up and show out. You've seen how women flaunt their nails: pointing dramatically at menus, directing traffic, nails tap-dancing on keyboards: I call it the Diva power trip. Gossip sounded juicier when a fresh pair of acrylics told the story. Nails is a ministry unto itself. This is why tweens beg to wear nail polish – they've seen how the aunties act when they come home from the nail salon.

As I prepped Jade's nail beds, she looked at me momentarily and then stared out the window. At times I'd get self-conscious about my hairy monkey arms alongside Jade's tanned, hairless skin.

'Which school do you go to?' she asked.

'Trinity Bay,' I replied. 'You?'

'Smithfield.'

I never saw Jade in uniform. I assumed she went to a private school, not public. I began to picture her at school. I imagined she'd belong to the *Clueless* clique, with an urge to break free from the shallow fuckery. But she was all class like Posh Spice – they both had similar features. Victoria Beckham will forever be my favourite Spice Girl. The little Gucci dress? Or the little Gucci dress?

Shortly after this, Mum did a workshop with Smithfield High students where Jade was one of the participants. Mum created a framed series of before and after make-up shots which later hung in the shop window, becoming a great promotional tool.

While I was wiping away the unrelenting streaks from the front glass windows – one of my jobs at the salon – my mate and his friends passed by, no doubt on their way to play Raiden at the arcade.

'Oi, do you know her?' he asked, pointing to Jade's image.

'Who? Jade. Sort of. Why?'

Busting out in a fit of laughter, he said, 'Yo, she's a slut.'

Anger rose inside me. 'Who told you that?'

'Everybody knows.'

I despised him for calling her that. There was nothing I could do but try and wipe away the filth on Jade's name. I didn't look at her any different. I just felt horrible for her because being a slut was far worse than being a bitch.

At 14, that's the last thing my friends and I wanted to be labelled as. We had already been indoctrinated into the culture of slut-shaming, which is ironic because if we didn't have so-called sluts nobody would get laid outside of commitment.

But even if you were virginal, all it took was a lie to ruin your reputation. Or, as I would find out, someone's perception of reality.

Dad had dropped by the salon one evening to pick me and Mum up. I waited on the bench outside the shop. Some of my mates I played basketball with at school came through.

'Ey, which way? What you doin'?'

'Nothing. 'Bout to cruise home.'

'Ey, true. You not stayin' in town?'

'Nah.'

It was Thursday, late-night shopping, and everybody hung out except me. Working at the shop meant I missed out socially.

Shooting the shit with my brotha boys, we were loud and obnoxious as teenagers are. I happened to catch my father's eye, and he was not impressed. At first, I thought it might have been too much Black Boy Joy on display. Our salon was situated around white businesses. And I knew the rules when it came to conducting myself in predominately white spaces – tone down your voice, expressions and music. Use proper English. Please, thank you and be on your best behaviour – the way you act reflects on all of us.

Surprisingly, it wasn't Black Boy Joy that had my dad bothered.

'Who are those boys?' he asked once they left.

'They're my friends from school.'

'You shouldn't be hanging around them boys like that.'

'Like what?' I honestly didn't know what Dad was getting at.

'It doesn't look good, a girl hanging with a bunch of boys on her own.'

Really? I'm right in front of the shop, not hidden in some alleyway, I thought. This is ridiculous. 'But I know them; they're my friends.'

My dad gave me a disapproving look, like I was playing games with him.

That's when it hit me: my father thinks I'm a slut. And that was the moment I wanted to unstrap my bra and burn it on site. It didn't matter if you were a classic beauty who didn't put a foot out of place. Or an insecure tomboy who happened to work in a beauty salon – you no longer belonged to yourself. What other people thought of you was far more damaging than who you really were.

I never got around to burning my bra. Instead, I bought Lil' Kim's debut album *Hard Core* two years later.

7

Dear Black Men

Now, I can only speak for myself. When it comes to any issues with the mob, I handle them privately. I'm from the 'don't be airing your dirty laundry' generation. As a Blak woman, I will never throw my people under the bus, particularly our Black men. But it must be said: Dear Black men, some of y'all have a lot of explaining to do. It seems some of you don't know how to make deadly choices. And others are quick to defend a Kardashian's honour then drag Blak women for filth. Disrespecting Blak women on prime time for clout and coconut juice – brothas, that ain't it. Yes, I know: not *all* Black men.

For the brothas who suffer from amnesia, let me remind you, it's Black women who make this world turn. In the words of Malcolm X but with two small insertions: 'The most disrespected woman in [Australia] is the [Blak] woman.'

Times are changing, and as the #MeToo movement has shown us, silence serves no-one. Speaking our truth does. If we speak up with love and intention, we have a lot to gain as Black women. It never was and never will be okay for Black men to slight Black women and have the audacity to think we will continually hold you down regardless of your transgressions. There are consequences, baby; we carry hot sauce in our bag.

As a Black woman, I am still trying to find the right balance on maintaining self-respect and accountability from others in my community when the colonial watchmen demonise our people for their self-hate and trauma-induced behaviour. I am walking my journey with compassion in order to understand the complexities of breaking generational curses while constructing borders that determine what I will and will not tolerate. It's hard. Black women, be kind to yourself in this process. Honouring your divinity and creating change in your community is a revolutionary act. You should be proud of that.

Not only does our spirit manoeuvre turbulent seas, but we also possess the most magnificent creation known to this Earth – our bodies. They are a vessel of inception, a beacon of inspiration. But our bodies have also been a battlefield, exploited and defiled. In this knowing of the trauma I carry, in my body, there is this constant longing in me to see its beauty glorified.

The art I was taught as a child, the art hanging in museums, the art widely appreciated, didn't include women who looked like me. The muses and masterpieces carved from marble and painted on canvases didn't worship Blak women like me who wanted to be and love fine art.

So, when my grand vision – to see Blak women's majestic beauty celebrated – collided with another Blakfella, it felt cosmic.

I'd spotted Dean's work in a sistagal's portfolio and some independent projects in the community, I didn't know any Blakfella photographers who had an eye for the style I liked. I loved how Dean's portraits made a stranger feel like a kindred spirit. The faces in his work seemed like lost souls whose vacancy reminded me of my own. I was more than eager to work with him.

When I called Dean to see if he'd be interested in collaborating with me, we instantly hit it off. It wasn't long before I was scouting locations or randomly coming across them in my travels. The excitement of it all. 'Do you see that?' I'd ask Dean.

Dean would rattle away a tornado of ideas, and away we went for the love of art. We shot sunrise to sunset, letting the flash own the night once the world faded to black. Dean tempered the mood with all those gadgets photographers carry with them. I'd ask questions about what such and such does, only to forget his answer soon afterwards.

The age-old cliché of the 'starving artist' finally made sense; making art is exhilarating. But all that fou fou, as Dad put it, wasn't paying the bills. Yes, photography is a gateway between you and me, a saving grace in a world marred by beauty and chaos. But for now, I needed a second job to make ends meet. I remember crying in the lunchroom at work out of frustration. I sucked at telesales and I was tired and penniless.

'Sis, I'm living off nuts and berries!'

My tidda bust out laughing.

'Bitch, it's not funny,' I moaned.

'I know, sis. I'm sorry … your face.'

She was right. I can be extremely animated when in distress. Ughhh! Just let me be great! All I wanted was to be able to pay my rent and breathe – not just air, but breathe life into something I loved and get paid for it.

So, when Dean and I had another cosmic epiphany to create a new series of work, it was my escape from the financial stress. We collaborated from the first creative ideation stage.

The concept was based on the beauty of an Aboriginal woman: how she is Mother Earth, imprinted throughout this Country – every blade of spinifex grass, squiggly gum to the scorched red dust. Her limbs branches; her legs rivers; her hands yam roots; her face dawn. My body was the canvas.

Dean presented the finished pieces to respected Elder Aunty Marlene, who blessed us with her language to title the photographic series that became an exhibition at her studio.

My first exhibition! I couldn't have been prouder: this was an All Blak affair: Blak photographer, model, Elder and entrepreneur.

Now, what to wear for the opening night? I did what broke girls do: bought a fab new Tokito halter-neck dress and returned it the next day. It helps when it's polyester. Liquid soap and a bit of warm water always does the trick, especially on the funky parts.

And no launch would be complete without my biggest cheerleader, my dad, with his expensive camera and tripod, rocking his gold chain, black suit, looking fresh to death. I love when my dad comes to my events. We like to work the room together like we're new money.

Clink, clink, clink. Aunty Marlene announced that the man of the hour was ready to open the exhibition. You could see the pride in Dean's eyes. We did it!

I let the champagne bubbles light me up like a chandelier as Dean charmed the audience with his words on how the exhibition came to be. But that light feeling didn't last long.

'I want to thank my wife, Sasha,' Dean said.

Excuse me?

Dean's wife, Bianca, was standing next to me. Remember the elevator incident when Solange tore into Jay-Z? Well, I was Beyoncé walking out calm as a cucumber with my 'nothing just happened' smile on.

Dean caught himself. 'I mean Bianca; my wife, Bianca.'

Dean's speech turned into waah, waah, waah after that. I stood still as a statue. Bianca and I had to play it off as dignified women do in sticky situations like this.

My sistagal, the journalist covering the event, gave me the side-eye: 'Sis, what's that about?'

I couldn't run from the truth even if I tried. Freudian slip much? I was just as discombobulated as she was. Fark, my dad is here, I thought. God only knows what he's thinking.

I wasn't going to let this faux pas break my stride. These photographs and the message behind them were sacred to me. I celebrated my body. I celebrated the woman who brought me into this world, the first women to be photographed – who were art but not captured as such. I offered my body as a declaration: shame doesn't live here anymore.

Artists and the faithful recipients that appreciate their gifts know the magic it contains. How can a movie, regardless of how many times you've seen it, render you to tears? How can a song transport you back to a time when you loved them, and they loved you? Heart and soul are poured into scripts, scenes and melodies that whisper melancholy in your ears.

Creative synergy is not enough. It has to be grounded in trust for it to take flight. I thought I had that with Dean. Not once did he trigger my spidey senses or leave me with doubts for concern. But in the end, the buck stops with me. I was grown but credulous. Verbal agreements mean nothing when money talks.

If someone asked me what advice I'd give my younger self: learn the power of the coin and contract, and sit with your Old People. I am thankful to Aunty Marlene for inviting me to have a drink with her one evening at the studio. Let's just say Aunty Marlene knew how to deliver truth bombs over a silky merlot.

Dean had the entire exhibition up for sale and had landed a significant sponsorship with an imaging brand. Dean hadn't mentioned any of this. And here I was feeling broke, busted and disgusted.

Of course, I picked up the phone and asked Dean what, pray tell, was going on. And that's when I learnt the harsh lesson of copyright. Regardless of whether you're in the photo, the copyright lies with the photographer unless an agreement stipulates special terms.

People show you who they are when you stop beating to their drum. Dean went from an endearing friend to acting brand new. He slapped me with, 'It is what it is.'

So, I took a page from *The Art of War* by Sun Tzu. I played the ordeal off and kindly asked Dean for high-resolution copies of our work for my portfolio. I hated walking into his two-storey house he'd just financed, appeasing him to get what I needed. The encounter was fake and I wanted to wash the bullshit off once I got home. But first, I needed to check the disc. I slipped the CD into the drive and clicked open the folder. There was only a quarter of the images – all were at low resolution – on the disc. When I tell you I was *livid*, volcanic Mount Yasur was timid compared to me. I sat in silence until the storm settled.

I called Aunty Marlene and asked if I could drop by the studio. She told me Dean had called her. Oh, I bet he did. On arrival, Aunty Marlene offered me wine. I politely declined: I was on a mission. Aunty Marlene led me upstairs; she knew what I'd come for. I did a 360 and contemplated which one I loved the best. There I was, the bare sheen of my body elongated as I stared over my shoulder: a mountain lit by a trail of fire. I pulled out a thick throw blanket from my bag and laid it on the floor. I unhooked myself off the wall, positioned myself squarely onto the veil and swaddled my frame. I met Aunty Marlene downstairs, and she called me a cab.

The next day, my phone blew up!

Revenge is a dish best served cold. Listening to Dean lose his shit via voice message was half the fun. Dean, you are the weakest link. Goodbye.

Dean's messages escalated from angry to threatening to call the police on me for stolen property. I was still a goody-two-shoes back then, so Dean's intimidation had me shook.

Who do you call in a crisis like this?

Daddy dearest.

I explained the entire fiasco to him. I hated the disappointment in his voice. 'Sash, how did you let this happen?'

I wasn't even embarrassed I'd got myself in this predicament. It was Dad's 'You're smarter than this' that hurt me more.

He also brought up the incident at the launch. 'Is there anything else I need to know?'

'No, Dad! Nothing is going on between me and Dean.'

'All right, now.' My father's go-to words when he means there'd better not be any surprises.

Just so you know, my dad is the negotiator you send in to get results. He's the 100 per cent satisfaction guaranteed or your money back – all parties are coming out shaking hands. He's a magician like that.

This time, Dad was going in to bat on my behalf. Dad called the imaging company that was Dean's new sponsor. Needless to say, they dropped Dean like hot potatoes.

I replayed Dean's distraught message for Dad and we bust out laughing. 'Oh, he *mad mad*!' It didn't erase what happened, but it was a lesson learnt.

As Blak women, I'm sure we can remember an experience that taught us to be vigilant. I don't know why Dean – knowing I was struggling – didn't break a young sista off with some chump change. Even if it were a sitting fee or 10 per cent of the profits, it would have helped immensely. The gem in this lesson is, when you know your worth, the price goes up.

Dear Black men,

I'm worth more than being a shoulder to cry on. An image you control. Something you possess. The sista that gasses you up so you can feel like a king in ivory towers. Your worth doesn't appreciate when you deceive the ones that love you the most.

I love you. Do better.

These days, I am happy to see Black artists banding together, sharing knowledge and opportunities so we are protected and can prosper together.

Oh, younger self, it's me again: hang around mob like this. And stay away from those who want to be the only Black person in the village.

8

Napranum

Word of Mum's beauty talents spread like wildfire from Cairns up to Cape York. Mum was requested to do a youth workshop in Napranum and we'd be travelling via Cessna plane. The flight up was so choppy, all I could think about was not going out like La Bamba. Give me a Boeing 747, please and thank you. I'd rather die with 40+ passengers: morbid, I know.

I may be grown, but I still get shame whenever I rock up to new communities. Especially when the local mob break their necks to see who dat der? I'm just lucky it wasn't a Murri Carnival!

Finding the local community centre was easy: we just followed the sound of Blak kids singing out top note. I looked around to see who was running the show. I eventually spotted a white youth worker oblivious to the chaos and Mum went to talk while I stayed put outside. I must have stood out like a sore thumb because the most precocious of the kids broke away on her bike to come find out who I was.

'Where you from?' she asked.

Her inquisitiveness startled me. 'I'm from Cairns,' I replied.

She circled me several times on her rusty BMX, sussing me out. Little Miss flashed me a cheeky grin and rode away, satisfied with her interrogation.

In the distance, Mum appeared from the office, tapping her wrist; she motioned we had to G-O before the local shops closed. Lucky we left when we did because the shops were shutting down in the next 20 minutes.

First stop, camera shop. I handed the clerk my roll of film, itching to get snaps developed from my boyfriend's Year 12 formal. When she rang up the price, I thought she was taking me for a ride. Little did I know remote communities paid two to four times the price for essential items than we did in cities.

And not a damn thing has changed. Cut to today, and the shelf price for baby formula is $50; eight-pack cotton nappies, $62; body lotion, $35; a pack of pork chops, $82. And forget about fresh fruit and vegetables – it's rotten at best. Oh, that's right. Apparently, Blak people get government hand-outs, free cars, houses and education.

I walked out of the shop staggered by the highway robbery.

Driving down a thin strip of asphalt, the skyline was awash with puffs of burnt orange clouds, a view too spectacular to waste. Arriving at our accommodation, we sat on the verandah, watching sunset meet dusk. Mum and I let the balmy breeze kiss our skin before we headed in for the night.

You know what they say: early bird gets the worm, and a big feed. Egg toast, Vegemite faces and Milo moustaches littered the stadium. The youth breakfast club made sure little tummies were filled, because we needed the kids' full attention.

Standing by our workshop station, Mum and I waited for our students to join us. Hmm, who could I choose for the icebreaker? Scanning the jarjums, I spotted my BMX bandit from yesterday. Catching her gaze, I asked if she wanted to be my guinea pig. She nodded and gave her mischievous grin.

I patted the massage table. I told her to jump up and lie down on her back. Grabbing her wispy hair, I tied it up and secured her cute face in a headband. Mum poured measured amounts of boiled and cold water into the hand basin, carefully dropping in some lavender oil. Little Miss fidgeted on the bed, her wide eyes surveying what would happen next. Plunging the hand towel into the basin, I let it swallow the water. Squeezing it out, I told Little Miss to close her eyes and began fanning the pleasing aroma from the hot towel above her and then swaddled her face. Little Miss had completely surrendered. By now, you could hear a pin drop in the room. Mum poured a small circle of her secret potion into my malas (hands). I rubbed them together and applied it in one clean sweep onto bubba's face.

In soft, circular upward motions, I soothed her facial muscles into relax mode. In five minutes flat, Little Miss was out like a light. A loose snore escaped her, and the whole group erupted in laughter. Despite the disruption, sleepyhead remained stiff as a board. So we let her get her Zzzs, placing a throw blanket over her for comfort.

Confident we had a captive audience, we got our mini troupers to partner up to do yidil (massage) on each other. Each pair concocted a secret potion from essential oils, based on how they wanted to feel. Did you want to feel happy, relaxed or focused? Some answered in shy whispers to a Tigger-style bounce: 'I want that one!' Pointing to the bottle.

I started a pair off with a demonstration to get all the teams ready. Once everyone was all systems go, Mum and I glided past to praise our pupils. 'Good job, nice and soft.'

Little Miss wasn't the only one knocked out. In the end, we had a congregation of glistening cherubs.

Once we finished, we ushered the jingins to get a feed. Some raced back to us to hand back their oils. I rubbed their tiny backs and said, 'No, bub, that's for you to take home.' Their astonished smiles and sweet thank-yous melted me.

I could see the youth coordinator chatting away to Mum near the canteen. Buggered, I grabbed a handful of sandwiches and found a vacant spot to rest. Believe me when I say I am the Pied Piper when it comes to kids. Some of the girls from the session headed my way, Little Miss leading the pack. Eating their lunch, they formed a ring around me. One hovered behind me, and I felt a gentle tug on my loose curls. I turned around and matched her grin. She slid on the bench beside me, swinging her feet back and forth. She stared up at me. Holding my gaze, she softly announced, 'You're gidar.' She actually said 'pretty', but my ears heard gidar. Her mundu (spirit) felt my gidar, and I felt hers.

Beauty rule number three: gigorou is mundu. Mundu speaks in an unspoken guwal (language). My mother showed me malas are mirrijin. Yidil is mirrijin. Majal is mirrijin.

Our trip to Napranum would be our last community workshop. When Mum told me she was closing the salon, I thought she meant for the holidays.

'No, we can't afford to stay here anymore,' she said.

Majal was my home. The place I did homework: hopped under the steamer and played relaxing flute music when I had 99 problems. Where I painted my nails to give me a pep in my step. It's the place where I derived my self-esteem. Where beauty was more than how you looked on the outside but how your light gave others permission to shine. It was my induction into Blak excellence.

So, it was tough accepting this was the end of an era, as short-lived as it was. Even more heart-wrenching was pulling down Mum's artwork, aromatherapy posters and nail station. Mum and I didn't speak about how we felt – like when my parents separated.

And like before, I filed Majal away in my scrapbook of failures along with the other perceived deficiencies I marked against my name.

I'd find out later that limited capital, marketing and foot traffic had contributed to Majal's demise.

I wish Majal had remained around a little longer; perhaps I might have discovered my worth sooner. Instead of seeking validation from dusty ole boys with dirty fingernails who couldn't spell Mississippi if their life depended on it, Majal gave me purpose, a crown on my head. Without the crown, I no longer walked in rooms poised; instead, apprehensive.

Closing the sliding door for the last time, I let all the laughter and memories cling to the pink clay walls and peered through the glass I'd made sparkle. No more bike rides into the city or waking up early Saturday morning to do a shift at the shop.

In the weeks to come, it hurt walking past the empty salon to the cinemas. I'd try to avoid that route altogether. I hated when my friends asked me ad nauseam, 'What happened to the shop?'

All was not lost. My mother had created a name for herself, and her former clients sought her out. That's how the granny flat downstairs became Mum's home-based salon. I'd peep out my bedroom window to see who was rocking up for a treatment. Majal version 2.0 restored the essence of the salon we missed dearly. I loved this for Mum as I watched her passion for beauty ignite inside her as it always did.

Now that Mum was going solo with Majal, I was free to find my own place in the world.

9

Jinnali

Our mob love a good doris in the *Koori Mail*. It's where Mum stumbled across a post from Jinnali Productions, a casting seeking models to be featured in Australia's first Indigenous women's calendar. Up until that point, my modelling career was at a standstill.

I had dropped out of high school two years prior and moved in with my boyfriend. He was three years older. I tried to finish Year 12, but he made it incredibly hard for me. Every morning he'd pick a fight before I left for school. In the end, coming home to my possessions smashed all over the floor and trying to hide my bruises from classmates and teachers was impossible. I had to let go of my dream of going to university. When I did manage to leave the relationship after multiple attempts, I moved back in with mum. I landed a job at the casino but hated it. So, it was a no-brainer when Mum encouraged me to apply for the

Jinnali casting. She thought it would boost my self-esteem after everything I'd been through.

The application asked candidates to supply head, full-body and profile shots. And once again, our living room became a DIY studio to capture the images. I seriously don't know how we waited for negatives to develop back then; even worse if you were Blinky Bill.

Satisfied with our final selection, I mailed off my submission and tried not to give it much thought. In a little over two weeks, the verdict was in. I had made the cut – finally, a breakthrough.

Jinnali Productions was based in Meanjin. The crew had scheduled my shots to be taken on Mulgumpin. This was my first domestic flight outside of Gimuy. Yes, I packed like I was leaving the country.

Donna and Lena, the brains behind Jinnali, met me at the airport. Donna oozed confidence and had a mystique about her. Lena was straight up bubbly and had the gift of the gab, squelching my initial unease. We jumped in Donna's Corolla and sped down the highway, heading downtown. I freaked. The tallest building I'd seen was the Cairns Hilton. Here was a full-fledged CBD. The ladies gave me a tour of Brizzy before dropping into their friend's stylish apartment. Everybody was older and more sophisticated. Content to be a fly on the wall, I took notes. Later that evening, I settled into my accommodation for an early night, the shoot was tomorrow, and I needed to get some beauty sleep.

The next morning, I met the dynamic duo to catch the ferry over to Mulgumpin. Slicing the waves, our ferry delivered us to blinding white sand. The charming heat started to pinch as we trekked across the beach. Donna introduced me to her cousin Betina, the photographer, and her friend Dave, Betina's assistant.

'Have you got your bikinis on underneath?' Donna asked.

I turned to Donna and stared blankly. 'No, I don't have them with me.' God, I felt so embarrassed. I left my Roxy bikinis back at the hotel. Seriously, Sasha, you had one job.

I thank Donna for sparing me a lecture. I was already ripping myself to shreds.

'What type of bra and panties do you have on?'

'A black strapless bra and black undies,' I replied, puzzled.

'Fine, we'll shoot you in that.' Not giving it a second thought, Donna was already on to the next task. By now, I was having a mini meltdown.

'I can't. Everyone's going to know I'm not in bikinis!'

By the grace of God, Donna rummaged in her bag and pulled out a slim see-through dress. I slipped on the dress, which literally saved my ass, behind the bushes.

Tense AF, my nerves were shot. Donna sploshed over to me and grabbed my hands.

'Close your eyes and feel the water. Let yourself sink into the sand. Take a few breaths and just relax.'

Everything went dark. I inhaled the sea breeze, letting the salt melt my anxiety as the waves washed it away. I opened my eyes.

'You feel better?'

'Yes.'

'Okay, let's do this.' Donna rallied up Betina and Dave.

Dave cracked out the reflector and bounced a force field of light into my face. The sunlight brought out the best in me; I smiled bright like its rays. The crystal waters splashing upon my skin calmed me. I'd been so stressed, I failed to appreciate we were on Quandamooka Country.

When you stop and reset, Country gives you what you need. The morning fiasco was now a distant memory. What you focus on becomes your reality. A moment of gratitude shifts the tides.

That's what Country does for me. It reminds me of my gigorou. Country offers what a studio can't: a connection to an ancestral bloodline. How can you not feel gigorou when all Country requires of you is to be YOU – nothing more, nothing less?

Shortly after my calendar shoot, the buzz Jinnali generated was contagious. Media outlets were vying for the latest scoop. Headlines such as 'Black with a vengeance' and 'Black Aussie models show 'em' caused a stir for all the right reasons. Here were two Blak female entrepreneurs challenging stereotypes and showcasing Indigenous women's beauty, which was hardly ever celebrated in the mainstream.

Some of the press coverage made me hurl. Opening lines like 'Drunk, stoned and on walkabout? Indigenous model agency helps the Dreaming come true and Aborigines take on whites in glamour stakes.' Not only was this revolting and irresponsible, but it also put us at the centre of race-baiting, undermining the positive impact Jinnali achieved in a short amount of time. Within four months, Donna and Lena booked nearly all their models for consecutive jobs: unheard of, considering most were first-time models, and tokenism was, and still is, rife in the industry.

When Jinnali snagged a spread in *FHM* men's magazine, they single-handedly pushed the blonde-haired blue-eyed bombshell to the left. The editorial, titled 'Dream Team, riding off Sydney's 2000 Olympics hype', hit newsstands in August before the big event.

Was I happy for my sistas? Yes! Jealous? Yes! Colourism had reared its ugly head again. Just give me light skin, straight brown hair and petite features, I begged the Colour Gods.

Jinnali's track record for overnight success proved they had the chops to represent me. I left my hospitality job to go on the road with my new agents. I promised myself I wasn't going back to emptying ashtrays and dealing with belligerent patrons at the casino. Jinnali would not be added to my scrapbook of failures. I was going to make it work if it killed me, said every Type A personality.

Besides, what did I have waiting for me in Gimuy: certainly not my name in bright lights. Leaving behind bad memories outweighed the discomfort of feeling like the middle child in the group. I found out more each day I was a city girl at heart. And with that, Team Jinnali flew from Meanjin to Warrang to Naarm and back; this was more travelling than I'd ever done. The jetsetter in me was getting used to flying high – in the sky and my career.

It wasn't long before Donna sent me off to my first casting at *Cleo* magazine. When I arrived, the panel asked me some run-of-the-mill questions to get a feel for my personality as they browsed my portfolio. One of the reps I started to develop a rapport with asked me what my background was. I said, 'Aboriginal and African-American'. I smiled and continued to sell the best version of me. I had fun at the casting and thought I did well, aside from a sprinkle of nerves.

Anxious to find out how I went, I prodded Donna for feedback.

'Sorry, bub,' she said. 'They were after an Aboriginal model.'

'What do you mean? I am Aboriginal?'

'Because you said you were African-American, they decided to go with Violet.'

In other words, my African-American heritage diluted my Aboriginality.

'They did say they really liked you.' Donna was trying to clean up spilt milk.

I was crushed. I didn't want to hear they liked me; I wanted the job. Desperate to placate my ego, I decided Donna was the fall guy: she could have told me they were specifically looking for an Aboriginal model. You blew my chance, I thought, as I stewed on it for days.

In hindsight, it wasn't her fault. Hiding my African-American culture was denying my identity. Exactly what my Ancestors did to survive persecution. I knew what being the *Wrong Kind of Black* was like, just like Uncle Boori Monty Pryor. Given the numerous racist encounters I'd endured, it was easier to avoid bigotry by hiding behind the 'right kind' of Black. You know, the culture where everybody wants to be Black until it's time to actually be Black? The type of Black that brings the world to a standstill, sparking a global uprise in May 2020 but leaving Blakfellas at home wondering why our Blak Lives don't matter, asking, *How Many More? (Four Corners)*; crying out 'Justice for Cassius'.

So here I was, having a hissy fit about the entirely wrong thing. I should have directed my anger at the colony – non-Aboriginal people defining Aboriginality – sounds very Andrew Bolt-*ish* to me. Newsflash, there's no such thing as a real or pure Aboriginal. If anyone asks me again if I'm 100 per cent Aboriginal, I'll tell them, yes, my dad's Ernie Dingo and my mother is Devon. Relax, fam, it's a meme.

Here we go again, I was either too pretty to be Aboriginal or not Aboriginal enough.

Thanks a lot, *Cleo*!

Speaking of the colony, 2001 marked 100 years since the Centenary of Federation formalised Australia's Constitution and brought former independent States together. And true to form, First Nations peoples were left out of Australia's Constitution, and it wasn't until 1967 that my people were no longer considered flora and fauna but recognised as human beings. Australia is consistent in breadcrumbing us, with artificial justice in increments of 50 to 100 years. A practice stealthily reinforced throughout its colonial subsets – take, for instance, fashion.

Jinnali was one of the cultural highlights for Melbourne Fashion Week's Centenary of Federation programs. An amalgamation of notable Indigenous personalities matched with Australian designers to illustrate reconciliation – that warm and fuzzy notion we call upon once a year or buzzword to absolve the colony from actually closing the infamous gap, which only gets wider. If I hear 'closing the gap' one more time, I swear. It's become bastardised like 'woke'.

Okay, so Melbourne Fashion Week organisers wanted to paint the Jinnali models up in dots and lines and parade us down the catwalk in the spirit of restoring friendly relations. Yes, you heard me. Like ancient relics flown in to replicate *The Greatest Showman*, Hollywood's insidiously whitewashed version of P.T. Barnum's Human Zoo.

First of all, these so-called dots and lines are sacred – they signify ceremony: birth, rites of passage, death, lore – our rituals. Our markings are powerful and distinct, inherent across Aboriginal nations. We don't paint up to entertain you. But this is the colonial way of thinking, and unsurprisingly it's embedded in the Birth of a Nation, the White Australia Policy and elitist structures like fashion. Who knew fashion could be so dark? But I digress.

Needless to say, Donna and Lena told the organisers, respectfully, 'Hell no!' (Sidenote: where was the cultural consultant in all of this?)

With that out of the way, wardrobe fittings for the show were simple because we were hardly wearing anything. Jokes aside, Jinnali was assigned to model Kylie Minogue's debut lingerie collection Love Kylie. Kylie's polarising ad Agent Provocateur Proof got banned and won an award for being too racy. According to BBC News, a spokesman for Elle Macpherson threw shade at Kylie's new range, saying it was, 'More tarty and a bit risqué.' But it was probably all a publicity stunt because Jinnali was also wearing Elle's Intimates as well as La Perla. Ooouuu, I love me some La Perla.

On the night, we were overwhelmed by the backstage chaos. Plus, this group of Indigenous models didn't quite fit the scene. A few male models flirted with us, which lightened the mood. Finding a corner in the room, we banded together in exhilaration – we were at Melbourne Fashion Week! In our little bubble, safely tucked away, we failed to see who had approached us, *E Street* soap star and 'Read My Lips' singer Melissa Tkautz. She must have felt out of place too, and asked if she could sit with us. Of course, we said yes. I don't blame her. I reckon Melissa could hear *Sesame Street*'s song 'One of These Things (Is Not Like the Others)' like I did, although geeked to be backstage at fashion week. I felt fugly compared to the celebrities with bright white teeth and perfect skin. Models who towered over me, legs long as stilts, with genes made from the fountain of youth.

With that said, we sat humbly in our clique, drowning out the surrounding façade until it was showtime.

Watching the other models during their collections was hectic. Several people changing one model into her next look within 10–20 seconds. Lucky, we only had intimates to get out of. Can you imagine couture? When it was my turn to hit the runway, it felt like my entire body was pounding rapidly like my heart. Omg, is this really happening? When I got the tap on my back, *fark*, here we go. The spotlight blinded me. I heard murmurs in the audience, but I couldn't see a soul; strutting through thick fog was easier than this. Don't slip, Sasha, don't slip. Some genius coated the stage in what felt like sheets of ice. To cope, I pretended my heels were arctic cleats trying to grip the slick surface. The wreath of flowers affixed on my head turned into a crown of thorns. The fort of photographers awaiting my arrival had me aflutter. Getty Images, did you get that? Okay, time to do it again. I turned and made my way back and did this three times for the rest of my looks. Each time more intoxicating than before.

The jubilation of the show bubbled out of champagne bottles into clinking flutes. And where there is Black Girl Joy, there is Becky waiting in the wings. Leading up to the finale, everyone was positioned in line by order of appearance. I had changed out of the sheer La Perla lingerie set into a lavender kimono. In front of me, a rather inebriated celebrity was merry as can be. Ms Thang turned around and hesitated for a second before giving me the shadiest once-over. Oh, no, she didn't! I thought. I couldn't believe she just did that. And I felt a case of déjà vu wash over me.

Leaning into my personal space, champagne in hand, Ms Thang abruptly interjected with, 'Why are you wearing that?' She laughed dead in my face and went back to drinking, banishing me from the kingdom of fabulosity. I stood there dumbfounded. Wtf just happened? Her behaviour was utterly nonsensical.

A sympathetic soul behind me saw the entire thing. She rubbed my shoulders and whispered, 'Don't worry about her. She's just drunk.'

What is it with mean drunk white women cutting me down to size? For fuck sakes, can I live?! But that's why the French made Moët & Chandon: so I could put Becky on mute, and get back to living my best life.

When Naomi Campbell says jump, you say how high. And that's exactly what the Australian fashion industry did.

On a visit to Australia, Naomi called out the Australian fashion industry for its lack of Indigenous models. Now I'm going to let you in on a little secret: BIPOC knows this, but the rest of Australia doesn't. Whenever an international celebrity graces our shores and speaks on the lack of diversity in fashion and entertainment, Australia goes into panic mode: people start running around like chooks with their heads cut off searching for a handful of tokens to demonstrate to the whistleblower, 'See, we're not racist.' But when the cats go away, the mice play: the tokens return to obscurity, and back to 'Aussie, Aussie, Aussie, oi, oi, oi' we go. The number of times the industry has pandered to foreigners instead of reflecting Australia's multicultural society reveals that those in power don't want it that way. And that, my friend, is systemic racism. But back to my story.

It just so happened that one of the Elders caught Naomi's headlines. Taking it upon herself, she contacted Melbourne Grand Prix's Chairman, Ron Walker, and Steve Cameron, Naomi's New York agent, to see if Ms Campbell stood by her words. Would she support the inclusion of Indigenous models at the Melbourne Grand Prix?

And just like that, calls were made, and casting agents searched the country for Indigenous models. Violet and I were chosen to represent Jinnali, and found ourselves suiting up as Qantas Grid Girls for the 2001 Melbourne Grand Prix. No sooner did the media announce the news, 'Role models: Naomi's dream team for Grand Prix Grid', I was holding the number two placard for Ferrari Formula 1 driver Rubens Barrichello. For 60 minutes, I stood on the roasting tarmac like the Statue of Liberty, with a classic Jim Carrey smile plastered across my face. High off the engine oil and fumes, the incessant revs kept me at attention. Until pit bosses saved us: they were ready to start the race.

Violet and I were definitely the oddballs. Most of the male fans took photos with the white grid girls. They weren't rude about it. No offence taken; it gave Violet and me the chance to slip off our heels and rub our blistered feet until, bless their souls, a group of Italian men barracking for Ferrari bounded towards us. Naturally, Violet and I assumed they wanted the white models.

In his thick Italian accent, the rowdiest one of the bunch said, 'No, not you; the Black ones' – so matter of fact, and shooing the white girls to the side.

I *died*!

So, Violet and I (the Black ones) obliged. That's why I love Italian men. There's no ambiguity; they like what they like.

Day four arrived, and we were officially relieved of being objectified for male sports. Hand on Bible, after that, I dared anyone to force me to smile or wear heels to glorify men.

Now, they do say, no pain, no gain. And the upside to all this was a smorgasbord of celebrities. Violet, the extrovert to my introvert, spotted the surfer Kelly Slater across the turf. Screeching his name, she ran straight at him like a rhino. Not my preferred approach, but I wasn't going to let my childhood crush, who I had plastered on my bedroom walls as a teen, slip through my fingers. I let Violet go gaga over him while I swam laps in his irresistibly pretty eyes. When he turned to acknowledge me, he stared right into my soul. I swear I heard SWV's 'Weak' playing in the background. Kelly turned me into jelly. I'm not going to lie; beautiful people make me nervous – especially the modest ones.

Either God was smiling on us that day or we had good karma. Because out of a crowd of thousands, Lena found Violet and me. And by the gigantic grin on her face, she was bearing the news we wanted to hear: 'We're going to meet Naomi Campbell.'

In all our excitement, Lena managed to brief us. Violet was going to present a copy of the Jinnali calendar to the Queen herself.

Words could never describe what it meant to meet my idol. Naomi made a nine-year-old girl have the audacity to think she could be Bad and Bougie. Naomi's British accent betokened Black women had a passport to unknown territories, where Black beauty was adjacent to the monarchy. Black women dated outside their race, flaunted their sexuality unencumbered, and showed how Blackness reclaimed lavish affairs and distinguished spaces, and that splendour was reserved for us too. Naomi showed me Blackness was not one-dimensional. Naomi epitomised Black, Bad, Bougie and British.

I was the fangirl who had all Naomi's books, editorial tear sheets, magazine covers. I collected them like coins. I watched all her appearances from George Michael's 'Freedom' and Michael Jackson's 'In the Closet' to Spike Lee's *Girl 6*, and loved her album *Baby Woman* despite the critics. Whatever Naomi produced, I preserved.

And here she was, her svelte 5'10" (1.78 m) frame, flawless complexion, edgy pixie cut – my muse right in front of me. I stood captivated, watching Violet give the Jinnali calendar to Naomi. She courteously accepted our token of appreciation, offered us words of encouragement, and snapped a group picture before being escorted to her next engagement. As quick as it was, it was a dream come true.

That wouldn't be the last time Ms Campbell would see us. Coincidentally, Violet and I ran into Ms Campbell at Melbourne's Crown Casino later that night. And all over again, we turned into two deliriously excited schoolgirls, stalking her as she shopped. We tried to be as incognito as possible, picking up tees we were too broke to buy and neatly placing them back on the shelves. The joke was on us.

Suddenly looking directly at us, her sweet smile surprised us. 'I met you girls, earlier?' Naomi queried in her posh British tone.

We relaxed when we realised she was human, just like us. We told her we'd come to get a bite to eat after a long day at the Grand Prix – making sure she knew we weren't stalkers.

Not an ounce of annoyance. She no doubt was more endeared by two young Aboriginal girls fangirling her. Can you blame us?

Naomi flexed her star power to create change in the winter wonderland we know as the fashion industry. It took my muse to open doors here in Australia. Doors usually closed off to models of colour. That's what Black excellence does. It speaks your name into rooms you don't have access to. It reaches back and pulls others towards opportunities that are beyond their reach because (we) know, if not us, who else is going to do it?

10

Cosmopolitan

At 24 years old, Mia Freedman was the youngest ever editor of *Cosmopolitan Australia* – across the 58 international mastheads. Under her tutelage, she commissioned *Cosmopolitan* magazine's first fashion spread featuring Aboriginal models.

Mia read a story about Jinnali and immediately got her team to lock us in for their May 2001 edition. In her words, 'So why not until now?' (Cosmo Diary, May 2001), Freedman said she'd never seen an Aboriginal face among the thousands of portfolios that came across her desk.

That opportunity I thought I'd lost when I didn't land the *Cleo* job? The universe handed me *Cosmopolitan* instead. *Cosmopolitan*'s call sheet beckoned us to a studio in Broadway, inner-city Sydney; our photographer, fashion veteran Simon Upton.

On the taxi ride over to the *Cosmo* shoot, I had butterflies in my stomach. In situations like this, I tend to go quiet.

I stared out the window to distract myself, which didn't help. I began reeling over things out of my control. I'd never shot for a magazine before. How does one even prepare? On the other hand, the other models were super hyped, squealing and laughing as one would expect. Oddly, it heightened my anxiety. That's why I could never be an athlete – I wouldn't be able to handle the pressure. A packed stadium cheering me on would put me off.

Arriving in front of the studio entrance, I was glad to abandon the taxi for fresh air and personal space. I drew a large breath in before we hiked up the stairs, suddenly blinded by an aura of natural light. The studio looked like one straight out of an episode of *Sex and the City*. I'd watched enough episodes to know a Carrie Bradshaw moment when I saw it.

This wasn't New York, but the racks of designer clothes screamed, 'Welcome, Sasha Fierce, we've been waiting for you.' With Lena's blessing, I flitted around the studio. I inspected bedazzled loafers to Sergio Rossi heels and accessories for every occasion: you want fun and funky or casual chic; how about boss lady extraordinaire?

I ran my hands softly across the lush collections. If only I had walk-in wardrobes as grand as Mariah Carey's on *MTV Cribs*. I could fit this entire collection in it easily. I had always dreamed of sitting on a director's chair with my name on it. Although my name was missing, I still hoisted my derriere into the chair. Staring into the Hollywood framed mirror made it official. I was shooting for *Cosmopolitan* magazine.

I heard my name called and joined Lena and the girls as she ran through the call sheet, running us through logistics, the shooting order, who was up for hair and make-up – then handing it over to the stylist to give us a brief on the look and feel of the shoot. I was last on the call sheet. Awesome, I thought, this will give me more time to watch and prepare.

As the girls got ready, I watched the stylist pull the first outfit for Shenade, a chocolate glitter lurex top, navy blue pants and coco ivory earrings – simple but glam. Shenade's hair was slicked back, her make-up what make-up? Shenade had satiny skin. Heck, all the girls did. A pink rose petal gloss lip was all Shenade needed.

Aurora and I stood on the sidelines watching Simon shoot Shenade. I listened intently as he instructed her, absorbing how the pizazz was created, what expressions and movements worked well in Simon's eyes. I was in my *Pinky and the Brain* mode – I wanted to take over the fashion world. I left Aurora's side to shadow the stylist. I politely asked how she got into the business of styling.

An internship, she told me.

I didn't have that type of internship on my high school careers list. But my father told me the best way to learn is to watch and ask questions. I prodded the stylist with a few more questions and pocketed her tips.

The next look was Sass & Bide, worn by the duchess herself. Kirra, slightly older than us, is who I idolised. She had a regal grace about her. I zoned in on Kirra: her pecan-coloured hair was silk pressed. With her pearly white smile, Simon didn't need to use the flash. Kirra was a dream to watch. If I hadn't been so engrossed in Kirra, I would have noticed that Aurora was missing from the set. When Jacinta came out in her ice blue satin gown, Dorothy Dandridge-styled hair and jewels, it was all over. Jacinta was the Blak Disney princess we never had.

And that's about the time the ugly duckling came out in me, reinforced from an earlier incident when model submissions were coming in to the agency like fan mail. Donna was trying to get a handle on them, so Violet and I jumped in to help sort through the head shots, piling them in order. Donna took it upon herself that evening to knock me down a peg, stating that when she came across my submission, she put me in the unsure pile.

'When I saw your photo, Violet, I knew straight away you were in.' Donna beamed at Violet as if I wasn't there.

I couldn't cry or remove myself from the table because that would prove to her she had won. I sucked it up and carried on piling the models' headshots in categories as if I didn't hear her. I wasn't going to let her get the best of me.

Unfortunately, she got the best of Aurora that day on set. I thought I was the only one Donna didn't like; Aurora was on her hit list too. I later found out Donna had chastised Aurora for eating a donut from the catering platter. Donna took her around the corner out of earshot from us and berated her. 'Should you be eating that? You're going to get fat if you keep eating that crap.'

Aurora had doe eyes, so I didn't notice she'd had a cry after Donna's hurtful comment. If anything, Aurora just looked a little tired on set. I tell you what: despite all that, Aurora worked the hell out of those Bettina Liano jeans, Charlie's Angel-styled top and nude heels. She didn't even have to try – she was a siren. The Blak Monica Bellucci.

How It Started

I was lucky last, and Simon decided to incorporate some action into my editorial. Styled in a Zimmermann '70s retro dress: swirls of fuchsia, hot pink and purple dripped down the fabric – a beaded flower hugged my wrist. The stylist handed me a pair of diamante stilettos to slide on my feet. She had taped the bottom of the soles so they wouldn't scuff, and told me not to walk in them. I wasn't going anywhere. I had $1K on my toes – far more cash than I had in the bank.

When Simon was ready for me, he called me to position and started testing the flash. The assistant flicked on the industrial fan, which allowed me to indulge the infamous Marilyn Monroe subway scene from *The Seven Year Itch*. Who orchestrated that scene anyway?

Simon encouraged me to dance and have fun with it! As I warmed up to the idea, I became one with the dress; she became one with me. I grabbed the deluxe fabric, a playful flick here and a tasteful grab there. God bless Zendaya. Have you seen her fashion flex? That woman should do a masterclass: you betta werk! No, I wasn't that good, but it felt like it.

I had a full audience watching me – the only downside to being last. I must have been doing something right, I thought. My camera time was longer than the previous portraits. I kept pumping it out with all I had. The girls cheering me on when I made a deadly move, which boosted my confidence. The ugly duckling eventually realises she's a swan, right?

In Beyoncé's *Year of Four* documentary, she said shooting her 'Run the World (Girls)' video reminded her of when she first started in the game – like she was 15 again on her first video set and didn't want to go home.

I didn't want to, either. I could do this forever, I thought. Sasha Fierce has left the building.

How It's Going

Madonna graced the *Cosmopolitan* cover, posed in an All-American tee perforated with bullet holes and leather cowgirl pants. Who better to introduce *Cosmo*'s sealed section: '35 Naked Bodies: What's Sexy? You Decide', along with 'Beautiful vs Bonkable' and 'Celeb Sex Positions'.

I bypassed all the sex and headed straight to page 90. Slayville. My sistas brought breathtakingly beautiful glamour, dewy glow and smouldering 'come hither' sex appeal as well as ethereal innocence. Now that's how you shoot First Nations women. Honestly, my Jinnali sistas could've easily passed for a superstar R&B group. They showcased a myriad of beauty that *Cosmo*'s readers probably hadn't seen before. Freedman's sentiments rang true – why'd it take so long for our beauty to be honoured?

And right there on the page was me. Cue Viola Davis's boy bye, grab bag and leave GIF.

So, here I was feeling myself, wind machine blowing, flowy dress, hot ironed curls, and a salsa-swaying Sasha twisting her body to the beat. Remember the Jim Carrey smile from the Grand Prix? Well, it showed up that day: wrong place, wrong time. Ughhh, and those damn gecko fingers clasping my thighs – spirit fingers, Sasha, spirit fingers!

I was trying too hard but having a ball. I felt I had a connection with Simon like in the movies – 'more chin – turn to the side – little smile, little more. Perfect. Beautifuuul!' Pity it failed to translate to film. The antagonising part was waiting for *Cosmo* to hit newsstands when you thought you killed it! But in reality, you crashed and burned.

Okay, if there was ever a time I needed Miss J. Alexander from *Next Top Model*, it was then. Sis was a hot ass mess. I blame it on the wind machine. Have you ever been in front of one? Sis thought she was Beychella. I was clearly bathing in delusions of grandeur.

Tyra Banks' *America's Next Top Model* is not just entertainment. The show provides a crash course to aspiring models on how to master their expressions, angles and smize. You have to learn your body – how to contort it. And the hardest of all is executing action shots. To be successful, you have to know your craft. Models born with the X-factor don't have to work as hard as others. For us mere mortals that do, it requires a lot of effort. Case in point, I needed to put in the work.

Why couldn't I be photographed like everybody else? A graceful and simple portrait.

Remember how I said it was an action shot? Well, in my editorial, I had my legs open like I was about to squat. Anyone coming across the image would wonder, *wth! Why is she posing like that?* And that's exactly what the mob back home thought. Some loved it purely because I was in *Cosmopolitan*. The other half asked my mother, 'Why she got her legs open like that?'

What was supposed to be the proudest moment of my modelling career turned out to be an *epic* fail. And to make matters worse, some of the Elders asked why they had included us in that filthy sex issue – touché.

On a positive note, five First Nations models claimed the pages of *Cosmopolitan* magazine. After the issue launched, one of the readers wrote:

I usually have to buy British and American mags if I want to see an image of myself: thanks so much for leading the way and showing a different face of Australia. G. Harris.

Twenty years on, there's been a sprinkle of progress in the mainstream. It's not enough for Australian women of colour to genuinely feel like their beauty matters. Thank our lucky stars for social media; it saved a generation from invisibility.

I swear the gatekeepers sleep with the key around their necks.

11

The Matrix

Due to creative differences, my journey with Jinnali came to an end. After six months I jumped ship. I had grand plans for the direction of my career. Strutting the catwalks of Europe and shooting for top designers was more my zhoosh – think Fendace. And with the ambition of Josephine Baker, I packed my bags and decided I could manage it from here. I was going to make a name for myself.

Breaking out on my own was exhilarating. I didn't know where to start, but an agent from Chadwick's male division planted the seed. Sitting beside me in an internet cafe, the booker turned and asked if I modelled. I said yes. At first, I thought he was suss. He handed me his card and encouraged me to attend Chadwick's open call.

'They represent only a few Black models,' he said. 'But I think you might have a chance.'

I appreciated his honesty, so I took him up on the invitation and attended Chadwick, CHIC and Priscilla's open calls.

The Matrix

Aspiring female models had to be 5'8" (1.73 m). Thinking I was slick, I wore sturdy pumps, stretching my body like a rubber band. I felt like a short kid trying to sneak onto a carnival ride.

When I entered the room, the CHIC agent called me on it. 'You're 5'7" (1.7 m)!'

'5'7½" (1.71 m),' I corrected her. How could she tell?

I had my heart set on getting signed but got knocked back by everyone.

And then there was ASM Models who represented multicultural talent. I chose them because no-one else was interested in me. ASM wasn't all that bad. I actually got work. It's how I landed the gig as an extra in *The Matrix Reloaded*.

When filming *The Matrix Reloaded*, I couldn't believe an entire movie set looked like the real Australia. Not the milky version you see on TV. I'd never seen so many beautiful people of colour under one roof. Working as an extra is the best; you get paid to sit around, network and eat gourmet catering. I listened intently to the highs and lows of being a talent of colour. I soon discovered big brands loved to cast Black people for chocolate and coffee ads.

For the love of God, Australia, can you stop profiting off Black culture in your advertising? It's hard to see your favourite rappers selling out the culture (for the bag) to give Aussie brands street cred. Baby Cupid break-dancing and moonwalking on clouds with toilet paper may seem cute to some, but to me, it's irritating, like nails on a chalkboard.

Aside from the diversity and inclusion dramas, there's a lot you can learn from showbiz. For one, there's no I in team. I get why Oscar winners get fidgety when they get the wrap-it-up signal: they don't want to forget to thank someone. There's a lot of people involved. And that's not including the peeps behind the scenes – extras. Without extras, you wouldn't have a city, a war or a nightclub to dance in.

After half a day lounging in extra camp, our group got escorted to wardrobe. The compound was massive – what seemed like chaos made sense to the crew. As we stood waiting, Nosey Parker, shall we call him, began sifting through a rack of costumes nearby. Talk about bold: he started inspecting the Polaroids attached to each garment to see if he could spot any stars. I was there to do my job and hopefully snag another. So, I did what I do best: minded my business. The lass beside me, Sophia, hissed at him to leave it alone. I'm glad she had the guts to relay what I was thinking. Because I wasn't losing my job for nobody.

Just then, a senior crew member popped out of nowhere with a folder and pointed to Sophia and me to follow her. The crew member opened two changing room curtains where our costumes were hanging up and instructed us to get changed.

As soon as we emerged – wearing drabs of mummy cloth – a seamstress came over, took the scarf from around my neck and fashioned it into a headband.

'Is that too tight?'

'No, it's fine, thanks.'

'Okay, turn around slowly. All right, you're done.'

She took a Polaroid of me and shook it like André 3000.

'Can you spell your first name?'

'S-A-S-H-A.' In seconds, my name captioned the Polaroid.

'Okay, wait over there.'

The Matrix

No shade, but shade: our costumes were as depressing as the YEEZY-2 collection. After the fitting, me, Sophia and a handful of extras – thankfully minus Nosey Parker, who was still one step away from getting us all fired – walked across the lot until we reached a gigantic studio probed by spotlights.

It became clear extras really were human props. A production assistant handed me a hessian bag, the lady beside me got a tin bucket and the dude up ahead was assigned a wheelbarrow. He kept lifting it up, telling us how light it was. Duh! I thought, rolling my eyes, my irritation interrupted by childlike giggling. We all looked around to find out where it was coming from.

'Okay, we're ready for Gina,' the PA said into her walkie talkie.

She motioned for us to move to the left to make room for actress Gina Torres and the cutest little boy and girl – the type of kids made from Black love.

Gina made tattered rags look Gucci. I was now proud to be a Zion citizen standing behind a star. For starters, Ms Torres has the most hypnotic pair of eyes. She could look you dead in your face, whisper, 'I'm taking you for everything you've got,' smile, and you'd let her, being broke and happy as you live out your days. Her aura alone was intoxicating. Imagine working with her every day? That, my dear, is called the X-factor. The reason co-stars fall in love on set. Heck, I was falling in love with Gina.

'All right, can I get everyone's attention?'

Everybody came to a hush.

The PA ran us through our scene. Pretty much all hell was breaking loose: the city of Zion was under threat. Our job was to recreate this by walking hurriedly, with enough space between us so we didn't trip anyone up.

Everyone's cue in the front was to start walking straight ahead as soon as Gina and her babies stepped inside the chamber door.

We all got in position. I could see Gina squeezing the kids' hands, checking if they were ready. They nodded at Gina with enthusiasm.

'QUIET! ROLLING.'

We ran through the scene at several different paces. After 11 takes, it was a wrap. Wow, nearly three-quarters of the day spent getting hair and make-up done; costumes; standby in the village; and bam, 20 minutes on set and finito. Sophia and I were a metre behind the Wachowski sisters watching the playback. We kept nudging each other, watching a fictitious set and a storyline come to life on camera. We made it real, right down to our props.

Sophia and I got lucky that day. I overheard the PAs talking among themselves. The Wachowski sisters wanted to keep shooting. A PA came up to Sophia and me and asked if we wanted to do another scene. Gurl, why you even asking? Hell yeah!

Take two, and your girl is now a priestess. This time dripping head to toe in a midnight blue dress and indigo beaded veil; a simple and elegant piece. Now, this was more like it. It was just the four of us ushered to a new set with a wide grated bridge, which would later have special effects applied turning it into a multi-tiered city. We were then guided to the end of the bridge, lined by shoes placed outside the temple. A new PA ran us through the scene we were going to shoot. As priestesses, we were about to enter the holy temple. Before going in, we had to take off our hessian shoes and slowly grab a round wire basket containing fake bread and mushrooms. The props were light as a feather, but we had to pretend they were somewhat heavy as we walked in pairs faking conversation. A candlelit glow illuminated the temple. Stalactites cascaded from the ceiling while stalagmites stood erected from the ground. It wasn't hard to pretend prayer was in session as an eerie silence dominated the air. We did a few practice runs, and the PA reminded us to place our baskets on the ground when we reached the top of the incline. Then walk and look past the camera, not directly into it.

Pleased with the run-through, a man shouted, 'PLACES. ACTION.'

By now, my bare feet were sweaty, and the steep decline was rather slippery. Great, I thought, that's all I need, to go ass up on a Hollywood set. I tried to shake off visions of me busting my face with blood pissing out and two teeth discarded on the floor. Talk about 0 to 100 in worst case scenarios.

It's safe to say none of this happened. I got through a dozen takes and lived to see our scene play out in cinemas. Yes, I bought *The Matrix Reloaded* when it came out on DVD and watched it a thousand times on slow mode. That's us, I thought, as the Kid, aka Clayton Watson, races into the temple for Counsellor Hamann's opening prayer.

When we finished up at the studio, I blew off drinks with Sophia and the gang. Instead, I splurged on a taxi ride home. I wanted to savour the moment alone. That night I lay in bed with a cheesy grin, like I was nine again; the little girl who won her first modelling trophy.

12

Perils of a Black Model

Back in the '90s and early 2000s, it was common for US and UK productions to film in Australia. One, it's cheaper; two, we can replicate their demographic. But the real slap in the face is when Australia can't cast the diversity of their society in their productions. Why is that?

Being on a blockbuster production put stars in my eyes, but it also opened them up to a nationwide problem. The lack of beauty products available to women of colour on Australian shelves. Before *The Matrix*, I had the luxury of having a mother who was a beautician and could import beauty products from international suppliers. When she left the industry, she also lost her beauty connections. I was rocking Maybelline's Toast foundation for a hot minute until they discontinued the line. Australian women of colour, you've probably been here before. You go to the section where your foundation lives, and it's no longer there. Perhaps they're yet to restock the shelves, you tell yourself. You politely ask the sales clerk if they have your shade, and the dreaded 'It's discontinued' rings the alarm. You want to scream, 'So what you're saying is Black women don't wear make-up?' but then you'd be labelled the Angry Black Woman. SECURITY!

Left to our own devices, we became cosmetologists overnight, buying and mixing multiple shades to recreate a DIY version of our perfect match. Even Miranda Tapsell weighed in on this dilemma in *Get Krack!n*'s final episode. Miranda's white ashy face says it all. Not only was whiteface happening due to unstocked department stores; it was happening via unskilled make-up artists in entertainment studios. Those who had the money to buy high-end foundations that matched our skin tones did while the rest of us placed make-up and haircare orders with relatives and friends travelling abroad to the US and UK; countries that stocked Black beauty.

Shout-out to Shanthi Murugan and Adore Beauty for initiating the Global Shades movement, to improve inclusivity within the Australian beauty industry by calling on global beauty brands to #StockAllShades. And hairstylist Chrissy Zemura, petitioning TAFE for courses on how to style Afro, textured to curly hair.

On the bright side, on the set of *The Matrix* I met Harold Perrineau – Murch from *The Best Man*. One of my all-time favourite Black movies. We were both waiting in wardrobe, and since he looked familiar, I struck up a friendly chat with him. The sweet-spirited Perrineau was eventually called away, and politely said goodbye. It wasn't until the African-American make-up artist who summoned me into her chair casually mentioned she'd just finished touching up Perrineau ... I can't believe it didn't click that I was speaking to Murch.

But if that wasn't Kinder Surprise, being rescued from Ashville was. This sista had every colour, brand, shade at her disposal. What in the Blackity Black was going on here? Cosmetics I'd never seen or could pronounce. If we had social media in the early noughties, I'd have been Elaine Welteroth on Insta stories showing off my B-E-A-T face.

I asked her every question under the sun: What's my colour? How do you apply that? Sorry, what brand is this? And that was the day I was introduced to MAC Cosmetics; MAC Studio Fix Powder NC45 was my perfect shade. This queen wrote down all the products she used on me. And for 20 years, I was loyal to MAC until Rihanna changed the game with Fenty Beauty, aka The Fenty Effect. RiRi brought us 50 shades and listened to starved consumers overlooked by lazy brands – tone and shape, I got you, Boo.

When it comes to Black beauty, Black women have been doing it all our lives; it's in our blood. Annie Turnbo Malone and Madam C.J. Walker became America's (first recognised) self-made female millionaires for their haircare empires. Christina Jenkins, inventor of the sew-in weave, and Eunice W. Johnson, founder of Fashion Fair Cosmetics – the first make-up brand for women of colour and once the largest Black-owned cosmetics company in the world.

Thank God for Black beauty brands that put us on game because a Black model had to be a jack-of-all-trades. You had to bring your own products and do your hair and make-up. I foolishly trusted Aussie hair and make-up artists one too many times and paid the price. Fool me once, shame on you; fool me twice, shame on me. I can't tell you how awful it is to be sidelined and completely forgotten about at a shoot. All because so-called professionals don't know how to work with Black hair and skin.

If that's not infuriating enough, being sent to castings only to be asked, 'Why did your agency send you here? We already have enough Black models?' or 'You don't look Aboriginal enough.' Well, Suzie, I wasn't expecting you to be so basic, but here we are!

Back then, models and talent of colour just wanted to be featured on Australia's most popular soaps, like *Neighbours* and *Home and Away*, but we've seen how realistic that is. All we ask is to be respected for our craft and the years invested in refining it. Not to be typecast by our ethnicity. We wanted to be considered for how well we can play a character and sell the shirt off our back. Skin colour shouldn't be a barrier to something as simple as that. It's really not that hard.

Pretty Hurts

> *When she is told her skin is too dark, I don't hesitate to offer that the sun loved her so much it kissed her more than the rest of us.*
>
> **Anonymous**

How do two young Blak women end up in a plastic surgeon's office? Simple. You got a minute?

Along with another model, I made a joint appointment with one of Sydney's top plastic surgeons. We figured we were both unhappy with our assets; why not give each other moral support. She wanted a breast enhancement. I opted for a nose job.

Sissy had the video vixen physique. Her milkshake brought all the boys to the yard. I pined for her curves. In my eyes, she was sublime already.

On the other hand, I had a broad nose that screamed young, Black and ethnic. You know, the type of nose that doesn't last long in Hollywood. I had succumbed to the whitewashing in fashion. If you were a successful Black model, you typically displayed what insiders termed the white model dipped in Black look: translation a Black model with Eurocentric features.

Sidenote: I loved Tyra Banks' nose pre-op. She made a hopeful Black model feel seen.

A born optimist, my Big Black Nose turned me into a realist – your beak doesn't stand a chance. So, when the surgeon asked me, why are you here, duh can't you see, this thing is taking up far too much real estate. No, I didn't say that. I told him I wanted a pixie nose like Halle Berry; she had one of those cute button noses I'd seen on so many Black models and actresses in showbiz. To get Halle's nose, I needed hella rhinoplasty.

The surgeon knew why, but he didn't know how I got here. It started with this thing called colourism. And it began one summer when I spent six straight hours in the pool. Despite my mother's warning to get out of the chlorine, hard-headed, I chose to laugh now and cry later. Sure enough, when I got out of the pool, my skin was burnt to a crisp. I was ashy grey, a lifeless prune. I bawled my eyes out as we walked all the way home under the scalding sun.

I'm pretty sure the pool saga triggered me, snowballing into my high school years. The Slip Slop Slap sun protection campaign was in full effect. And I thought sunscreen would protect me from, wait for it – not skin cancer, but getting darker. Sis, you live in Far North Queensland, a hop, skip, jump away from the equator. But sure enough, I'd duck into the bathroom right after school and lather up on sunscreen before riding home. Mind you, my plan backfired, and so it should. The oily ingredients acted like suntan lotion and baked me like a rotisserie chicken.

I was back to square one, and here came the skin shade hierarchy to rub salt in my wound. In the '90s, Hot Girl Summers were reserved for the light-skin gummas with green eyes. So, when my high school sweetheart happened to be a Hot Boy with Michael Ealy eyes, it brought out the green-eyed monster in me.

First and foremost, I didn't know why my boyfriend chose me. I wasn't a light-skinned girl. The way our caramel-toned sistas were exalted, I assumed my boyfriend would prefer that instead of plain old brownie me. And the narcissist in him used this insecurity of mine to his advantage. The irony is, in California, I was once the light-skinned girl. Now, it was me who was putting the shoe on the other foot.

Knowing his golden-boy charm and good looks had the upper hand in our relationship, my boyfriend got his brother to make me jealous telling me he had only dated light-skin girls before me. That girls were persistently blowing up their landline or trying to push up on them at parties. Did all this obliterate my self-esteem? Bloody oath it did. He drove me insane, to the point I felt I couldn't do any better and that I should be thankful he was even going out with me.

Well into our relationship, we had one of our numerous lovers' spats. I chose to leave my bedroom where my boyfriend remained. Intent on not letting the argument get the best of me, I decided to watch a comedy. Engrossed in laughter, I failed to hear my boyfriend leave the house. I returned to my room only to find my notebook lying on the desk. I don't know what told me to open it. Flipping through it, I stopped at a coon-like caricature of me. A stick figured body with squiggles of curls, over-the-top clown lips, and there it was, my *big black nose*, outlined several times over in blue pen to make it more pronounced.

He was so cruel about it he wanted me to stumble upon it unexpectedly, plunging the knife in that much deeper. Somehow, instinctively, he knew. And there it was: what I loathed the most – my *big black nose*!

Later, vitriol like 'boong' and spitting in my face became the norm before it turned physical. Without warning, after a disagreement, he smashed the back of a tablespoon against the bridge of my nose. My nose swelled to epic proportions. Miraculously, the damage to my nose self-corrected over time. Although the physical pain was excruciating, it eventually went away; it was the emotional scars that remained. My childhood sweetheart now the devil in disguise was one *Mortal Kombat* move away from finishing me.

That's why, when Lil' Kim explained in an interview her transformation over the years, I could relate. Abuse can lead assertive and accomplished women to the dungeons of reconstruction. When you are criticised incessantly about your appearance and identity, it breaks you down to nothing. Lies become weapons of mass destruction, and internalised racism and colourism show up at your door.

Modelling exacerbates weeping wounds. And before long, it becomes body dysmorphia. My self-loathing hid out in the gym, exercising for hours to eliminate fat that didn't exist. At 20, standing 1.7 metres tall, weighing 50 kilograms, liposuction was on my wish list. Staring in the mirror, all I could see was cottage cheese clinging to my bony thighs like rock oysters. For goodness sakes, I was a baby. I hadn't even fully developed into a woman yet. And here I was trying to alter God's work in progress.

For what? I was trying to be the pretty Black girl I saw on the television, in magazines, music videos and in advertising. What he and they wanted me to be – everything I wasn't.

So that's how I found myself in a plastic surgeon's office. As I watched the surgeon etch out my nose in black marker on the paper, he explained how he could morph me into somebody else. I told him I had to give the surgery some thought and asked if I could take the paper with my new nose on it. The nose that was going to fix all my problems. I stuck the avatar on my wall, and we stared at one another. Weeks passed, and something inside me couldn't bring me to take the next step.

People say they can feel their Ancestors guiding them. Mine steered me away from the chopping block. Away from abolishing the precious symbol of my tribes. To my sistas struggling to love their nose, know this. Your nose is a mark of your legacy. Let it enter the room boldly – let it sing, 'I'm Black, and I'm proud' upon your face. Don't contour but highlight it, so it shines bright, and adorn it with jewels. Rub it with the finest of oils.

When you see Black women go hard on social media, it's for you. Remember, we are upholding Black Is Beautiful, an affirmation lovingly created by Black women who came before us. They've handed us the torch. That's why we have #BlackGirlsRock and India.Arie's 'Video'.

You're pretty for a ... what?! You are not pretty, you are gidar for everything that you are and represent. You create trends. You are the culture. You are the descendent of royalty.

Modelling 101

Who's watched *Toddlers & Tiaras*? Creepy, right? It's fascinating how we nab our children straight out the womb for critique, cash prizes and fame. I get it, raising children is expensive. Parents who thrust their kids into this billion-dollar industry say the financial gains and perks are worth it. But for who?

Some parents use the child pageant circuit to build their kid's confidence. Heck, Mum did it with me through modelling. Understandably, if your child is a natural-born superstar, why wouldn't you capitalise on a goldmine? Now I'm sounding like Kris Jenner.

I'm not a parent, but I have been in the room when a newborn is labelled ugly. Harsh? Absolutely, but it's the nature of 'beauty' and the beast. We enter our bundles of joy into baby competitions to show everybody little Erica has good genes.

So, what lengths do pageant parents go to? You can start with barrels of hairspray. Toddlers' hair teased to the heavens, fake hairy caterpillar eyelashes, Oompa Loompa tans, and bucketloads of make-up that would make a drag queen blush. And don't forget the flippers (fake teeth) – though we might as well call them dentures, since these children are adults.

Don't get me started with the costumes. It's not the bedazzled baby-doll dresses that I'm concerned about. It's the talent show. Contestants aged four years and up shimmy across the stage in

Perils of a Black Model

Dolly Parton padded derriere and chest, Madonna cone-shaped bra and Julia Roberts' *Pretty Woman* streetwalking outfit.

It's just harmless fun, you say. Mothers and daughters bonding over dress-ups in a room full of other like-minded families.

But it's beyond disturbing when a mother admits to injecting her eight-year-old with Botox because her daughter asked for it: because she didn't like theced the wrinkles. Now, who's the child and who's the parent? But hey, that's just my opinion.

How far is too far? Where do we draw the line when it comes to over-sexualising girls?

Are we putting our children in harm's way through exposure? I think of the unsolved murder of six-year-old beauty queen JonBenét Ramsey. It makes me think about what goes on behind the scenes that we don't know about. Is beauty a sinister pastime – not only for our kids but for us? I say yes. Young girls are dressing up as fully developed women. And grown women are shrinking into prepubescent bodies. It's warped. Even the toy department is on board. We went from Barbie to Bratz to L.O.L. dolls. Those dolls are way too sexy for my liking.

Beauty is predatory, a money-making machine that grooms us from baby contests, child pageants to scouting for fresh faces as young as nine years old. Yes, I am one of them. I've got the trophy and pipe dream to prove it.

Modelling agents scour continents for young new talent. Promising hopefuls are chucked into the deep end; with model bootcamp. Some are encouraged to lie about their age to scouts. Depending on how unethical the agency is, they're in on the lie too. By law, many countries don't permit models to work if they are 14 and under. If shady agents can get a 13-year-old to pass for 15, they'll pocket an extra two years of revenue. Once a young model crosses borders, they're usually crammed into sub-standard accommodation with other models and chaperones. Knock on wood that chaperone is a decent person who will look out for your child abroad. Can you imagine what it's like for a child who's never flown to another country where they don't speak the language?

Fortunate are the new models whose guardians can accompany them or provide additional support – emotional, financial and life skills – until they build their careers.

There are horror stories where models are introduced to a glamorous life then start hanging out in the wrong circles – fuelled by drugs, sex and alcohol. If circumstances get out of their control, they could find themselves mixed up in escorting and sex work.

The opportunity of a lifetime doesn't pay for itself. Models are paying their dues every step of the way. Where do you think the money comes from to fly them across the world, feed and house them? The kicker is, it may take models years to pay off agency debt and start earning. That's why castings are their bread and butter – no castings – no work.

Now let's talk about the fine print. Clauses in your modelling contract can vary and stipulate you must maintain a certain weight, body measurements, hair colour and style. They can also switch up the contract terms whenever they want. Teenage models have been sent home for gaining a couple of inches on their growing bodies. That's why models are prone to suffer from anorexia, bulimia and other unhealthy disorders. The industry often gives them no option, especially when you're in debt to the agency and financially support a family back home.

Modelling is not all glitz and glamour. It's getting up at 3am for a 6am editorial. Shooting a summer collection in winter, a spring campaign in autumn. It's plunging into an ice-cold lagoon concocting a grandiose expression underwater. Patiently smiling through chattering teeth until the photographer is ready for you to do it another 15 times. If the photographer is super chill, you might get a, 'How you holding up, kid?'

Oh, it gets better. Nothing like being whipped by a sandstorm in a pair of bikinis: nipped on the heel by a toy poodle and holding in your pee for hours during a bridal show. No, no, Boo Boo; you ain't wiggling out of that corset and bridal hoop and ruining hair and make-up. You're wearing the show-stopping piece.

Shooting an editorial in the rainforest is fun. Just watch out for the bloodthirsty leeches you discover in the weirdest places. Did I forget to add that you're required to be a good sport? No attitude, just sweet and responsive. Lest you be considered difficult to work with, no back-talking, though clarifying the photographer's directions is permitted at a pinch. Any issues on set are relayed back to your agent. And, for godsakes, no chitchat unless the crew engages. And if they do, keep it brief. How successfully you perform determines whether there's another job waiting for you. Good luck, kiddo!

The fashion industry sometimes boils down to 'Did I make the cut?' or being cut-throat, depending on which side of the scales you're on. Whether you're a creative or the talent, you can shoot for a magazine, and your work may never see the light of day. You're only as good as your last tear sheet, showreel, campaign, by-line or celebrity you've worked with. Those accustomed to the industry have learnt not to boast about working for a renowned masthead or somebody who's a pretty big deal. Rugs can be pulled right from under you. It's best to wait until you have the receipts before making that 'Big Tings, Stay Tuned' Insta story.

As a model or actress, what are you willing to do to recreate the fantasy or land the job? What are your dealbreakers? In this industry, you have to figure out what's a hard pass. Or where you'll make an exception. Are you bothered by what your community thinks? It's all part and parcel of the job.

Sometimes you have to bring your Ancestors, family members or faith in the room to make the right decisions. On the other hand, you may decide to push that thought in the back of your mind because this is an opportunity you can't pass up. The image you pose for or the character you play lives on, just like the photos and tweets you post on the internet. It's difficult to ask your 18-year-old self if you'll have a problem posing for *Playboy* 20 years from now.

This is where good management is crucial. Finding the right agent and team has to feel right, like trying on shoes. There's nothing worse than buying an ignorantly fire pair of Louboutins that's not your size. Trust, those blisters hurt more when they're lost earnings and a damaged reputation. The process can be hit or miss, but the gut doesn't lie.

Some agents treat the business like a pick-up playground. If you want to keep it strictly business, your team needs to project that. Let them know, godammit, I came to win. By no means should a model be hanging out in a seedy bar at Kings Cross with their agents; dangled like bait in front of powerful men to land a job. Or sitting in a lobby – your agent hiking up your dress just shy of your cooch, 'Show more leg.'

Perils of a Black Model

Oh, don't worry, I pulled my dress down back where the hem belonged and caught a taxi home. The prospect of being pimped out didn't sit well with me.

Wth, Sasha? Where did you find these agents – a dumpster? No sis, lousy judgement. Remember, when it comes to dreams, if you're buying, they're selling. Word of advice: Put everybody on a 7–90-day trial period. Stay away from lock-in contracts. You're a money maker. Yes, I'm talking to you – you're a star. Before you go exclusive, they have to earn you. This applies to any business, whether it's modelling or life. Loyalty doesn't mean issh. Not until they show you the money and integrity.

Just because someone introduces you to modelling, takes your pictures, and introduces you to industry reps doesn't mean you owe them your firstborn child. People who genuinely want to see you win do it out of the goodness of their hearts. They're upfront about how much support they can offer you. And then point you in the right direction when you both come to the end of the line. Others do it because you are a meal ticket, and if they can make you feel guilty or gaslight you along the way to eat, they will.

Ike didn't make Tina. Anna Mae Bullock did. Don't forget that.

When I left the modelling industry and became the founder and editor of *Ascension* magazine, I met an agent who represented one of our top First Nations talents. When I met him, he expressed an incessant fear of losing her to a top agency. He'd be with her on every shoot – ball and chain, whisking her away between breaks so nobody in the industry could build a relationship with – ahem, poach – her. He was constantly interrupting shoots to control the creative direction. And had bad-mouthed her to anyone who'd listen; burning bridges with sponsors.

If it wasn't for her divine character, it could have hurt her career in the long run. Ultimately, her star power could not be hindered, and she eventually cut ties with him. Sis is now a cover girl, brand ambassador and editorial Queen. I share this not only because this applies to everyday life but, as Blak women, it's a thousand times more important because we live in a world where opportunities to work in elite industries are few and far between. Blak women need superb agents – people who will speak our names into rooms.

13

Cattle Call

I never slept well before a casting. 'Go sees' are the worst: the butterflies, cottonmouth, sweaty palms and practising in the mirror the night before. For those who don't know what a 'go see' is, it's when your agency sends you to interview for a potential job. Brands and productions send agencies casting calls: potential jobs, inviting them to send their best candidates. If you're all that and a bag of chips, brands request you specifically to attend their casting. Then it's up to you to be your own cheerleader on the day to land the job.

Picture trying out for *The X Factor* or *Australian Idol*. Just lose the number on your chest and replace it with a black book known as your portfolio. The resume you carry containing tear sheets and composite cards; a snapshot of your best work to leave with the panel for consideration. I don't know what's worse, competing on *The Bachelor* for one man's love or castings.

The modelling industry has been known to refer to models as human coathangers. Our job is to sell clothes, products and services. A downside to modelling is becoming a decoy to bamboozle consumers into seeking a lifestyle they can't afford and provoke FOMO among the masses. Models are the human element of advertising. The masterminds behind the scenes are testing subliminal messages and imagery to evoke the desired response from their lab rats, my bad, potential consumers. In turn, hoodwinking us into becoming life-long customers of flashy cars, sparkling diamonds, gadgets and credit card debt plus interest. Take Apple, for instance, they've mastered the formula. They release a new phone nearly every two years, and you buy it. I'm still discovering functions on my iPhone when I accidently swipe or double-tap.

Now, ask yourself what compels you to buy stuff you don't need? Need a hint: Men & Companies who profit from selling us dreams. Google Edward Bernays, De Beers and Victoria's Secret.

The buck doesn't stop there. It would be remiss of me if I didn't note today's influencers – the brand foot soldiers. The new kids on the block, have a new bag of tricks: Facetune, filters and flat tummy tea. In reality, some of us are hip to the game, and are okay with all the smoke and mirrors. Those who like the finer things in life know it takes two to tango in this dance of buyer and seller.

All I'm saying is, be cognisant of how you're manipulated into keeping up with the Joneses. Essentially our purchasing power has always remained with us. It's a question of whether we use it wisely or not.

I got a call from my agent to attend a casting at a posh tennis club. On the bus ride over I felt the reflux of intimidation leaving a bad taste in my mouth. Uppity neighbourhoods and well-to-do people made me nervous. Historically I didn't belong in these parts, and its residents often made me feel like I was trespassing. But my inner Real Housewife felt at home. I was a young Black woman who was taught from a young age that everything I do in life must be executed 1000 times better. Regardless of how Charlotte, Tammy or Liam performed.

I remember asking Mum, 'Why?'

'Because you're Black.'

I baulked at how unjust it was.

But all I got was, 'Life isn't fair.'

Could I at least get a lollipop for my troubles? Now that I am grown and know better, this was Black parenting cemented in love. To raise me otherwise would be negligent, setting me up to fail. The same rules apply no matter how old you get; your parents' commentary plays on repeat. I sure was going to need it going into this casting. Bigger, badder, better than ever drummed in my mind to quell my self-doubt.

Stepping into the foyer, my eyes swept over the gold lettering on wooden plaques and gargantuan trophies guarded by glass. This establishment seemed to be home to a lot of champions, and members who I suspect ate cucumber sandwiches and spritzed their face with Evian.

'Can I help you?' asked a scrawny woman who immediately gave me the vibe she ruled the roost.

'I'm here for the casting.'

Cruella de Vil raised her eyebrows, her eyes asking me, Oh, are you now?

I volleyed back with a 'Yes, I am; don't play with me' smize. We stared at each other to see who'd crack first. Game, set, match: that's what I thought.

Accepting defeat, Cruella rattled off the directions.

I followed the hum of voices down the corridor until I found a wide door with 'Sydney Fashion Week Casting' on it. I pushed it open and spilt into a room of lily-white faces and tans from Ibiza. Not one model of colour to be found.

Standing there like a deer in the headlights, I freaked! Fark, it was too late to turn around and walk out. I'd look like an idiot. I was prone to panic attacks in those days – though I didn't know what it was – but I felt one coming on. My heart rate accelerated, and a hot flush engulfed my body. I started surveying the room like a meerkat searching for a hole I could crawl into. There it was, a sliver of wall I could anchor myself to. I crossed the room steadily, with a poker face. The last thing I needed was to collapse in a room full of white people.

When my back was now up against the wall, I could breathe easier. Stable enough to slide down and take a seat on the floor. I pretended to check messages on my Nokia 8210; the nearby chatter helped centre me. All right, Sasha, get it together.

I scanned the room to check out the competition. Jesus, these models were perfect 10s dressed in their smart casual outfits from Sportsgirl, Esprit and Jeanswest. I looked down at mine: smart casual from Bargain Buys. Just shoot me now.

I rustled through my purse for my compact. Of course, frizz shady came out like Jack in the Box. Bloody hell, I just straightened my hair. It was paper thin when I left. I squirted frizz control into my palms and attempted to pat down the tumbleweed forming like a crown.

And then a redhead in an emerald dress plopped down beside me. Ahhh, really! Gurl, can't you see I'm busy?! And, of course, she wanted to shake my greasy hands. 'Hi, sorry I've got gunk on my hands.'

She didn't mind a bit. I quickly jerried she was the only person in this joint with a pulse.

By now, I was over it. I didn't want to be here. So, what better way to pass the time than kick it with Red. I don't know what it is about redheads. The ones I've met had a bit of flavour. And quite a few told me they were considered outcasts in their circles. Join the club. Anyways, can't nobody rock the colour green like redheads and Black people. How bout that.

As the hour passed, the room got smaller until the casting director came out and told us we were up next.

No sooner did Red talk me down from the edge, my anxiety came back like The Flash. Red noticed I went all quiet. She smiled and respected the process. I watched Red disappear into the room. I already knew she killed it. I really wanted her to get the job. She deserved it. The sweetheart that she was whispered, 'Good luck.' And flashed me a go-get-'em smile on her way out.

Soon, the casting director nodded at me, 'Your turn.'

Entering the mini ballroom, I was met with paisley-patterned carpet with Victorian light fittings hanging from the ceiling, and a U-shaped panel lined with faces. Wow, okay, I wasn't used to this many judges to determine my fate.

'Okay, when you're ready,' a baritone voice called out.

I could hear the bookers whisper among each other, 'Where is she from? Where's her comp card?', which completely rattled me.

Did the agency send it to them or not?

I was auditioning for Sydney Fashion Week, so the girly catalogue smile wasn't necessary – just the 'I don't get out of bed for less than $25K' strut. Whenever I hit the catwalk, I fall into a trance. I don't know how I get there so fast, but it sure is marvellous.

Yes, the convulsive jitters are horrible initially, but to feel extraterrestrial is unreal. The anticipation is why castings and auditions are so nerve-wracking, but it's the dopamine hit you get after that is the reward. Panic attacks and dopamine highs. No wonder your gurl was a basket case in her 20s.

Phew, I had gotten through the casting without throwing in the towel. Some might say calm down, that's what models do, but what about the models chasing something outside themselves? Models who think they need this job because that's how you become a somebody as opposed to a nobody. On a merry-go-round chasing campaigns or spots on guest lists and billboards.

Are models masochists? Why would anyone subject themselves to a revolving door of critique?

Walking out the casting doors, I made my way to reception. Dammit, it was pissing down rain, and I hadn't brought an umbrella. As I waited for the rain to pass, I watched raindrops chase each other down the windowpane until they became one. I pretended the anxiety over the job was raindrops, and let them disappear into the gutter, down a drain, never to be seen again.

I heard a high-pitched shriek only Black people make. Spinning around, I saw four African models joshing each other. They looked at the rain, then at me.

'Did you do the casting?' asked one of the sublimely tall models.

'Yeah. Did you?' I was grateful for the distraction.

'Yeah. We just finished.'

I wondered how I'd missed them. I know if I'd seen them there, I might have felt more confident. I don't know how to explain it. It's the initial awkwardness I feel as a Black person visiting another country for the first time – for instance, Vietnam, where I am not the norm. I receive constant stares, innocent giggles and whispers. I am a novelty by default. Walking into rooms where I am one-of-a-kind takes its toll. Some days I just want to see a friendly Black face smiling back at me. That's why the only Black employee is delighted when another Black person joins the team. Black camaraderie in predominately white spaces is rare and must be treasured.

'What are you doing now?'

'Nothing,' I said.

Two of the models I hadn't met yet were kekeing behind us, which delighted me when I saw the irritation plastered on Cruella de Vil's face. I think the girls did it to piss her off, and I was here for it.

'Did you want to grab something to eat with us?'

'Yeah, that sounds good,' I said as I joined the Bold & Beautiful.

Black Models & Co. grabbed their umbrellas from the rack. And off we went, on our merry way, leaving Cruella de Vil behind with a few extra wrinkles to laser off.

We chose a cafe at Central Station so everybody could catch public transport afterwards. I studied the menu, searching for the lowest calorie item I could find, which was pointless because everything was dripping in cholesterol.

We finally realised we hadn't officially introduced ourselves, so we did your usual: my name is, my star sign is, in my spare time I like to ... just joking.

With the formalities out of the way, I saw an opportunity, and asked, 'May I?' gesturing to Fatima's black book, which I had been eyeing off since we met. I already knew Fatima stayed booked, busy and blessed; her portfolio was busting at the seams. Not only did sis have tear sheets, she tore them up. Page after page: campaigns for Coke, Fiorucci, Missoni and Steve Madden. I bet Fatima was chuffed AF handing over her credentials at castings. If you haven't twigged, portfolios are a model's portable trophy case. And sis was *winning*!

'Is this you?' I asked, pointing to her Sachi editorial.

Fatima's nude silhouette was turned into a Sachi bag. She was photographed looking into a mirror; one Fatima became two. Uhhh, so Mario Testino meets the Y2K. Fatima's skin was flawless: human silk. There was clearly graphic design employed to superimpose the bag onto her body. But I, along with many others, didn't know about airbrushing used to smooth out her skin, along with the other tips and tricks of perfection known to the Adobe Creative family.

Had I known about photoshopping, it would have saved me wincing over every new scar or blemish I acquired that could be captured on film. Oh, and the cellulite that could be erased. Who needs the trauma of liposuction when you can sit in front of a computer and vanish it away? Can you imagine the number of women who underwent cosmetic procedures without being fully informed?

There were no 'This image has been retouched' disclaimers

in the magazines I read. Had publishers and advertisers been upfront with us, it would have alleviated a lot of heartache. So many young girls and women ridiculing their skin for birthmarks, moles, stretchmarks and battle scars from falling from a tree, winning the hockey championship sporting a busted shin; heck, the marks from living your best life.

As advertising's unspoken motto goes, what you don't know can't hurt you. Wrong.

I wanted to know Fatima's secret. 'How did you get all this work?'

'You have to have thick skin … I go out and find jobs.'

'What do you mean? You have an agent?' I knew Australia's top agencies signed these girls; their portfolios were branded accordingly. 'Why are you hunting for jobs?' I asked, perplexed.

'I'm a Black model.'

The girls all nodded in agreement. Ohhhhh, sis, say less.

To me, everything about the business was down to luck – making sure your assets were in tip-top condition. Right time, right place, yada yada. Now I was hearing, we had to find our own jobs too? Sis just passed on the best piece of modelling advice: you have to go out there and get it for yourself. I admit I was naïve; I assumed you were set once you got an agent.

I scoffed down my burger and chips, wondering how these girls hoed down double what I ate. The girls wrote down their numbers to stay in touch. We bid each other farewell, with European kisses and tight hugs that felt so good coming from sistas.

Pulling up to my hostel, I was happy to see my brotha boy dragging on a durry out front.

'How'd you go?'

I scooted beside him and grabbed his smoke and took a puff.
'Good, darlin'. I'm just glad it's over.'

Seeing Fatima's portfolio was the motivation I needed.

All gassed up with a new strategy, I arranged a meeting with my agent, Lee. We had business to discuss. I wanted Lee to be my Jerry Maguire, my Ambassador of Quan. Mind you, snagging the meeting took weeks. I seriously needed a Marcee Tidwell on my team. Like Rod, I was on the bottom rung in the pecking order when it came to models. But I didn't let that deter me because I knew I was somebody.

'To what do I owe the pleasure?' Mischa asked when I visited Lee's office.

Some damn work might be a start, I thought.

'Oh, I just wanted to touch base with Lee. Is he available?'

'No, he's in Japan'.

Now I was pissed. Does it look like I'm here to play games? Marcee!

Time was money, and I wasn't making any, so I launched into my master plan. I started listing off brands and campaigns featuring diverse talent. To see if the agency could keep their finger on the pulse for castings and put me on the company's radar. In my heart of hearts, I really wanted to snag high-end fashion campaigns like the Black Supermodels I admired. Regardless of all the ambition I possessed, I had to be realistic. So, I decided to piggyback off the urban movement. Some work is better than none. My only concern was being pigeonholed into a category I wasn't passionate about.

Cattle Call

'Sounds like a good idea. I can look into that,' Mischa said after hearing my pitch.

Yes! Mischa squizzed through my portfolio, 'How about we get you some fresh photos.' Mischa handed me a business card.

'Give Tomas a call to organise a test shoot. I'll let him know to expect your call.'

Low-key Mischa was trying to appease me, but what else was I supposed to do. I could only hope she'd keep up her end of the bargain.

I called Tomas, and he told me we'd shoot at Coogee Beach, Surry Hills and Circular Quay. Bring something casual, smart and semi-formal to wear.

That night, I packed the essentials: a nude strapless bra, face scarf, make-up, frizz control, the outfits Tomas suggested and footwear.

The following day I met Tomas at an apartment block in Surry Hills. We began shooting in front of an '80s glass block feature straight out of *Miami Vice*. As a rule of thumb, photographers say your first roll of film is your worst. It's when you're getting a feel for the camera and your surroundings. I can vouch for this. I am taut 20 frames in.

Tomas was a short and meek man. The silence made me uncomfortable, so I asked him, 'Why photography?' as he changed his lens.

'I loved watching my uncle take photos. I guess it grew on me,' Tomas replied, rummaging in his backpack.

This intrigued me. I loved learning the exact moment when someone discovers their passion. Tomas was a struggling photographer who moved to Sydney from South America. He loved high fashion as much as I did and would never make the big time where he was. Ditto!

As we began to flow with more ease, we snapped another roll of film at Circular Quay and then headed to Coogee Beach. Lunchtime had approached; we were starving. Since Tomas lived a block away, we bought sandwiches to eat at his place. This way he could change his equipment while I slipped into the final outfit for the day.

Tomas shared an apartment with his cousin; it had a South American touch. His peach terracotta walls were decorated with tiled crucifixes. *Monstera deliciosa* guarded the corner walls, and rosaries hung around the Virgin Mary's neck. Tomas's bookshelf revealed an avid reader. None of the titles were familiar to me. I hoped one day I would have my own little place. Sydney's rent was sky-high. Until I made it big, the hostel it was.

You can tell a lot about a person when you're in their space. My eyes traced his apartment for more clues.

'Herb Ritts?'

Tomas glanced over to the book in question and smiled. 'You a fan?'

'Oh, my God, yeees!'

I flipped through *Notorious*, Herb Ritts' iconic collection of photography. I always thought it was Madonna's mouth on the cover. Come to find out, it was Sandra Bernhard yelling at us this whole time. Who invented multi-hyphenate? Ritts, my friend. Herb dominated an era of fine art and commercial photography. He's the genius behind Mark Wahlberg grabbing his crotch for Calvin Klein underwear. Ritts captured a softer side of Madonna, snapping her wearing an adorable pair of

Minnie Mouse ears, and the mystique of Prince and Cher in portraits for us mere mortals to appreciate.

But when it came to hallmarking the '90s, the cultural renaissance that it was, Ritts achieved this by directing Janet Jackson's 'Love Will Never Do (Without You)' and Michael Jackson's 'In the Closet' music videos. Ritts hit us with the sepia and splashes of black and white.

Ritts inspired me to explore photography in high school. I heard everybody made out in the class darkroom, and I'd daydream about my crush whisking me away for some of that TLC red light special. Ughhh, darkrooms are so hot. But the class was always in high demand, so I didn't get the chance to see if my eye was as good as my shutter game.

After lunch, Tomas and I made our way down to the beach. Tomas positioned me up against the sandstone. My white off-the-shoulder señorita top and blue jeans were the perfect combo. Hours flew by, and we shot until the sun disappeared underneath the sea. It's a wrap, we both chimed as we packed up and headed to the esplanade.

Since the shoot went over time, Tomas kindly offered to drop me off to save me lugging everything on public transport at night. Throughout the day, I didn't get any odd vibes from Tomas. So, while dropping me off, the question to grab dinner threw me. Luckily, I told him to drop me off one street over.

I put on my 'be nice' face. 'Umm sure,' I said, politely swerving him.

'How about Friday?'

Dammit! 'Umm, I can't. I'm busy Friday. Can I let you know?'

Tomas was cool with that. I shrugged it off as nothing to worry about. Yes, it did strike me as unprofessional, but he seemed harmless.

A week went by, and I called Tomas to see how my photos were coming along. He said they'd be ready for Mischa tomorrow.

'Hey, are you free for dinner this week?'

Ugh, here we go again. I made up another excuse, hoping he'd get the picture. A few days passed and I got a text message from Tomas: Dinner??? Stalker much! I left him on read and called Mischa to see if Bug-a-boo had sent her my proofs.

'No, he hasn't,' Mischa informed me.

I decided to sleep on it. Tomas had me hot. The next day, I gave Tomas a bell. It went straight to voice message. I wanted to give Tomas a piece of my mind. Instead, I did what nice girls do: play nice. I left a sweet unconcerned 'just checking in' message on his answering machine. And for the next two weeks, Tomas dodged my calls.

This charade had gone on far too long. He forced my hand. I had to call Mischa and explain I'd been trying to get my photos to her, but I couldn't get a hold of Tomas.

Tomas feigned busy with work as his excuse. Yeah, right! You had time for dinner. How about you focus on your job? I was slightly hurt. Not by him asking me out but by his attitude afterwards. Usually, I could sense a man's interest and curve him gently and still get the job done. But it was the switch up from Tomas that threw me off. I replayed our shoot over in my head to recall if there was anything about my behaviour that could have led him on. I mean, why would he act this way?

In the end, my snaps made it to the agency. Not only was this situation embarrassing, but it had also been unnecessary. I was glad I didn't have to see Tomas's receding hairline again. Not that he would be the last creep to pull this type of stunt.

Tomas was what some might call one of the harmless ones – passive-aggressive – compared to the Harvey Weinsteins of the world. Where there is women, money and power, there's a Harvey enabled by an industry that turns a blind eye. One of the most humiliating things I have endured as a woman is abuse: every type, from physical, sexual, psychological, verbal, emotional, mental, financial and spiritual.

Abuse usually comes pre-packaged; with a lot of the methods I mentioned above utilised to gain complete control of the victim. Not only is enduring the abuse something I wouldn't wish upon my worst enemy, it's tossing up whether to report it or not. The decision to speak up entails you sitting in front of a stranger and reliving the trauma by making your statement, looking into their eyes after they put their pen down, wondering, 'Do they believe me? Will justice be served? Will I be blamed? Is the career I worked so hard for in jeopardy? Will I lose family and friends?'

It's a lonely road when you have to go it alone. In a separate incident I experienced five years later, my perpetrator and I lived and worked near each other and had mutual friends. A couple of acquaintances knew about the abuse but didn't want to get involved. I couldn't tell anyone else; it was futile to do so. My abuser had a high-standing position in his profession and within our community. To speak ill against him was a battle I didn't have the fight for. I just wanted to get out.

I found myself in a courthouse with a support worker reassuring me everything would be okay; left scanning the doors and exits to see if he would turn up or one of his representatives. Taking the stand in a desolate room, hearing my shame echo in a chamber, avoiding eye contact to disassociate myself from what I stated for the record. Going home alone, checking my doors were locked repeatedly and sleeping with a knife on my bedside table, because what if this pushes him over the edge?

There are levels of abuse and harassment. It's a wolf-whistle from a colleague in the lobby as you walk by, a slap on the ass with briefing papers. It's servicing drinks to a group of men, a coaster falling on the floor. As you retrieve it, you hear, 'While you're down there …' Feeling the breath of your boss brush the lobe of your ear, the gentle squeeze of your shoulders. The management meeting you're invited to as a junior, but the rest of the team hasn't arrived yet – it's just you and him.

If I had a dollar for every woman who just wanted to pursue her dreams in peace, void of sexual harassment and abuse, I'd be a millionaire. So many of us, prior and leading up to the #MeToo movement, were trying to traverse safely through landmines without us even knowing it. Can you imagine the women sitting next to each other in the same room, with the same shame, the same secret, the same perpetrator?

Times are changing, thank God, but if it were easy for women to speak up, we wouldn't be where we are today. If we didn't rationalise the abuse, it wouldn't be what it is today. If the system supported victims, there wouldn't be an epidemic of abuse. If enablers turned into whistleblowers, abuse wouldn't have a place to hide. If we raised men and shaped a society that valued women, we might have a chance.

If …

14

Yarrabah

I could taste the sea breeze sweeping in, the morning light drifting before the sun opened its eyes. Today marked a celebration of love. A young couple was getting married. Mum and I, the faithful servants, were there to adorn the bridal party with make-up. The modern-day tradition we adopted.

I wonder what our traditional bridal ceremonies were like before they took them away. Did we paint up in gaba, magirra or gunggu ochre?

Sitting around the patio one afternoon, my Aunty Bella told her daughters and me that she had been promised to an older man when she was 15.

'Really? Back then?' I asked. 'Do you know who it was you were promised to?'

'No, I never found out. Good go, I'm not marrying no old man.' Aunty Bella chuckled.

I loved the softness that blossomed on Aunty's face; her natural blush whenever she shared her stories.

She said the Old People chose a husband for you by looking at the bloodlines to see if you were connected. They considered if he was a good hunter and if he could look after you. If he was older, it wasn't all about passion like when young people get together. He taught you the right way when it came to intimacy and how to be a bride.

Young girls from the age of 10 went to live with their promised husband at his camp. Learning her role in the tribe from his family.

Across the paddock from where we sat with Aunty Bella was a bevy of wild horses. What a spinout, I thought, as I recalled Aunty Kym's tales of the cattle stations and travelling far and wide to attend rodeos. That's so country, I mused. I wasn't about that life. I didn't inherit a penchant for saddles, stirrups and an Akubra. Not after getting on a horse at 14 without knowing how to trot. That horse nearly ripped my susu's clean off my chest. I swear my pelvic bone almost smashed like glass.

Once, Aunty Kym asked me to go to the rodeo with her, but it was too hick for me. So, Aunty Kym, the Carefree Blak Girl, hopped in her aqua green Mazda, and burned rubber – kitted out in her peasant top, jeans, hiking boots and a flannie to block out the cold. Destination the Mt Isa Rodeo.

She liked knocking back cold ones, snacking on treats and perusing the festivities: barrel races and the women on horses were her favourites. When she'd return, she'd tell me about the cowboys she met, and the buckles strangers gave her. That's what I admired about Aunty Kym. She could talk to anyone. She had an air of familiarity as if you'd known her your whole life.

I'd worry about Aunty Kym way out in woop woop travelling alone. She told me that out bush she occasionally saw hairy men and strange lights, and heard noises along the highways. Some of the spots she passed were no-good places. But Aunty Kym had a friend – a little man, her protector – who followed her from our Country on the Tablelands.

'He's been with me for a while,' she said.

That's where I draw the line. I don't do spirits. Even if little man was a bodyguard.

For a while, I assumed Aunty Kym enjoyed the rodeos because she had Grandad's stockman genes. Come to find out, she was once a jillaroo.

'Grandad said if you don't want to go to school, it's either work or TAFE,' Aunty Kym said. She only lasted two weeks at TAFE.

'So, what did you do next?'

Aunty Kym went into the CES Job Shop where Aunty Fiona worked.

'Where do you want to work?' Aunty Fiona asked her.

'Anywhere out of Innisfail.'

Aunty Kym took a pencil, closed her eyes and pointed somewhere on the map; it landed on Richmond. Aunty Kym snagged a job as a baker's assistant, earning $348 per week. Not bad for making dough rise. She sent Grandad some money and spent the rest on shoes and handbags. It wasn't long before teenage rebellion took hold: underage drinking and getting into trouble, leaving her boss no choice but to call Grandad, who said, 'Send her out to a station. That'll fix her up.'

The boss's friend needed some help, so the former baker's assistant became a governess (a bush au pair) to three children under 12 while she completed half of Year 11. Every now and then, she'd argue with the boss – because isn't that what teenagers do?

'I didn't back down,' Aunty Kym remembered. 'Not even for my own good.'

As a jillaroo, Aunty Kym had to check on the water pumps for the cattle. She'd back her truck up under a tree and camp out overnight with only the wild dogs to keep her company. Exploring and getting lost on her way back, which she tends to do.

After a year, the family bought a new property at Springsure and asked if she wanted to come with them. Aunty Kym said yes. 'But something told me it wasn't the right idea.'

She decided to return home for two weeks. On her way there, she found out Nana Joseph was sick. Aunty Kym made it just in time – two days before Nana passed away. After that, she didn't want to go back to Kalda Station.

'So, what did you do after that?'

'At 21, I was an offside roo shooter, skinning kangaroos.'

In South Australia, there was a big market for roo meat and skins. And only so many licences given out. You were only allowed to shoot roos over a metre tall.

My stomach got queasy when Aunty Kym said her knife got stuck skinning her first roo. Her boss told her to jump on its head, which caused the head to fly right off. She eventually got used to hanging the skins on the side of the LandCruiser and piling the roo carcasses, which she called the big pyramid of death.

After working from 3pm to 5am, she'd have a shower, go to bed and get up and do it all again. A day off if she hit her quota.

'It was interesting. I don't know if it's something I'd recommend – it's not for everyone.'

'Did you know how to shoot?'

'Yeah, but I didn't want to shoot the roos. Instead, they taught me how to skin and carry the roos a specific way, so I didn't hurt myself. I didn't think I could, but I did.'

Aunty Kym got a black eye from a roo when she was opening a gate. As her boss drove through, he told her to watch out for it. Even though it was dead, its nerves were still moving around. The tail swung back and hit her in the face. Just her luck. Half an hour later, she had to pee. She was wearing overalls. Ughhh, we all know how awkward that is.

Squatting down behind a prickle bush half a metre high, all she heard was, 'Stay still, don't get up.'

As her boss reached for his gun, Aunty Kym yelled out, 'What are you doing?'

'Shhhh,' her boss warned her.

A big boar had snuck up behind Aunty Kym, mid pee.

'Omg, it would have got me straight up my arse,' she told me.

Her boss shot over her head to scare it away.

Just another day at the office. And this is precisely why Aunty Kym is scared of pigs.

For the rest of the day, they'd place the roo skins in a box for salting, lugging away well into the freezing night. As morbid as it sounds, Aunty Kym kept warm by laying against the dead kangaroos. 'It wasn't a pretty sight. I'd get back to the station covered in blood like I had slaughtered people.'

I tapped out when she told me the battery for the skinner, the button they pressed to rip the skin from the roos' heads, went dead. When her boss went to get a new battery, Aunty Kym's torch started to flicker.

'Don't start this shit,' she cursed, tapping it to work. Then came the growling. Feral cats started climbing the pile of roos. Lucky, her bossed showed up a couple of minutes later.

Is it me, or does any of this scream *Wolf Creek*?

After telling me all this, Aunty Kym pondered, 'I don't know how other women feel working in male-dominated industries?'

Gee, I wonder? There's no way I'd last.

'So, how did you navigate it?'

'I didn't pay people or things much mind.'

To me, Aunty Kym was fearless, the epitome of drama-free. She treated everyone the same, going about her business, taking a hot shower, chucking on her thermos and scooping up the friendly feral cat to keep her warm at night.

But it was Aunty Kym's story about the poddy dodgers (unbeknown to her) she used to work with, who eventually got caught by the stock squad for stealing unmarked cattle and cars. That story made me think of Nana Brackenridge.

Jarrugan, Nana Brackenridge, was born on Woodleigh Station in the Tablelands. As soon as she could walk, she learnt how to ride horses. At nine years old, she mustered cattle. Working for the station boss, the rule was if you come back home with one cow missing don't come back at all. During her travels cattle duffers stole some of her cows. Nana had a special call for her herd, yoooohooo she sang out to them, and in the distance, her cows cried back, yoooohooo. Following the sound, she found them in a fenced-off paddock. Jarrugan loved watching the black and white films starring Annie Oakley. Mimicking Annie, she grabbed a rock and started gashing the fence open with it. Nana got her cattle back all right and alerted the authorities. The cattle duffers were caught, but of course, they weren't happy with Nana. They cursed her out – 'You little yellow bastard' – as they were hauled away.

In our language, light skin is jirri jirri. And this is the reason Nana was sent to Townsville to work as a domestic.

That stint didn't last long. The boss's son was sweet on Nana, and because she was the Blak servant, the parents were having none of that. So, they sent her to the mission on Palm Island. Nana made it clear she'd done nothing wrong. 'I was there just to do my work.'

On Palm Island, Nana and Uncle Ginger's mother were best mates. 'The prettiest girls on the island,' my great-grandfather said. He said Nana walked around with her nose up in the air, her thick plaits falling down her back. Grandad would watch her from the hill.

'Eerrr, she wouldn't even look at you, Dad,' Aunty Ruthie teased.

'But I got her in the end,' Grandad boasted.

And that's how Nana met and married Blak ole Grandad, as Aunty Ruthie put it.

It was always a commotion doing bridal parties, especially with a gaggle of women and children scattered around the house. This time, in Yarrabah, Mum and I were the eye of the storm keeping it all together before chaos descended. We'd seen our fair share of bridesmaids scrapping like cats among pigeons. The mother of the bride fussing about before bridezilla launched into a tirade.

Unpacking my make-up kit, a bouquet of flower girls gathered around me.

'What's that?' one of them pointed to a brush.

'It's for putting on blush.' I picked up the brush and lightly dusted the flower girl's cheek. She recoiled in laughter. I reached out and tickled the rest of the girls on their cheeks – causing an uproar of giggles loud enough to break a dam. The girls watched me intently as I placed every item on the table in order of function.

We had a bit of time up our sleeve, so I made a game out of the Dermacolour palettes. 'What colour do you think you are?'

I let each flower girl guess their shade, half the fun was when they got it wrong. I turned to their cousin for their suggestion, and they'd rejoice when someone got it right. Dabbing the make-up sponge into the palettes, I blended foundation into their skins – letting the second last flower girl have a turn blending while I arranged the blushes and eyeshadows for the second stage of the bridal look.

You could tell these tiny hibiscuses were new to the enchantment of make-up. Their eyelids fluttered like butterflies as I feathered stardust on their lids. I'd catch them assessing themselves in the handheld mirror, sneaking glances at their mothers and aunties as Mum beautified them in the same fashion. Yes, bub, you're going to look glamorous, just like them, I thought.

I was once one of them, stealing glimpses of my mother as she got ready to bestow her beauty onto the world. I never got caught playing in Mum's make-up, but I did study her. Perhaps, I knew I couldn't create art the way she did.

Sitting at her champagne vanity with the gold English trimmings, to me, she was royalty. Her dresser homed: pomade, her compact and mulberry lipstick that appeared like a genie out of a bottle, with nothing but a twist. I remember Aunty Ruthie had a vintage perfume bottle with the puffer like the Hollywood actresses. Lifting my head and closing my eyes, I pretended I was Eartha Kitt squirting my neck as divas do. I was obsessed with that crystal bottle. I asked Aunty Ruthie if I could have it. 'Oh no, not that one,' she said. Instead, she offered other treasures from her glory box, but nothing could compare.

What did compare were the gifts we all shared, the features that bejewelled us. Aunty Lydia and Aunty Ruthie wore rich melanin from Mauritius. Mum and Aunty Bella had onyx stone eyes in the shape of Java, passed on to me; Soraya carried their high cheekbones shaped like the Seven Sisters standing tall on the Tablelands.

'Aunty Ruthie, what do you wear on your skin?' I asked one day.

'Oil of Olay.'

I asked my nana on my father's side what she wore to keep her face supple. She said Vaseline. I wanted a youthful face with wisdom beyond my years, just like them. It's fascinating how we eventually become our mothers. We inherit their femininity dashed with our own mannerisms – authentic beauty unveiling itself in the petals of new flowers.

Tabu was my mother's scent: a vintage fragrance passed down to her from the women in our family. Its spicy citrus notes became my allure. As I matured, the floral and woody musk captured me, as did hints of vanilla, jasmine and amber encased in Red Door, Obsession and Sì. Anything to be close – to smell like my mother.

My West African lips now wear the pigment Dionysus by MAC, similar to my mother's mulberry shade. My skin is now radiant like Aunty Ruthie's, thanks to Palmer's Cocoa Butter.

My heart fluttered as the baby princesses twirled in their white frilly dresses with a satin burgundy bow.

Mum stepped back and tossed her head to the side, lips pursed, as she critiqued her work. I suspected Frida Kahlo did the same. My mother is a perfectionist, so there's always room for improvement. But what really mattered was whether the bridal party was impressed, and they were.

The bridesmaids were a garden of bougainvilleas: their lips, cheeks, eyes and gown. The men dashing: from footy shorts, singlets and thongs to distinguished gentlemen in suits. And the bride, well – of course – she stole the show. She stood before us in a pearl-encrusted bodice: her gown cascading down in an illusion of ivory mist. No veil, just a crown of baby's breath.

I wonder what happened to Mum's pearl V-shaped veil that I promised I'd wear when my turn came around. Maybe it wasn't meant to be. Perhaps I'd take after the mob who reclaimed the feathers of guyumbula (white cockatoo) and bimbirri (shell) as their headdress and lined their face with ochre instead.

Standing together, the bridal party looked similar to the black and white photos I'd seen of our Old People when they got married on the island. These days, photos are in colour; and we no longer seek permission from the white man to marry.

As Mum said her goodbyes, I took one last look out at sea before we left Yarrabah. I didn't know when I'd be back.

'Your grandad was born in Yarrabah,' I remembered Aunty Kym telling me one day.

'Really?'

'He used to ride a horse to school … Remember that photo I took of him before he passed?'

'That one of him looking out past the inlet?'

'Yes.'

'He was looking out at Yarrabah.'

15

Shame Factor

Being shame began at 10 years old. My girl cousins and I wore large T-shirts and shorts over our swimmers, to the pool, waterhole – wherever there was water. To us, it was normal. Even though the extra fabric clung to our bodies, the comfort outweighed the embarrassment of exposure.

'Where does shame come from?' I threw the question out to the women in my family while writing this.

'It started when the white man came,' my cousin offered.

'In our culture, there was no shame; nakedness wasn't a thing.' Aunty Bella confirmed what I was thinking.

'Once again, here comes the white man with all his perversion,' I said.

I sipped my tea to wash down my disgust, but I wasn't finished. 'The shame factor must be generational trauma – all the rape and abuse of our women had to have been passed down to us.'

We all nodded in agreement, letting the wind chimes clear the bad juju in the air.

As a kid, I hated walking past the photo of my nana, Doreen, hanging on the wall in my house. Her expression was sombre, somewhat eerie – and it gave me chills every time I saw it. Whenever I entered the living room, I'd acknowledge her and pray under my breath, please don't do anything. I know that sounds stupid – she's my grandmother, for godsakes, but somehow, she frightened me. I felt bad about it and asked my cousin if he felt weird too. He did. I told him I ran past Nana whenever I had to go to the toilet at his house. I dared never to look in her direction at night. But when I broke my own rule, shadows formed around Nana's face, turning her into a witch.

It wasn't until I got older and saw the photographs of unnamed Aboriginal women, the ones taken by white ethnographers, anthropologists and purveyors, that I understood. Hopelessness etched on their faces seeping from their eyes, just like Nana.

From the photos in our collection, I knew Nana was beautiful, but her life, not so much. Doreen Florence Brackenridge was born in 1931 on Palm Island and assigned certificate number 46/43 under Native Affairs. In September 1943, Nana – along with other members of our family – was granted exemption to leave the mission:

Her affairs are not being controlled by this Department
Yours faithfully, Acting Deputy Director of Native Affairs.

Although in principle Nana was free to move and work as she pleased, living in so-called Australia as Aboriginal people, are any of us really free? Nana still slept with one eye open: a piece of paper didn't stop the Aboriginal protectors from stealing your babies. Maybe a clean house and children, depending on fate.

I grew up bathing in diluted Dettol: a capful – no more, no less. Hospital-grade cleaner to mop the floors and eucalyptus oil for surfaces. These are the smells that greeted Saturday mornings – not eggs and bacon. These smells are nostalgic, and they wake me up at 3am when Mum goes on a cleaning binge. And now I begin to wonder, do these smells trigger Mum? Do they take her back to 1962?

Nana had six children; my mother was in the middle. Aunty Kym told me Grandad walked into the RSL, won a game of Two Bob, and walked out with 900 quid and Nana on his arm. Grandad and Nana had a volatile marriage from what I've heard, and when it ended, it was definitely for the best.

It was hard for a single mother of six children with not much support back then. And history seemed to have a habit of repeating itself. Mum and my aunties would band together and try to smooth over rough times, just like Nana and her sisters did.

Aunty Ruthie told me men were enraptured by Nana's beauty – she was ethereal – but her anger could sear you like a hot iron; her words, like my mother's, could cut like a knife. And like a moth to a flame, Nana had to fend off a lot of unwanted attention. It had its advantages for my aunties: men flocked to them in attempts to get close to Nana. But you weren't getting a foot in the door unless the drinks kept flowing. The aunties made sure of that. Gin Jockeys were in full supply.

'Hanging around for a bit of Black Velvet, they were.' Aunty Ruthie sparked up her cigarette as we were yarning.

Shame Factor

'What's Black Velvet?' I asked.

'Black like velvet, smooth to the touch.' Aunty exhaled her smoke and gave me a look, leaving me to fill in the blanks.

Mum told me how much she hated men buzzing around her mother. How she would play up and hang off her mother to fend off admirers. Kids can always sense unscrupulous characters. They would try to coax Mum with lollies to go play, but it never worked. It only made her stick to her mother like glue.

I, too, hated the thirsty ole captains fishing around Mum and my aunties as a kid. There was one who drove a Black & White taxi; his beer gut protruded over his belt buckle. Two shirt buttons were left undone, revealing his silver chest. He seemed to always pull up just as we entered the taxi rank after we finished grocery shopping.

I'd roll my eyes and chuck the groceries in the boot. Ughhh, let's get this over and done with. I'd wind the window down because his nicotine breath made me want to gag. But I kept my eye on him through the rear-view mirror in case he got too friendly. My aunty could handle herself, but I still shot him the evil eye: You mess with her, you mess with me. I couldn't wait for the taxi ride to be over. Of course, until next fortnight when the dirty old bastard happened to be there, same time, same place, offering a free ride home.

And this is why it tickled me to watch Tracey Moffatt's film *Nice Coloured Girls*. Swindling white men out of drinks, dinner and a night out on the town suited me just fine. It was I who would have the last laugh. There will be no partaking of Black Velvet tonight, not on my watch. I carried out my revenge because I never forgot how the lustful ole captains made me feel as a little girl, those randy eyes objectifying my kin. I knew how it felt to walk around with a bright white dress with a black stain on it.

I guess you can say Aboriginal women inherit conflict with the white gaze in one way or another. It's not as if we asked for it or sought it out; it's just how it is. And for years, I've tried to reconcile darkness. Why did Nana's story have to be so tragic? Why Aboriginal women?

This relentless quest to find answers led me to write and direct my first documentary for National Indigenous Television titled *Too Pretty to Be Aboriginal*. Nestled in the wings of the State Library of Victoria, I became more intimate with salacious content depicting Aboriginal women: articles, film, music, literature, advertising to bric-a-brac. There seemed no limits to the colonial perversion that sullied our women; there was no room for her dignity.

I scrolled through century-old Australian newspapers like *The Bulletin*, *People* and *The Age*. I couldn't believe how they mocked and ridiculed us for the nation to read. In everyday Australian vernacular, terms like Black Velvet, Gin and Lubra – colonial tropes – rolled off their tongues. Degrading language specifically assigned to Aboriginal women, publicly branding us as promiscuous, sexually available, 'there for the taking'. Right before me in black and white, Australia's depravities; our nation's psyche.

One has to ask themself, what inspires Australian comedian Charles Vaude to write and compose 'My Little Lubra' with lyrics: 'My little Lubra ... want you to be my Gin'?

Or renowned bush poet Henry Lawson's 'The Ballad of the Rouseabout': 'Where falls the half-caste to the strong, "black velvet" to the weak.' Lawson elucidates: 'The surface of the skin was smooth, a feature that gave us bushies the saying of "Black Velvet".'

Without batting an eye, a Victorian establishment acquired and affixed a portrait of a young bare-breasted Aboriginal girl made out of velvet to the wall of the Fitzroy Union Hotel.

Journalist Harry Cox had an article published on 14 November 1956 for *People* with the headline 'Black Velvet: It's a name for seduction in the outback and means degradation for a once-proud people'. Cox wrote:

> *Black Velvet, as the seduction of aboriginal women is known all through northern Australia, began with the first white settlers.*
>
> *Black Velvet has not been stamped out, but it's not nearly so prevalent as it once was. One reason for the decline is simply that there are fewer gins.*

Then there are Top End tourism advertisements featuring Native Belles, cartoon-like illustrations selling deplorable ideas of what you can expect visiting the region. Culturally sensitive items – what seem to be the artist's attempt at burial poles – are sketched in the background. Advertisements like 'McCarty's Lubricants Always Lubra Kate' encourage consumers to 'Use Lubra-Kate for all your farm machinery, motors and vehicles.' D. & W. Murray Ltd Lubra Boot Polish promotes the tagline: 'Dis Lubra Polish make boss's boots shine good as that big feller sun.' Execrable appropriations of Aboriginal women marketed to the masses.

These advertisements are reminiscent of cartoonist Bill Leak's more recent controversial depiction of Aboriginal fatherhood as nothing more than deadbeat alcoholics. And as we always do, Blak Twitter countered such mendacity with #IndigenousDads to take back their honour.

But as we know, the colony doesn't let up. In the past, and even now on eBay, kitsch Aboriginalia floods the market: dolls, boomerangs, tea towels, salt and pepper shakers, plates and ashtrays. Yes, Aboriginal women painted on the bottom of ashtrays outfitted in scantily clad clothing; lingerie and heels, tribal markings; her hands tied behind her back. Cigarette butts ashed out on her porcelain body. My stomach turns after seeing such atrocities; some I can't even bring myself to write about.

Once again, Aboriginal people claw our way back to reclaim the narrative – our lives, through what we know best: Blak Liberation; Blak Art.

Destiny Deacon, a K'ua K'ua (Kuku) and Erub (Mer) contemporary artist renowned for coining the term BLAK, gives the middle finger to the coloniser by dropping the C from BLACK to reinstate self-determination. We are the architects of our contemporary Indigenous existence as a culture and a people.

'I feel sorry for those little dolls lying in trash and treasure markets … looking all forlorn and stuff. I don't know why – I just seem to rescue them.' (Destiny Deacon, 1996 Asia Pacific Triennial, Queensland Art Gallery & Gallery of Modern Art)

Through Blak humour and Koori Kitsch, Deacon combines photography and her affection for dolls to grab at Australia's jugular. Decapitated doll heads placed on top of watermelons, axed off and made to mimic despondent eyes with a boomerang smile recreate the unsettling and morbid truths hidden in plain sight.

Girramay and Kuku Yalanji contemporary artist Tony Albert turned his childhood pastime collecting Aboriginalia, an innocent fascination he says was 'looking at pictures of family', and repurposes the ill intent behind the objects. Albert does this by emancipating kin through social and political messages and his reimagining. As Albert says, 'There is elements of rescuing objects giving them a life they weren't able to originally have – they're about revoicing the objects.'

Albert's piece *Expulsion* from his exhibition 'Conversations with Margaret Preston' had me transfixed: in the middle of Sullivan+Strumpf envisioning paradise before our people were cast away from our culture and Country like Adam and Eve from the Garden of Eden.

But it's also Albert's stunning image of a young Aboriginal girl – aptly named *Girl* – emblazoned on bendy plywood, shredded from her shoulders to the footer of her image. A perfect analogy, how the system tears us from the core leaving just enough to exploit whenever they see fit.

Deacon's and Albert's interrogation of the white gaze through their art repositions Blak people where we belong – at the heart and centre of this Country – no longer on the fringes.

Jedda, Australia's first feature film – directed by Charles Chauvel – was not only the first in Australia to be shot in colour, but it starred two Aboriginal lead actors, Rosalie Kunoth-Monks and Robert Tudawali. *Jedda* even went on to compete at the Cannes Film Festival's prestigious Palme d'Or award.

The portrayal of *Jedda* is bittersweet. Here is an Aboriginal woman featured on the silver screen in 1955, an Australian classic, shot through the white gaze. That good old slur Lubra and

Blackface make a cameo. And nothing like a bit of enticement to get bums on seats with hypersexualised promotional material such as 'Jedda the Uncivilised: The Magic of the Native Mating Call'.

But I still love *Jedda*. Rosalie Kunoth-Monks and Robert Tudawali always bring me to tears when I watch the film because, goddammit, representation matters, and *Jedda* will forever be iconic to me. This film, cinematically speaking, is magnificently shot. It is the first iteration of Blak Love in film, as problematic as that depiction is. I don't know what motivated Charles and Elsa Chauvel to centre the story around a tragic romance between a First Nations man and woman. But ultimately, it's a storyline created through the white gaze and therein lies the core issue. Blak Love perceived by white eyes and minds.

That is why Blak people must be the authors, writers, directors, photographers, cinematographers and creators of our lives and stories, who we are destined to be. It is our only redemption.

'I cannot stress the importance of us as Black people need to be able to tell OUR own stories without the white narrative. Being a Black woman in a racist and sexist industry which is dominated by white male photographers I won't be silenced, my work will be seen and I am not going anywhere.' (Instagram: @marleymorganphotography)

Fiona Foley's photographic series *Badtjala Woman* (1994) unshackles our Ancestors from nameless exotica tropes and brings us back to being the authority unto ourselves. Foley centres herself as the ethnographer, researcher and subject. She reinstates Blak women: we are majestic; we are sovereign.

With the rise of self-representation, Blak photographers such as Fiona Foley, Marley Morgan, Bobbi Lockyer, Colleen Raven

Strangways and Leicolhn McKellar reveal who we truly are. Seen through their lens, we are divine, purposeful, infinite and unforgettable.

And it warms me ever so that our Blak men have replaced the colonial purveyors to capture Blak people, culture and landscapes in all its gigorou. Rob Hookey, Luke Currie-Richardson, Trent White, Michael Jalaru Torres, Luther Cora and Lowell Hunter are among my favourites. There's something about a Blak man who honours their sistas' regalness in a world that chooses to suppress it. It's a comfort; I don't have to worry if they'll misinterpret me because they come from us – Blak women.

When we leave our stories to be told through the white gaze, it will permanently distort and detract from the truth of who we are.

Such views of Aboriginal women often reflected more about the European men themselves than their chosen subjects. The creation of such female images also shows the destructive nature of colonisation when European art, made for a European audience, perpetuated denigrating attitudes to Aboriginal women. (Anita Heiss, quoted in 'Exploring Aboriginal Identity through Self-Portraiture', Bianca Beetson, thesis for Doctor of Visual Arts, Queensland College of Art, Griffith University, 2017)

I refuse to watch Black colonial and slavery period pieces or rejoice when Black actresses win awards for trauma porn – exploited as slaves and servants rather than exalted as nurturing, wise, gentle, fierce, vulnerable and lovable.

It's why I cling to classics like *Radiance*, a story set in Far North Queensland, a place I call home, because it's storytelling I can relate to. Like Mae, Nona and Cressy, characters similar to the Blak matriarchy I come from. The cheeky and feisty Nona, played by Deborah Mailman, pushes everyone's buttons. She loves hard and is too young to know. Cressy (Rachael Maza) is a flash Blak who leaves her small town behind, only to come back to face the music. I see Mae (Trisha Morton-Thomas) in my sister: solid like a rock. But who's looking out for Mae when it becomes too much to bear?

Stories made possible by veterans Rhoda Roberts and Lydia Miller. Unintentional as it was, *Radiance* became a Blak story, which many women could relate to. Kismet saw *Radiance* become Rachel Perkins' directorial debut for a feature film and Deborah Mailman to be the first Aboriginal woman to win an AFI award in 1998 for Best Actress in a Leading Role. Aboriginal Girl Magic at its finest. These are the hallmark stories I grab on to and never let go. Blak women telling their stories, our stories through whatever medium they see fit.

Over the years, I've asked where is Aboriginal women's #MeToo movement? I now see it's already upon us: Blak Liberation through Blak Art.

As awful as these last two years have been as an Aboriginal and African-American woman persevering through the tragic death of George Floyd and the uprise of the B-L-A-C-K and B-L-A-K Lives Matter movements – same story, different soil – the silver lining is that it sparked a reckoning. Enough is enough. We can't keep going down this path. And now a new wave of truth-telling has begun, and Blak women are at its forefront.

16

Gin Jockey

I hate to say this, but Black Love is a unicorn I can't seem to catch. Hell, a Pegasus. No-one talks about Pegasus these days, do they? All I'm saying is I tried. I vividly remember the first time I dated a white man. As a mutual friend put it, Michael had a thing for Black women. Embarrassing as it is to admit, I was geeked a white man found me attractive. See what happens when you don't know Black is beautiful.

Pop quiz: How do you know you're being fetishised? Hmmm, I know, I know. When he asks you to talk Blak to him in the middle of Blockbuster. Yes, fam, here I was gearing up for a movie marathon, and out of the blue, Michael leans in and whispers, 'Talk Blak to me.'

My eyes abandoned the movie synopsis. I stared blankly at him. I'm being punk'd, right?

Michael asked again, 'Talk Blak to me.'

I pretended it didn't happen and continued to peruse the shelves.

Then Michael's caucasity went into overdrive. He screeched out, 'Eya, which way?'

I fricken died, and immediately fled the scene. I didn't even look up to see if anyone heard him. I couldn't live with myself if I locked eyes with another Blak person who did.

You see, guys like Michael are the usual suspects when it comes to dressing up in Blackface.

Back then, I didn't know how to handle a situation like that. But I do now …

[leans into radio mike] Dear White People. I don't know what possesses you to pull stunts like this. I've read the white papers on this phenomenon. But no matter how it's explained, I can't seem to wrap my head around it.

Fancy that! Tap dancing in the middle of Blockbuster for this fool's entertainment.

Man, I was naïve. I gave Michael a pass – because no harm, no foul, right? Michael was just a silly white guy, trying to be down. So, I let him love bomb me and invite me to family gatherings. A guy who isn't serious about you wouldn't introduce you to his mum and dad, right?

On one occasion, I accompanied Michael to a Christmas barbecue with his close friends.

Taylor, our host, greeted us when we arrived, escorting us through the stained-glass doors onto her sparkling white tiles. Michael's friends spotted us from the pool and raised their beers, calling us to join them. I felt Michael's hand on the small of my back, ushering me gently towards the verandah. I was grateful Ivanka, a friend of mine, was there. Breaking the pack, she bounded towards me and wrapped me up in her arms, planting a kiss on my cheek. Ivanka whisked me away from all the testosterone to grab a drink and a bit of privacy. Even though I didn't know Ivanka that well, she had a knack for reading people and making them feel at ease. But she also wanted to get the 411 on Michael and me.

Ivanka and I sat on the front steps nursing our beers.

'Sooo, how are you and Aaron going?' I asked Ivanka. I always felt comfortable shifting the focus on others.

Ivanka hesitated. There was trouble in paradise. She didn't have to go into details. I knew it was Ivanka's flirty nature that pissed Aaron off. I overhead Michael and Aaron chatting about it. She made a few cheeky comments to Michael, but I didn't feel threatened because he preferred Black Queens.

I tried to soothe Ivanka's angst with lies. 'Everything will be all right. I'm sure it's just a phase you two are going through.'

Ladies, we need to stop lying to each other. When a man wants to know where you are 24/7, tells you how to dress and complains you go out too much … hunny, it's not a phase. That's control.

'Do you have feelings for Michael?' she asked me.

A ridiculous grin spread across my face. 'Yes, I really like him.' She couldn't see it, but I was Black girl blushing.

Ivanka pulled me into her side and gave me a soppy hug.

Men always know when you're talking about them, I swear! My Nokia beeped.

Michael: 'Where are you? We're about to eat.'

Spicy steak meat and Crown beer wafted from the patio. The once rowdy bunch were shovelling down barbecue as only grown men could.

As the itis set in, Aaron broke out a bottle of Jägermeister to keep the party vibing. I was already on top of the world, nuzzled beside the man I was falling in love with.

Michael squeezed my hand intermittently to let me know he was thinking of me. I smiled back with stars in my eyes to let him know I thought he was the one.

Bryce, the man of the house, stumbled into an impromptu story about a night out in town with his girlfriend Taylor. I could tell the liquor had mellowed him, and as he edged further into his account, an uneasiness gurgled up in me. Bryce explained how Taylor had gotten shit-faced off two wines. He said he'd been agitated at the scene Taylor was making and told her to pull herself together or else he was leaving town without her.

As he spoke, I looked over at Taylor who was squirming in her seat. Bryce, being Bryce, didn't seem to read the room and proceeded, nonetheless. And this is where I inadvertently joined the story.

'... And then we pass a group of drunk Gins. You know them Gins that sit in the park uptown?'

He said it with such contempt, like they were – *we* were – the scum of the Earth.

Bryce's voice started to fade. My body went numb. Humiliation scrambled over me like a thousand spiders with no destination. I stared down at my drink and prayed no-one realised there was a Gin in the room.

Gin Jockey

Michael gently squeezed my hand, forcing me to face reality. I refused to acknowledge him and committed to watching the ice melt in my cup.

I felt my phone vibrate. I slowly reached for it. I don't know why; perhaps to help me escape this ...

Michael: 'Are you okay?'

Wooow!

And that's when I knew I was nothing more than Black Velvet to this Gin Jockey.

17

Archetypes

As a child, anger frightened me. I'd seen its ferocity between my parents. Holes in the walls, the smell of burnt gifts and polyester, photographs ripped into confetti pieces, and mosaics of broken crockery on the floor. Notes in my mother's handwriting with the words 'Attention Please', directed at my father, would be pasted to kitchen cabinets. And the air would be so thick you could cut it with a knife. I was a flower child born in the '80s, the decade of greed, the rise of the yuppie. Peace, love and harmony is my mantra. You can find me in the 'good vibes only' section. So, when conflict shows up, it feels like sandpaper scraping against my glossy veneer. Fight or flight? Hmmm, I'll take flight for 300, thanks, Alex. Unfortunately, life isn't *Jeopardy*, and love didn't seem like a prize I could win.

I was the eldest, and my strength was fixing things. It made me feel good to make everything better. I did this by consoling my younger siblings when my parents argued. Back then, I didn't know wounds weren't just physical; they were also emotional, psychological and financial. And the ones we love can attack us without using their hands or wielding a weapon. As peaceful as I was, anger brewed inside me. I miss how, when I was young, it lashed out unexpectedly when I needed it the most, especially when my ego was bruised.

Like the time, when living in the US, I lost a championship game of tetherball. My fellow competitors booed me off the court – even my best friend. Furious, I pushed her and told her to fuck off. And when the clock struck 3pm, Dawn and I were scheduled to fight, according to my classmates.

This marked my first fight, and it was against my best friend. I didn't know a damn thing about brawling. I was a church girl with no street smarts living on a Marine base within a gated community. Walking out of class, the student body of Oceanside Elementary waited for us on the vacant bitumen adjacent to the school. You could have easily thought New Kids on the Block was performing that afternoon. There was no backing down. I couldn't; I had a beehive of students escorting me to a fight I never commissioned. I pretended like I knew what I was doing. I took my position in the ring and started to mean mug Dawn. Thinking it was a fair fight I passed my backpack to a mutual friend, and as I turned around to fight, Dawn had swung her bag – batting my face for six. She cleaned my ass up on-site leaving me clutching my face with a sweet little cut under my eye. I was totally blindsided. How could she? Not only was it a cheap shot, but she was my best friend. I know Dawn felt bad as I recoiled in pain nursing my eye. I glared at her unforgivingly with the one eye I still had intact. She stopped the fight by storming off, leaving me there and the rest of the spectators wondering wth just happened. I snatched my bag in humiliation and made the walk of shame home with a trail of agitators roasting me. 'You let her,' they said.

Chanting 'Rematch, rematch, rematch' like a pack of hyenas.

But that was the least of my problems. Maria, the school bully, caught me from behind. All I heard was, 'Maria's coming!'

I spun around, and there she was, her brooding face burning into mine. Maria swooped me up by the scruff of my neck.

'Leave Dawn alone,' she ordered.

I didn't even know Dawn and Maria were tight like that. There was nothing left to do but crumble in her hands in a deluge of tears. Maria's anger broke me, right there in front of everyone. When she released me, I ran straight home.

My Dad was chilling with another Marine in the front yard and immediately went on the offence. 'What happened?'

I told Dad the entire story, and by the end of it, he told me to wash my face because we were going to Dawn's house. And our parents did what they did best – patched things up for us. We were forced to apologise to each other, and Dawn and I were friends again before my funky ass brang the heat.

Of course, the annual class photo was scheduled later that week. And guess who sported a crusty scar under her eye wearing three ponytails, ribbons and a church dress. They should have just given me the mugshot placard and called it a day.

It was some time before I let my anger get the best of me again. My defiant streak broke out when I stuck bubble gum in a school mate's hair because she annoyed the issh out of me. I scribbled in turquoise crayon on the white church pews because we worshipped far too much: five times a week to be exact. I decided in a bout of boredom enough was enough. God, if you don't know how much we are committed to your word, I really don't know what to tell you.

Oh, and then there was the time I shot daggers at my aunty's new boyfriend. I gave him the evil eye from the top of the staircase when they came home. My aunty wasn't having it. She put me in my place – reminding me she was grown. And told me to lose the attitude. That made it worse. Every time lover boy came around, I'd excuse myself from the room, letting everyone know I may not be grown, but I didn't have to be there.

Apart from the occasional beef with siblings and friends, I can't remember any other incidents where I woke up and chose violence.

Until I found my voice again at 13, when puberty sheds the charm of My Little Pony for Jodeci posters, SWV-styled bandanas, snapbacks and a Sony Walkman. The age-old moment when the combative sense of self breaks out of its cocoon, hormones race, and sneaking out the house at night came with the territory. Although I was too scared of the ass whooping and being grounded until 18 to lie about going to parties. Despite the wonder years, I didn't raise my voice like the ungrateful teenagers in *Beverly Hills 90210*. Because I knew better.

I chose to speak up in anger when violence was perpetrated against someone I knew. It wasn't conscious but reactive. No sooner did the words 'Leave her alone' crack out of me like a stock whip than I suddenly felt his hand squeezing my throat – my back pinned against the wall with nowhere to go. I was forced to lock eyes with the beast inside of him. I searched the black pit of rage for a sign of hope. He had the power of life and death in his hand. And when the rush of oxygen flooded my throat after a deep gasp, I realised I was still here.

After that, I kept my mouth shut. It was easier that way. Safer. Besides, what did I have to say that was so important – worth risking my life for? At the same time, the heroine inside of me wanted to kill the beast that lurked inside broken men. So, I subconsciously sought the beast out to slay it once and for all.

Following that fateful night, I began to choose my words carefully. The hairs on my arms could detect a threat naked to the eye. I let insults roll off me like water off a duck's back. I walked on eggshells and balanced on tightropes. I even performed flips and tricks like a trapeze artist without a safety net to prove how resilient I was – that I had everything it took to be a beast slayer.

But after a while, I got tired. I got angry. The meteorite inside me eventually came crashing to Earth. I had some close calls trying to tame the beast.

After one pointless argument with a boyfriend, I found myself clutching my hand to stop blood from gushing out. I stared at the pair of scissors jutting from the side of my palm. Dizzy, I tried to recall how it happened.

Another time my anger showed itself was during a night out. The following morning, a friend called to check in on me.

'Are you okay?' she asked.

'Yeah, I'm good.' Apart from an excruciating hangover and a sore neck.

'You scared us when you fell.'

'Fell?'

'Yes, off the table.'

Archetypes

The previous night slowly started to play back. In a fit of jealously, I'd drunkenly jumped on a tabletop and begun to gyrate *Coyote Ugly* style.

I don't know if I'd just been fed up with the abuse, being shown up in public by the other woman or all the above. Though, it seemed making him jealous didn't go to plan.

'We thought you were dead. You fell head first. You smashed into the floor so hard you didn't move.'

What if I did die? What would he do? I wasn't willing to find out. I looked death in the eyes one too many times to know anger can kill. But it also can be a life jacket that saves you.

We'd be lying if we didn't admit living vicariously through someone else – as fictional as they may be – is much easier than facing your own drama. There are so many make-believe heroines to draw inspiration from. Sometimes watching them play out the raw and complex sides we're too scared to acknowledge is what makes us human.

I feel satisfaction when Alex Irving in *Total Control* comes in like a wrecking ball and shoots my nerves to shit because she takes Total Control in a country that hates ballsy Blak women. Who clutches her hand after she's stabbed outside Parliament House, taking her place on the chamber floor because it's our turn for a Blak prime minister?

It's Quentin Tarantino's *Jackie Brown* when Samuel L. Jackson comes to kill Pam Grier, but she turns the table on him – pistol pressed up against his junk ordering his raggedy ass to take a seat. Duping the ATF and LAPD and jetting away half a million richer – minus Max Cherry's cut.

It's boss lady Jacqueline Broyer from *Boomerang* wearing a red power suit who finesses womaniser Eddie Murphy – giving him a taste of his own medicine, seductively blowing an eyelash out of Eddie's eye. My 12-year-old self decided: businesswoman and vixen – now that was my ministry.

We can't forget Angela Bassett's role as Bernadine Harris in *Waiting to Exhale* when she learns her marriage is over. Her tirade throughout the house as she yells, 'Get your shit, get your shit and get out.' Collecting all John's shit, dumping it in his BMW, and pouring gasoline on the luxuries she helped him obtain, famously lighting a match and tossing it in the car after lighting her cigarette. She takes a draw from it as we, the audience, wait for Bernadine to exhale.

Beyoncé's album *Lemonade* is a masterful culmination of these very characters (the dark feminine energies) hitting breaking point. When we wake up and remember who the fuck we are. The stages of denial, anger, pain, apathy, forgiveness and rebirth, the emotions women know all too well.

Lemonade is a reminder that the goddess within you is always present. Whether it's the river goddess Oshun bursting out of town hall through rapids of water. Flaunting her sensuality in a yellow ruffled dress, unbothered. Or fucking shit up with a baseball bat down the street with mischievous glee. Watching Beyoncé unleash her anger and revel in it is so gratifying. She is the avatar which Black women can embody – permitting us to do the same. Although ploughing a Monster truck over parked cars may be difficult; nonetheless, it's not impossible.

Archetypes

I should warn you; an avatar can only take you so far. There's a danger in abandoning oneself to play the victim or victor in a storyline that is not yours. Our own story needs our attention. Funnily enough, we might have to go back to where our story begins.

Sometimes I need to be reacquainted with the abandoned rebel. I miss the feisty girl that took her Year 8 report card home with the comment, 'Sasha is sassy.' Much to my father's dissatisfaction.

With stern words, Dad demanded I 'concentrate on maths instead of being sassy'. How I gloated afterwards because it ticked my father off. I wanted to be the strong-headed girl who walked five kilometres from her friend's sleepover, making it home before dark because I refused to be a little Blak nobody the other kids barely tolerated for the evening.

I missed that little Black girl before I was made to believe anger isn't pretty. Because the patriarchy knows our anger is power. That's why they are happy to appease us with storylines to fan out our flames.

As much as Jung's archetypes inspired me, he was a white man – just like the ones who are a cog in a system that doesn't serve me. What can Jung teach me that my Ancestors didn't figure out already? The only difference is one set of teachings and analysis is widely known – highly revered. That's why we have bronzed statues of white men who apparently did extraordinary things.

More importantly, my Ancestors didn't endure everything they did for me to sit on a couch in a bubble of escapism getting shit-faced. Sometimes we forget we are so much more than punchlines and avatars. You only need to look back in herstory to find out who you are.

I started to think about the alchemy of the Creation stories, how some stories saw our Ancestors exiled from our bodies, transformed from humans to animals, elements, the landscapes – from mountains, wind to stars. Was expulsion a time and a place for the Ancestors to do what we today call shadow work?

Uncle Darren yarned with me about how our mob used telepathy; how we sensed each other's passings and other unexplainable occurrences.

But nothing is unexplainable in our culture. Uncle thought about how Nana Jarrugan used to tell him the Dreaming stories just before he went to sleep. Uncle Darren said our mob already knew about the best time to retain information (psychologically) and why it made sense that jujuba – Dreaming (the white man's word for it) – funnily enough was spot on.

If you sit still long enough, you'll appreciate what the Old People left you. You'll hear their wisdom like the pitter-patter of rain on the leaves.

At school, I was taught about Hollywood's version of Cleopatra, Joan of Arc and Queen Elizabeth, but my people had our own goddesses: Barangaroo, Walyer, Truganini and Patyegarang. The Blak Matriarchs. Before Jung we had Oolana, Majal, Brolga and The First Rainbow to reconcile the divine and dark feminine archetypes.

The First Rainbow

Long, long ago, Nargeearr the Rainbow lived in a tiny mija (house) with his two daughters and their sons, not too far from Dooburrah (Dallachy Creek). Weak in his old age, Nargeearr relied on his daughters to feed him. They had to go hunting and travel further away from their camp as the dry spell had made nearby game scarce.

One day the two sons declared that they were too tired to travel the long distances with their mothers and wanted to stay at home with their grandfather. The sisters agreed and allowed their sons to remain at the camp, making their way to Dooburrah to gather fish. It took the sisters two days to collect enough fish for the entire family to eat. Although they were weary, the anticipation of seeing their beloved sons carried them safely home.

When the sisters got closer to the camp, they noticed it was unusually quiet, and their boys were nowhere in sight. Confused, they saw there in the corner of the mija lay their father. Desperate to know where their boys were, they woke their father up. For a moment, their father remained silent and refused to tell his daughters the whereabouts of their sons. But eventually, the horrific truth came out. The father had become overwhelmed with an insatiable hunger, and assuming his daughters had encountered an accident or even worse, death, he killed and ate the two children.

Immediately the two sisters dropped to their knees in grief until hatred consumed their hearts and revenge coursed through their veins. The daughters concocted a plan to wait until the sun went down to creep into their father's grass mija. Inside the humpy, their father lay snoring, sound asleep. The older sister twirled her firestick until smoke escaped into the evening air. Taking her firestick, she set her father's mija alight. Both sisters ran away from the blaze as fast as they could. Finally coming to a stop, the sisters looked over their shoulders and saw their father erupt into a fireball. He was hurled into the sky in a smouldering arc until he reached Gould Island, sinking into the ocean, never to be seen again.

Whenever we see the rainbow, we are reminded of the fury and sorrow that overcame the two daughters and their retribution against their wicked father. In the jujaba, the two sisters honoured their anger – never holding back the devastation they felt.

When we acknowledge our anger and trauma it is alchemised to become gigorou, The First Rainbow.

Barangaroo

If you've lived predominately in servitude of others like me, you probably have weak boundaries and feel guilty saying *no* to others. Some of us have created the version we think others prefer. Stiffing ourselves out of divine greatness. So, you've found yourself at the fork in the road. Are you going to follow your heart? Or perform in the circus?

For the best part of 15 years, I called Naarm home. Professionally, I had achieved all I could. I was stagnant; my zest for life all but lost. Was I on the brink of a mid-life crisis? All I know is that my body ached for adventure. I wanted to feel alive again. I fulfilled this yearning by bedding a younger lover and secretly revelled at my newfound cougar status. God, I hate that word. My sex was better than it had ever been. I had entered the golden age where I craved for fly-by-the-seat-of-my-pants escapades. I had a voracious appetite for everything I'd previously denied myself out of shame. I had robbed myself of the better part of my years.

Archetypes

Goddammit, I wanted my own *Eat Pray Love*. I wanted an Italian lover to cook me seafood scialatielli pasta and pour glasses of vino bianco with the sealine of Capri before us. I wanted to lick the cioccolato gelato as it melted down my hand while we lounged on the spiaggia. I wanted to write love letters on my terrace in Assisi after visiting the Basilica of Saint Francis. And let the rain baptise me for all my sins, and the ones I was about to commit as I prayed in Rome's Pantheon. I wanted to live my best life.

But I couldn't do that if I continued to colour inside the lines: being the good girl and the martyr. So, I took a leap of faith and placed my bet on *me*.

Four months later, I relocated to Warrang. I stayed with friends until I found a place in Balmain: a 15-minute walk away from the glorious views of the Sydney Harbour Bridge.

By then, I was pursuing new professional endeavours and found many of my business meetings were held at the Barangaroo precinct. I had an inkling Barangaroo was an Aboriginal word – the meaning and who I did not know.

When I was living in Naarm, I desperately wanted to live near the water. I'd walk the Williamstown esplanade when the weather was kind. I couldn't afford to rent in the area so I'd make a wish, hoping to get closer to the open seas. So, you can understand why I felt like a kid in the candy store as I glided across the emerald waters bordered by million-dollar homes and the impressive shipping vessels docked in the bay in Sydney. I inhaled the crisp sea breeze and let it tussle my hair like a whirlpool. Back and forth from Balmain to Barangaroo, Circular Quay to Manly.

I wondered about the stories these waters held – their secrets and the tales I simply didn't know. An early bird by nature, I'd arrive an hour before my meetings, content to watch the ferries – Bungaree and Pemulwuy pass me by. And stare at the Sydney Opera House, thinking how on earth did they build this iconic landmark situated on Dubbagullee (Bennelong Point).

And then there was this compelling urge to find out about Barangaroo. I asked others to see if they knew, but they didn't so I typed 'Barangaroo' into the Google search bar. I began to read about her, and it all made sense. Why her name stood out to me the most and how I could feel her gentle and insistent spirit beckoning me.

Barangaroo was a fiercely independent Cameraygal woman who held cultural authority in her clan – along with the other Eora women, who were the main food providers for their tribe. A skilful and patient fisherwoman, Barangaroo – and the other Eora women – traversed the surrounding waters of the north shore.

Through the wonderment of herstory, I transformed the landscape to when it was just us – our people, delighting in sovereign splendour. I'd sit on the concrete bench and let my mind erase the bustling hub of tourism and commerce and reimagine what her life was like.

What did they talk about during their fishing journeys as they navigated the calm to rough waters in their nawi (canoe) – breastfeeding their babies and setting up clay plates to cook on the open fire to eat and keep them warm well into the evening.

I thought about how the Eora women conducted women's business on the waters. How the waves were witness to their counsel, the songs they sang and the fishing and canoeing lessons taught to their young girls. Teaching them how to twist and bind fibres from the kurrajong tree and flax plant and using grass and animal fur to make carrejun (fishing lines). And how to prepare the bara (fishing hook) out of the turban shell.

I began to admire their freedom to come and go as they pleased. How the waters were their domain, and the immense pride they must have felt. I mulled over what Barangaroo would have endured at the height of colonisation, the change and challenges it brought to her and her people, how it took away their autonomy.

Even though Barangaroo survived the smallpox outbreak, sadly, she lost her first husband and two children from the ravaging disease that took the lives of many of her people. As one of the few women left who retained the cultural knowledge, lore and rituals, she became invaluable – not only among the women but also to her tribe.

Barangaroo also had the foresight to see the devastation colonisation would bring to her culture even when her second husband – a younger and ambitious Bennelong – succumbed to the charms of the colonial way.

The more time I spent in her space, the more I could feel her. Barangaroo's energy danced with mine – the interplay of her essence and mine became my newfound superpower. When I was preparing for my meetings, I would think about the outcomes I wanted to achieve and the actions I needed to take. If I needed to lead, I knew I could. If I needed to be neutral, discerning, I would. And if I needed to stand in my power, I did – just like Barangaroo did all those years ago.

According to British journals, Barangaroo frightened the colonial officers by her sheer presence – combative, she did not back down in her convictions. This was evident when Barangaroo was invited to watch a public flogging: disgusted by such abhorrent behaviour, she confiscated the whip from the officer – a gesture that extended empathy towards the matter at hand.

Barangaroo's distaste deepened when she saw British colonists trawl 4000 salmon off the north shore in just one day, then gifting some of this catch to her husband and some of the other men from her tribe. Barangaroo knew such a wasteful act would threaten the Eora women's cultural authority within the tribe, destroying their traditional way of life.

So Barangaroo rejected British laws and customs, their food, drink and social etiquette, even when her husband decided to conform. When Barangaroo and her husband Bennelong were invited to dine with Governor Phillip and the British party, Barangaroo stayed true to who she was. Instead of wearing colonial attire – a tight corset and a gown layered in silk finished with pearls – she came sporting her traditional wares: white ochre and a bone through her nose. In her defiance Barangaroo demonstrated her sovereignty was non-negotiable.

This remained a constant cause of contention between her and Bennelong. Barangaroo was displeased with Bennelong's burgeoning relationship with Governor Phillip. They fought over this, and she made her feelings known, breaking his spears when he'd visit Warrang.

Despite the pressure from Bennelong to adopt a colonial lifestyle when it was time to give birth to her baby girl, she

Archetypes

objected to his request to deliver her at Government House. Instead, she went bush and gave birth to her daughter alone. Not long after childbirth, Barangaroo made a fire to enjoy what would be brief moments with her newborn wrapped in soft bark nestled in her arms. Sadly, Barangaroo passed away shortly afterwards. Bennelong had Barangaroo cremated with her prized fishing tools in a ceremony. Unfortunately, against her wishes, Barangaroo's ashes were buried in the gardens of Government House.

I started to think about the intense feeling to be close to the sea. And the longer I pondered on this I wondered did Barangaroo call me through the waters. Did she call me here to learn her story – inspire me to learn many others – to link me back to stories of my matriarchs to realise my own. And how serendipitous it was to be sitting directly across from where her ashes remained with no idea – just a feeling.

I thought about what Aunty Bella said to me once, 'Country calls for us – you can feel that spirit. You know them Old People are out there looking out for you.'

When Aunty shared this with me, I interpreted this to mean my traditional Country, the place I return to remember who I am, to gather strength when I am weak and disoriented. But in Warrang, the message became so much clearer. Who was I to think the Ancestors are bound to one place, that their messages aren't carried by the southerly winds to meet us where we are, to lead us to where we need to be.

For now, Warrang feels like home. I love it here, in a rock pool of bliss, carving out new memories in the confidence of my newfound womanhood that I fought to protect. The decision to choose *me*.

Boori Plain

I cackled watching parodies of Cookie Lyon from *Empire* on TikTok. It dawned on me that I was once Cookie, desperately clinging to remnants of myself.

That scene teleported me back to when I hit 30 and every fibre begged for me to put myself first. I was getting married, but deep inside I knew I was making a big mistake. I rationalised that I'd come this far. Worst case scenario, I could get divorced if it didn't work out.

We were 48 hours out, and my fiancé was unaware that my Mizuno Waves were laced up and ready to go. This runaway bride was about to hightail it from the promises of marital bliss to the fields of freedom.

You see, what had happened was, Jodi, my fiancé, had stepped off a plane from Miami. My shoulders slumped sitting in the car as he bounded towards me, because he was here, live in the flesh. His dazzling smile greeted me through the car window. Jodi lightly pounded on the car boot for me to open it, which annoyed me. Who did he think he was bringing his stuff to merge his life with mine? I sat anxiously waiting until he got into the passenger seat. I did my best to exchange pleasantries. I used concentrating on the highway as an excuse to buy myself time. Jodi didn't seem to notice my unease as he reclined his seat back. Please make yourself at home, why don't ya, I muttered under my breath. I unintentionally became Jodi's tour guide as he gestured to a building or an Aussie phrase on a billboard asking what it meant. Note to self: rekindling a summer fling you had at 19 in Miami via Facebook ain't cute.

I let 24 hours fly by, hoping I'd ease into the life-changing decision I was about to make. My self-soothing wasn't working. Dad had rung and told me to 'drop that boy off' because he wanted to talk to him. No doubt the father of the bride and husband-to-be premarital talk. I breathed a sigh of relief. I needed to be alone to think. I dropped Jodi off, returned to my house, and burst into tears.

When you're searching for something, you're going to find it. A little voice inside my head told me to look in his phone. I couldn't believe Jodi had left it open. The exit door I was praying for was served to me on a silver platter.

Jodi had pulled a Tiger Woods on me.

Scrolling through his gallery of conquests, I immediately sized up who was pretty, cute and trash – trying to figure out why he would cheat with all these women. I don't know why we fall into the trap of comparing ourselves to the other woman. It seems to come as a complimentary side dish we specifically told the waiter we didn't want.

Great! Now I'm left pondering: maybe Pam had a bomb ass personality and made my man laugh in ways I didn't. Ludicrous, right! Through clenched teeth, I critiqued each woman. DMX's raspy bark reeled in my head. There was Cindy, Aiesha, Bonnie, Tameka … and the list went on.

My coochie began to twitch. Oh great, what if he gave me something? Believe it or not, the possibility of catching an STI or HIV was more aggravating than Jodi's cheating.

After gathering all the evidence I needed, I drove over to Dad's and asked Jodi to come outside for a chat. I flatly asked him, 'Have you been cheating on me?'

'No, I haven't.'

If I hadn't had the dirt to prove it, I would have believed him. He was so convincing. I took the L with dignity and turned on my heels, leaving Jodi standing in the driveway, left to explain to my dad what was going on. I jumped in the car and sped off; my mother would be landing soon.

From the West Gate Bridge to Tullamarine, I cried me a river. Mum hopped in the car, took one look at me and didn't say a word. I drove for five minutes before I blurted out, 'The wedding is off!'

Officially a woman scorned, I cursed and spluttered as Mum absorbed my fury like a sponge. When we got home, I sank onto the couch, defeated. My mother scooped me up in an 'It's going to be all right' bear hug. I let my tears of betrayal soak her shawl and allowed my face to puff up like the Michelin Man. When there were no more tears left to cry, Mum went into 'What we gonna do?' mode.

'I told you, Mum, the wedding is off.'

'Okay. Have you told him?'

'No!'

'Well, you gotta tell him. Where is he?'

'At Dad's.'

'Call him and your father up and tell them to come over here.'

I made the call. I didn't know how to break the news. Best believe Mum was taking no prisoners. She didn't even wait for

Jodi and Dad to get settled before her miniature frame paced the floor. 'Okay, Sash, tell him.'

Thanks a lot, Mum.

I can't remember what I said, but I was the most honest I had been in a long time. I had known this was not the man I wanted to spend the rest of my life with. I wasn't ready to admit I had settled because Father Time was knocking on my door. The incessant tick of my biological clock kept me up at night. And Jagged Edge's 'We ain't gettin any younger' convinced me to meet Jodi at the gates of holy matrimony.

Jodi sat emotionless when my truth gushed out of me and stained the crème carpet like red wine. I glanced over at my father, now a mind-blown emoji.

Later that night, Jodi and I lay in bed. I was too tired to fuss. I told him to cut the act. I knew all about his scandalous ways. The silence that divided us lasted an eternity. Jodi tried to grab me in his arms, but I turned my back to him.

He meekly whispered, 'I'm sorry.'

I let his half-ass apology lie between us in the middle of the bed. I closed my eyes and fell fast asleep, my confession no longer a burden I had to carry.

My father gave me the silent treatment the next day as we sat in Degani's as one big happy family. I felt it was my responsibility to be upbeat; trying to mop up this sombre mess like The Cleaning Lady. I watched my father order delicious little desserts and eat them depressingly with a teaspoon as if his dog had just died. He acted as if I'd left *him* at the altar, not Jodi. My father had no idea why I called the wedding off. It would be a year later when Dad got the whole story. By that time, I had grieved and made peace with the ordeal. But at that moment, I chose to protect Jodi from Dad. I should have thrown him to the wolves.

Ruby, my best friend to this day, still laughs when I bring up the time I almost got married. I ended up inviting sissy to live it up in the Honeymoon Suite at the Grand Hyatt. I may not have had a husband, but I did have a sista for life. We drank Captain Morgan and mused, 'Where to now?' Taking in the midnight stars and Melbourne city lights as they twinkled and danced for us.

A few drinks in, I laughed heartily; now I didn't have to worry about how horrible the wedding photos would have turned out. My biggest fear, apart from marrying a man who wasn't the love of my life, was our forced relationship captured on film. I can tell you a Madame Tussauds wax figure was more convincingly real than our relationship. I knew the wedding photos would be evidence my marriage was a sham. The camera doesn't lie. People do.

The only regret I had was not being there for my brother when he really needed me. I was still tender and hadn't broken off the relationship with Jodi. Numb and somewhat delusional, I didn't want to end things on a bad note. So, it was my idea for Jodi and me to enjoy our honeymoon. It didn't seem right, all that money going to waste. Besides, I might get the closure I was hoping for.

Tired and dishevelled, I dropped by my sister's house after making it to Gimuy. I ducked into my brother's room: he was listening to beats, drinking a Bundy. There's nothing more comforting than wrapping your arms around your soulmate when life just kicked your ass. But bittersweet when your brother is holding on by a thread. I could see in his eyes he had a lot to get off his chest. I was still emotionally drained and knew I had to leave to make the long drive to Palm Cove.

Before I left, I told Jr we'd talk later. Later never came, and we never got to have that talk. Three weeks later, my brother passed away. I blamed myself. The one time I wasn't there for him. His cry for help plagued me.

Would he still be here if we'd talked? Was it my fault? What if …?

In the end, none of that matters. Spirit chooses to go, and we can do nothing about it. All we can do is accept it – grieve and get on with our lives. I know for a fact my brother doesn't want me blaming myself while he's experiencing his new journey with his Ancestors.

I move differently these days, especially when it comes to people and time. I'll always have the conversation I didn't have with Jr in the back of my mind. Not to torture myself, but to remind me tomorrow isn't promised. A constant checklist: Who or what am I entertaining that isn't worthy of me?

The silver lining is that I trust myself. I know what I'm made of. I'm brave enough to choose me. I know what I want and what I don't want. Everyone might not like the decisions I make, and that's all right. At least I can go to sleep at night with no regrets and a full heart.

Like they say, when one door closes, another one opens. Don't settle. You never know what's waiting for you around the corner.

Boori Plain was a luxuriant jungle that thrived with every green plant, vine and fern known to the tropics. Scrub hens and bush turkeys diligently scratched up the ground and made nest mounds. Grand displays of black bean, milk pine, pencil cedar and lawyer vines dominated, and to the north, where the jungle met the dense forest, towering blue gums and Moreton Bay ash claimed the lands.

One evening, Boori, the margoi (python), slid down his mountain hill to see a special lady. The lady's home was nestled in a huge fig tree by a bubbling stream. During lazy days, she'd curl up and rest, and when winter arrived, she'd stretch out her sylphlike body to bask in the sun's rays. Her physique glistened under the morning light.

Boori watched her from afar and fell in love with her. She was fond of Boori too, and agreed to marry him when he declared his love. He raced home to prepare his mija for his new wife with much delight. While Boori was away, his rival slid in and began to court the young lady. When Boori found out, he was infuriated and set out to kill his enemy.

Boori tracked his rival down to the bottom of Boori Plain. The pythons wrestled, their bodies coiling and releasing – battling it out for seven days and seven nights. Their jaws locked on to one another, dragging each other across the land. Knocking down trees, leaving a path of destruction: broken trunks, branches and piles of vegetation on the jungle floor. Boori, the victor, killed his opponent and reclaimed his love. And together, Boori and his wife lived happily ever after.

Today, when you visit the battleground, you'll see a large clearing where the trees no longer grow. The only thing that remains is the scrub hen mounds to remind us of the lush jungle that once stood.

Sis, this is what 'I don't chase; I attract' means. You are worth the fight. If they don't move heaven and earth for me, I don't want it.

18

Louis vs Jawun

Nothing can describe walking into Louis Vuitton to purchase your first LV. It's as if you've arrived, strolling past security, like Joanne the Scammer. It was my 30th birthday, and I was there to buy the brown monogram canvas Speedy 25, launched in 1930. They called it the express because peeps had places to go and people to see in those days. I could appreciate that, along with its iconic rolled leather handles, cowhide leather trim, gold engraved signature padlock and key.

I did several laps of the boutique pretending I still hadn't made a decision. But I already knew what I came for. I had researched everything about the Speedy 25. When you're forking out nearly $1500, you want to be 100 per cent confident. I wasn't sure when I'd find myself in LV again, so I basked in the ambience: the plush carpet, leather seats and intimate lighting that complemented your skin tone. Ahhh, the smell of expensive leather. I can't tell you how many times I'd walk past the designer boutiques on

Collins Street on my way to the train station. As 50 Cent put it, I was a window shopper: Salvatore Ferragamo, Chanel, Prada, Fendi and Balenciaga were all on my route.

I wanted to wear Burberry poolside, sport a Birkin bag filled with Benjamins. I wanted to be the Christian Dior and Gucci loafer diva. On red carpets rockin Marc Jacobs. A Versace hottie with diamond-tipped toenails. I grew up on rap: Jay-Z, Foxy Brown and Lil' Kim's lyrics, along with other rappers who introduced a housing commission teenager to designer fashion.

As soon as I could get my hands on anything designer, I did. My first pair of designer shoes were Fendi. One day, I met with a potential modelling agent who said she modelled for Fendi in London.

'Do you know Fendi?' she asked superciliously.

I pointed to my shoes haughtily. 'Oh yes, I know Fendi.'

That's what designer fashion does; it gives you the confidence to check a bish.

The LV assistant hovered before asking me if she could help. I got her to show me a wallet and some small leather goods. I mulled over the items as if I had options, before beelining it to my dream bag. 'Yes, thank you. I'll take it.'

I patiently listened to the assistant as she ran through the care instructions, certificate of authenticity and how to fold my Speedy 25. I floated out of LV down Collins Street, ostentatiously swinging the apricot bag inscribed with Louis Vuitton in dark chocolate lettering. Look, mama, I made it!

The allure was short-lived: owning a Speedy is impractical. I had to walk around with ashy hands because wearing hand lotion damaged the leather handles. I forgot on multiple occasions. Fark! Splotches of Palmer's Cocoa Butter ate through the leather. Oh, that's why they wrap scarves around the handles, to preserve the patina. I had to find clean surfaces for Louis to sit on. I checked the weather to see if Louis could join me for the day. You'd think I was taking care of a child. And where were the goddamn compartments? I spent another $50 on a purse organiser and hand-cut a cardboard base. Every time I put anything in the Louis, it weighed the bag down like a sooky child's bottom lip. What feels more ridiculous: paying $1500 for a bottomless pit or digging through it for your credit card in a line of impatient customers?

In the end, I sold Louis on eBay, along with my Tiffany & Co. Heart Tag bracelet and the Anna Campbell wedding dress Jodi never got to see me in. I booked a trip to Vietnam with the proceeds – a gift to myself after I called off my wedding.

At least I have memories of parasailing hungover, enjoying the best pho and iced coffee, watching my life flash before me crossing the streets of Hanoi and canoeing in Halong Bay.

That sure beats the illusion of luxury – by a long shot.

When it doesn't work out with one design house, try another. I swore off designer bags when I broke up with my Louis Vuitton Speedy 25. I was reluctant to dust myself off and try again. But I had to get my confidence back and remember what it felt like to fall in love. I took it slow, ditching tubs of Connoisseur chocolate ice-cream in bed for dinner with a friend. Brunch and an afternoon at the gallery rolled into a weekend away at the vineyard with the girls. I flirted with a suitor here and there, satisfied to bask in a bit of enticement from afar. Gucci's Dionysus emerald leather mini and Saint Laurent Lou camera bags did catch my eye.

Crawl before you walk, Sasha, was my motto when the urge to impulse-buy nearly had me in foetal position. You are a complicated woman with luxury taste; do not settle. I stayed the course, but nothing prepares you for the day you lock eyes with your first love: John Galliano's Dior Saddle Bag. The closest I'd get to equestrian, when riding a horse nearly killed me at 14.

Genius, Galliano, genius! I wasn't the only one who had eyes for Galliano's classic. I saw her with Carrie Bradshaw on *Sex and the City*, under the arm of Paris Hilton. (The only exception I made for her was Foxy Brown, Galliano's muse. The pair's proclivity for controversy made sense, a creative affair of the new millennium.) So, when she disappeared, I was heartbroken. I didn't get to look at her one last time or even say goodbye. Until the Autumn/Winter of 2018, when Christian Dior's creative director, Maria Grazia Chiuri, brought her back out of exile. Her charm ceased to fade: how I longed to trace my finger over her kidney-shaped body, C&D curves. The only thing that had changed was a minor enhancement, a messenger strap. Galliano's classic had grown into a better version of herself; she had the practicality, a fancy new strap that I needed and could respect.

Why do fools fall in love? They rush in as I did with Speedy. I didn't give it time to see if Speedy and I were compatible. Had I known better, I would have held out for the LV Twist. I know it's presumptuous, but I thought we could have great chemistry.

I had a reverence for Dior. John Galliano brought the House of Dior into the 21st century. As did Olivier Rousteing – by merging luxury into the digital age, generating relevance with an online demographic. As the creative director of Balmain, Rousteing was the second youngest to lead a French fashion house. It was Yves Saint Laurent for Christian Dior, at 21, who was the first.

Rousteing's notoriety could easily fill a novel, a Harry Potter box set, so I'll keep it brief. One word: Coachella. The Queen Bee herself (the first Black woman to headline the event) commissioned Rousteing to design a series of outfits for her. That gave rise to the unforgettable *Homecoming* yellow and pink sweaters, paired with COAL N TERRY cut-off denim shorts and custom-made holographic fringe boots by Christian Louboutin. It paid homage to the Civil Rights movements, historically Black colleges and universities, and Black culture. And we can't forget Beyoncé's showstopping Egyptian Queen Nefertiti-inspired costume.

To date, one of my favourite collections is Rousteing's 2014 Balmain Fall/Winter Ready to Wear (inspired by Africa), starring three of the most iconic Black women on the planet – Rihanna, Naomi Campbell and Iman – with fashion direction from Edward Enninful, now editor-in-chief of *British Vogue*.

Galliano's C&D monogram found a home in rap and R&B at its height, in videos, lyrics and live performances. Rousteing is emulating Galliano's fashion crossover but taking it out of this galaxy. And he's just getting started: picking up from where his predecessors left off, launching Balmain Army #BalmainEnsemble – echoing Bethann Hardison, Naomi

Campbell and Iman's (Diversity Coalition) call for more diversity and inclusion in the fashion industry.

I deeply admire Rousteing's candour in his documentary, *Wonder Boy*. I think children of colour searching to find their roots and who they are harbour huge voids to fill. It appears Rousteing's antidote is plunging himself into fashion, refining his artistry – impeccability – like he has something to prove.

But not everyone is like Rousteing. The entry to luxury fashion could be destiny or the inheritance of a dynasty, as in the case of the Fendi sisters.

How did the Fendi sisters learn? Was it watching and listening, hands-on, or all the above?

What makes a designer legendary? Technicality, instinct, or both? Rousteing strikes me as an intuitive designer. I believe this is what makes him legendary.

Then I think about Aboriginal art. It is instinctive, as is fashion; made legendary by the artists from many nations and signature styles. Strikingly beautiful pieces: our practice originating from ochre, blood, rock, bark, sand and the body long before schoolteacher Geoffrey Bardon encouraged the transference of traditional storytelling onto new canvases and the start of the Papunya Tula Art Movement.

Instinct is what keeps art, fashion and culture alive. Uncle Abe Muriata, a Girramay master weaver, is the only man and one of roughly 20 weavers across 26 tribal groups in Far North Queensland (the Wadjan Bama) who carries the knowledge and craftsmanship of our signature bicornual basket design; the jawun, a cane dilly bag. Uncle Abe taught himself after watching his grandmother weave. Not formally taught by his grandmother through technique, Uncle Abe took trips to the museum and studied our ancient artefacts to gain a keen eye for the intricate lines, symmetry and texture; its sacred geometry. Uncle Abe's passion for reviving his grandmother's knowledge of weaving has seen the master craftsman's works exhibited in galleries and museums across Australia, Aotearoa and London.

You won't find our design anywhere else in the world; it is entrusted to us – an exquisite artefact of cultural and spiritual significance to its descendants.

Jawun is made from two materials: lomandra from the open forest and black palm. We use fire to heat the cane to help strengthen it. A knife, quartz stone or your nails can be used to split the cane. It takes precision to carefully split the lawyer cane. That's why identifying the right piece in the forest is an essential step of the process. And, of course, the cross-hatching weaving technique that creates our splendid, timeless, signature design. Weavers are known to use their whole bodies – from the mouth, teeth, hands and feet. The artist's energy is harnessed in each piece.

Jawun has a multitude of purposes: food collection and processing. Jawun is used to leech out the poison of food like mirrayn. The bicornual hooks of the basket are lodged securely between rocks in a stream. We let the continuous rushing water flush out the poison over a few days. Babies, at one time, were carried in the basket. The wide and long handle would sit on the mother's forehead while the baby rested in the basket against her back.

The bones of loved ones who'd passed were placed in the jawun and carried when mourning. These jawuns were specifically painted in colour to signify there had been a death. You can't do that with a Louis Vuitton. Yes, carrying money, credit cards, make-up, perfume and a daily planner. Not a traditional piece symbolic of life, death and purification. We may not have had special edition designer collections, but our markings and pigments signified its sacredness.

I thought about the Louis Vuitton, Coco Chanel, Yves Saint Laurent and Fun Fur double monograms being synonymous with luxury. When I look at jawun, I see cultural opulence – its immanent rarity. I thought about the small Fendi fur charms and Maria Grazia Chiuri's Dior Saddle Bag's modern messenger strap.

We had miniature bags too: mindis, small woven grass baskets traditionally used to carry small personal items, gifts and message sticks across Country to trade and communicate with other tribes.

Why do designer bags hold so much significance? Is it colour, style, texture, architecture or symbolism?

What makes us fall in love with a designer bag? Is it simply that beauty is in the eye of the beholder?

All I know is fashion wouldn't be fashion, art wouldn't be art, and culture wouldn't be culture if there weren't a resonance – an appreciation. One person's eyes meet another's at the same vantage point of recognition. A fervour to keep its inherent cultural legacy alive.

19

Ascension

When confronted with death, you quickly understand what they mean by 'Life is short.' Why do we wait for tragedy to find us before attacking life with urgency, grabbing destiny with both hands, and refusing to let go? Why was I so distracted? Why did I neglect myself? My dreams, my desires. These were the questions that plagued me as I grieved my brother and failed engagement.

Who am I? What is my passion – my purpose?

I knew I hated where I was at. In the last six years, I had bounced around from corporate, private, not-for-profit until settling down in the government.

Did it make my heart sing? Hell, no! Did it pay my bills? Hell, yes, and benefits. Safety and security were what I was raised to value. From a young age, high-profile jobs like a lawyer, doctor, accountant – pretty much six-figure careers – were the occupations of success. I came from a generation of Black parents who had our best interests at heart. But the conversation about living out your passion didn't make it to the dinner table.

It went down like this. My father asked to read my course selections for Year 10. Shortly thereafter, Dad announced I was taking business management, accounting, secretarial studies and Japanese. I got to choose one subject; I chose commercial art – one of the two classes where I got to explore my creativity and engage in healthy debate. I told Ms Strosvsky how absurd it was for her to critique my art. How you gonna judge what pours from my heart onto construction paper? My art is my art.

Since the significant piece up for debate was worth 50 per cent of my grade, Ms Strosvsky's opinion did matter regarding technicalities such as texture, balance, colour and unity. Considering the arguments I presented, I haggled Ms Strosvsky to a B+ instead of a C.

English was the other subject that helped an awkward Black girl escape brutal ledgers that didn't balance and who'd failed to count past roku in Japanese class. I did master 'Toire wa doko desu ka', the most important question to know when travelling in Japan. Where's the toilet?

Ms Jenson's English class is where stories jumped from the page and crystallised, taking me wherever I wanted to go without a passport. Fiction turned into non-fiction, if I believed it. My anxiety soared through the roof when red pen graffitied every page – a place where I had to trust my pen game to claim victory over writer's block. Where Martin Luther King's declaration, 'I have a dream', Sojourner Truth's question, 'Ain't I a woman?' and Oodgeroo Noonuccal's 'We Are Going' meant I still belonged. Words of affirmation that gave me back my humanity and promised new beginnings.

So, when it came to answering the question, what is my passion? It was writing and creativity by way of beauty and fashion. Although I'd turned my back on modelling, due to the lack of opportunities for diverse models, a love like that never goes away. I grew up in a beauty salon and dreamed of being a Black supermodel. So, no, I wasn't going to throw all that away. Fashion: you and me, we have history.

And I wasn't going to tolerate women of colour's invisibility in Australian fashion, beauty and media. Importing *Ebony* and *Essence* magazines to see a reflection of me was no longer going to fly. Nor was I paying a fortune for beauty products that weren't available for us on Australian shelves.

How many times do I have to fill out customer feedback forms and remind you my beauty matters? Lodge complaints to the Australian Communications and Media Authority, Australian Press Council, and rant in letters to the editors of Aussie mastheads.

But at the end of the day, I knew who I was. I am the child of James and Delphine. Oh, and let's not forget my Ancestors' wildest dreams: they didn't fight for me to come this far just to let the gatekeepers keep on keepin'!

So, when the Ancestors conspire with the universe and take inventory of all your dreams and plant a seed. That right there is called an epiphany.

Why you over here fussin' when you can ... wait a minute ... create your own magazine.

By golly, that's a great idea!

I fired up the internet and began attacking the search engine with: Black Australian women's magazine, multicultural women's magazine, Indigenous women's magazine, switching up the keywords.

There were no active publications. Not one that represented me: a First Nations, African-American, Javanese and Mauritian woman.

What? Shut up. You mean to say my magazine is an Australian first?!

Hallelu, won't he do it!

But what to name my magazine?

I didn't want to name her something bland like Jane or Cleo. No shade, but who are these women? I'm not a Cleo, certainly not a Sarah, but nearly every second person addresses me as her in an email, on prescriptions and my coffee order before I bought a KeepCup. Do I look like a Sarah? Once again, no disrespect, but why can't they let me be great?

After the death of Jr and letting Jodi go, I had to repair my spirit: which led me on a spiritual journey. I started doing the work. Part of that work was cutting ties to social, family and religious programming to get to my core. I had to release the fear of God's wrath by fire and brimstone to discover who I was. I went through my own kintsugi, the art of precious scars.

It began with salvaging all the broken pieces I could find shattered on the floor. Dusting them off and placing them carefully on rose pink tissue paper. Each day I would sit with a broken piece – relive that moment – honour the pain, and let the saltwater burn my eyes and heal my wounds. Sometimes I'd spend days, weeks, months on just one piece. And when I was ready, I'd forgive myself and set that piece aside on a new table, on a new sheet of green tissue paper.

When all was forgiven, the same process happened all over again. This time around, I had fun. I felt lighter. Binding the foundation of me back together into one whole piece with glue and sealing it with fine gentle strokes of gold powder. It signified a renewed love for self – imperfection at its best.

I believe brokenness can be temporary. Oftentimes, we are quick to cast judgement or claim we or they are broken, leaving one in a state of victimhood. Courage knows the wound only remains open if we don't tend to it.

Part of doing the work was finding what spiritual practices meshed with me. Ruby asked if I wanted to try out meditation. I'd never done it before and said yes. She handed me a flyer. It had the word 'Ascension' emblazoned on the cover.

Ascension. I liked how it glided on my tongue and sat in the back of my mind.

That first meditation session was crazy: I was an African goddess who was the mother of three boys; Jodi was my husband. The story didn't end well. Jodi betrayed our tribe. As his wife, I had to banish him from the tribe. But I got some good karma back, reincarnating as a Greek goddess who had all the admiration and riches I could dream of. My last journey was with Jr, a vision I still carry safely with me. In silence, we watched the desert glow from the balcony of an Egyptian temple. Telepathically, I said all I needed to say. I made peace with my baby brother and said goodbye – no words – as he handed me over to my husband, a pharaoh. It turned out that session was the closure I needed.

I knew exactly what I was calling my magazine: *Ascension*.

Golden Ticket

I had the hottest ticket to Australian fashion's most anticipated event – Australian Indigenous Fashion Week (AIFW) 2014. This event was setting the industry's tongues wagging and carving itself into Australian fashion history and the fashionistas' diaries.

I contacted AIFW's founder Krystal Perkins the minute I got the press release. I needed to be there. Krystal emailed me back, congratulating me on the upcoming opening of *Ascension*, and invited me to pre-launch it at AIFW. The fashion gods were smiling down on me; everything was aligning. My official invitation and the run sheet came through soon after. I'd be presenting just before former *Vogue Australia* editor-in-chief Nancy Pilcher. She had recently retired from the role, handing over the reins to June McCallum.

Are you kidding me? *Vogue Australia*, the fashion bible I grew up with, stacking my monthly editions in order of molto bene to cosi cosi? Christmas had arrived a second time that year. I glossed over the fashion line-up again; so did Imposter Syndrome. It even had the audacity to ask me, 'You sure you're supposed to be here?'

I idolised *Vogue*. To me, it was the fashion monarchy: its models, editorials, September editions and editors – everything. I knew I had no fashion pedigree; my CV mentioned no interning; no assistant or secretary roles; no moving up the ranks or swimming in their tight circles of exclusivity. Heck, I didn't finish high school or get a degree in journalism, which niggled at me over the years. What did a high school drop-out and former model have to offer?

I didn't have a mentor or business coach I could confide in, either. In many respects, I was on the outside looking in when it came to the fashion industry.

You've probably heard 'Find your tribe' – which is problematic, so let's rephrase it to 'Find your squad'. For sure I had that. When you choose the right people to share your life with, they become your professional wingpersons – raising you up and refusing to let you be mediocre. They're behind the scenes helping to peel the potatoes so you can serve up your lip-smacking buttery mash. In my case, they were also throwing my name into the ring at functions when I didn't pipe up about *Ascension*. Or introducing me to people I should meet. Schmoozing was never my thing. I thought it to be too braggadocious. Though, now, those old reactions of mine sound like tall poppy syndrome to me.

So, yes, a lot of my journey was governed by the ideology of 'fake it till you make it' until I realised the path I was on wasn't happenstance. I believe a lot of our success consists of how good our manifestation game is. The trust we possess to hand over control. There is only so much hard work, dedication and technique we can apply to the equation until we eventually have to let go to allow the blessing to find its way back to us.

I think of what Cathy Freeman said in her documentary *Freeman* about how she'd visualised winning gold at the 2000 Olympics, and knowing her competitors didn't stand a chance when she ran the race of her life. Rightly so. We are the First Peoples; our Ancestors' footsteps have already paved the way to victory.

As much as we physically train to finish our race, we also have to do the spiritual work. My spiritual teacher gave me homework to do, which I procrastinated over because I felt stupid looking in the mirror every day repeating the mantra: I am safe to be seen, to shine, and be fully in my power. If you can't confront the person staring back at you, that's part of the problem. I had my 5D L-plates on. While I was learning how to drive, I started telling people about *Ascension*, a handy tip a friend suggested to make me accountable to everyone I told. It also helped deter me from chickening out or downplaying the magnitude of my dream. That's why you've probably heard people say speak it into existence or write it down on paper; that way it becomes real.

My other major hang-up was all the moonlighting I was doing to launch *Ascension* into the market. I was also working a full-time job, like most entrepreneurs do until their capital game was tight. I found myself pumping out a 70-hour workweek on average. I don't think anyone can describe exactly how it feels to wake up and love what you do. But I can tell you how much I hated dragging my ass to a job that didn't set my soul on fire. When your determination outweighs taking orders from greaseball Larry, you do whatever it takes. Even if that means taking your business calls in the lobby, having multiple tabs open to review modelling portfolios when you're supposed to be updating the assets registrar. Reading beauty articles placed in your notebook when you're supposed to be reading the corporate plan. Taking power naps in the breastfeeding room (sorry) or praying to the Lord to stop you from snapping your team leader's neck because she tried you one too many times this month.

The highlight reels you see on social media – Look, everybody, I'm living my best business life – may be legit or hammed up for the cameras. Funny, I've never seen posts where you're one step away from throwing your laptop across the room, breaking down in tears like Jaden Smith in *The Karate Kid* – 'I too hate it here, I wanna go home' – with only five minutes to spare before you have to put your big girl panties back on. These deadlines aren't going dead themselves.

The highlight reel rarely paints the picture of you pitching to investors and advertisers for 24 months straight and being rejected every single time. Then concluding that middle-aged white men don't care whether women of colour are seen and heard in Australia's fashion and lifestyle sectors. Nowadays, I detest the word 'resilience' – the Black woman's gold star. Foolishly, I believed that if I refined my pitch, made the financials leaner, my 'why' more heartfelt, the 'ask' more confident, I'd have all it took for them to take a chance on a Black woman – in the same way, white men get money for being average at best.

If the statistics are anything to go by in Australia, of the record-breaking $10 billion of venture capital funding raised in 2021, only 0.03% of Black women and WoC were recipients. (*The State of Bla(c)k Women and Women of Colour Founders in the Start-up Ecosystem in Australia*, report by The Creative Co-Operative, March 2022)

Early on in the history of *Ascension*, I was interviewing a business duo, both of them women's glossies veterans. We were talking about financing when one so casually said, 'I don't know how any start-up can make it without substantial investment.'

Yes, but how? I thought, with a tinge of envy – inclined to ask, what aisle do I find my silver spoon in? I was barely making it, struggling tooth and nail to make ends meet. Now I wish I'd taken the opportunity to ask the pair for business advice outside of our interview. It had been enjoyable and both businesswomen had extensive experience in magazine publishing. My failure to do so revealed my inadequacies: the fear of showing my hand, my lack of knowledge in publishing and investment, my expectation that I should know all the answers in these areas. On reflection, my diffidence was a result of cultural and social conditioning. I was raised not to show incompetence; rather, to pole-vault over the high bar every time. My worry was that asking a question of two successful white women would make me look inferior.

That comment about my needing substantial financial backing to succeed as an entrepreneur once again reiterated a vast divide. It's exasperating for women of colour trying to prosper in spaces not originally designed for them.

I can't speak for all Black women, but all I want to do is skate a free program like Surya Bonaly, who did a backflip on one blade during the 1998 Olympics, despite it being an illegal move. But she was the first and is still the only female skater to land it. Then refuse to stand on the podium at the 1994 World Figure Skating Championship to receive a silver medal. No! I skated my ass off. I deserve gold.

I want the right to wear a killer black catsuit post-childbirth, as Serena Williams did at the 2018 French Tennis Open. Even though it's to prevent further blood clots, I'm not allowed to wear it? Okay, Giudicelli. I'll be back wearing a black Nike one-sleeve tutu.

I swear it feels like the world enjoys attacking Black women. Cue Jane Campion being 'thoughtless'. You will never be a match for the Williams sisters.

In an episode of *Braxton Family Values* (ciao, Braxtons!), the sisters took a trip to Italy and had lunch at a monastery. One of my favourite parts of the episode was when Toni Braxton started to do the river dance to ward off a bee. When the shenanigans were over, the sisters shared who they had been in a past life. Towanda chose to be a rich white woman, arrogantly taking a sip of her drink. I fell about laughing along with her sisters. Apart from a white man, what better position is there in life socially, politically and economically – culturally, not so much: Black women have that on lock. How much easier would life be! But it's the enormity of Towanda's choice, off the rip, that speaks volumes of the privilege we don't possess. Don't get it twisted: if given a chance to walk in a white woman's shoes, would I take it? No, I'll watch it play out when Wunmi Mosaku's character Ruby Baptiste drinks the potion on *Lovecraft Country*.

Yes, you're on to me. I have a copy of Chelsea Watego's *Another Day in the Colony* on my bedside table. And you know what, it feels so goddamn refreshing to share out loud what I hold back on the daily. All those 'that's not fair' moments I complained about to my parents as a child are now routine. I never want to lose the kid in me that constantly asks, 'But why?' And doesn't accept that that's just the way it is. I don't want to turn into stone, forever jaded, with no fight left to get on the mic and yell F**k Australia because I, along with other Blak women, still stand with Tarneen, and all our other sistas positioned in front of the firing squad for speaking our truth – the truth they don't want to hear.

If I had a dollar for every non-Indigenous person who told me when I started *Ascension* that there should be a grant for that –

like there's a pot of gold waiting for Blakfellas at the endless supply of rainbows – omg, I wouldn't need a grant. I'd be rich. Ten, heck 20 years ago, the funding available for Blakfellas wasn't supporting young Blak women who wanted to build a fashion and beauty empire.

All this to say, invest in Blak women. Want to close the gap? Invest in and pay Blak women. I am tired of seeing us struggle. We deserve to enjoy the upper echelons of life, to live, work, play and prosper culturally on our land. Even as I write this, I feel a tremendous amount of guilt as the old-school doctrine kicks into gear. Just get on with it, pull yourself up by the bootstraps. Stand on your own two feet. Shame: don't play the race card.

So, about that life jacket we call resilience: let's be honest – it's a straitjacket. If you've been raised in survival mode, as I have, you know it's gotten you where you are today. Our modus operandi has played red light, green light with the system. There's been no room to reflect, release and recalibrate: heal, focus or ask, is resilience working for me or my mental health?

Black women, do we know how to ask for help?

Today, I want to do things differently. I call for a day on the calendar, Black Women Ask for Help Day. A day Black women come together to vocalise where they need support, and our family, loved ones and allies step in to assist.

Black women, it's our time now.

Meeting *Vogue*

If you're raised by a Marine, you arrive an hour early no matter the occasion. As my father would say, just in case. That's what

I did for AIFW. I did a final once-over, checking to see if my make-up was on fleek. Eyeliner: check. Contour: check. Red lips: uh, not so much; I could use another coat. I pulled out my MAC Ruby Woo and applied the colour all women wear before overtaking the throne, RED. Believe it or not, I didn't start wearing red lipstick until I hit my 30s. It says a lot about my state of mind. The colour scared me, or should I say I wasn't entirely in my power to embrace the shade.

I fixed my Fulani earrings and wiggled in my vintage pumps to get a snug fit. With my Boss Bitch Flex in check, I was ready to secure a seat at the table. *Ascension* was a new masthead on target to officially launch in the spring; AIFW was definitely the place to be seen.

Coming out of the restroom, I could see Nancy Pilcher, the former editor-in-chief of *Vogue Australia*, up ahead. I wanted to do what I always do: turn on my heels and jet off in the other direction. I had a bad habit of getting tongue-tied when I was starstruck. But logic said, 'Wait, you might not get a chance to talk to her.' You're right. I only had seconds to think of what I was going to say. I dug in my purse for my business card.

'Sorry, excuse me. I'm Sasha Sarago.' … whatever else I said to Nancy is a complete blank. When I'm nervous, my mind automatically shuts down, and words rush out like Niagara Falls. I'm sure I mentioned I was launching Australia's first lifestyle magazine for women of colour and gushed about what a huge fan I was of hers.

'Here's my card', handing it to Nancy. 'I'll see you in there.'

God, I was so glad that was over. My heart was beating faster than an electric egg beater. What the hell did I say to her? I couldn't tell if I overwhelmed her or if she was trying to comprehend my word vomit. Too late, what's done is done.

I found a seat in the front of the room where the screen read The Australian Indigenous Design Initiative Creative Lab: Story, Style and Sustainability. I scanned my notes, making sure I had memorised each section of my speech. I was still tossing over whether I should share the *Ascension* manifesto. I was scared it would go over people's heads and sound too woo woo: picture Jerry Maguire's 'It was just a mission statement'. Oh God, what did I just do?

It's incredible how we second-guess ourselves, because we worry about what others might think, and block our blessings. Undecided, I folded my notes; I was beginning to stress.

The session started, and I tried my best to concentrate on the panel discussion. I'd dip in and out of the conversation and go back to visualising my speech. My body started to perspire more as my session got closer.

And then I heard my name. Taking my place on the stage, I looked to my left to check my presentation was ready to go. A strikingly beautiful Noongar model stared back at me.

I heard a whisper in my mind; *Ascension* is more than just you.

Ascension Manifesto

Spirit speaks to us. She guides us in an unspoken language. Spirit whispers softly in our ears.

Ssshhh ... Listen! Can you hear her?

Spirit urges us to listen to our intuition. But we hardly ever do. Why is this? As women, we're conditioned to ignore our power. To play small and conform to a foreign ideal that places us in constant conflict and turmoil with ourselves and the world.

Ascension *magazine is a spiritual revolution. Right now, we are in hot pursuit to reclaim Spirit. It is time to give ourselves permission to transcend everything that no longer serves us.*

This is called emancipation.

When we realise that we're infinite beings, we become capable of everything our heart desires. The universe never meant for us to act in desperation, but in faith, expecting abundance.

Our Ancestors are aware of this wisdom.

They watch and wait patiently for us to understand this universal truth. Culture beats like a drum in our hearts. It runs deep through our bloodlines. It's the glue that binds us to each other. Our language, totems, dances, songs, our spiritual home is where we derive strength and purpose.

Culture is never lost. From all parts of the globe, we Australian women share a common reverence for culture. With many new dialogues of ancestry, tradition and contemporary expression these are signs of a cultural renaissance.

What sets Ascension *magazine apart from every other glossy magazine is our courage to see the world in colour rather than in black and white.*

Ascension *is the magic that happens when women dare to be fearless and release the goddess power within.*

Welcome to Australia's first Indigenous and Ethnic women's lifestyle magazine.

Ascension

My heart was full, and I had poured it all out. I had just given one of the most vulnerable speeches I would make in my career. I swear I floated off that stage. Everything I had envisioned for *Ascension* since its inception was in that presentation. Nina Simone's 'Feeling Good' carried me off the stage, and as I took my last step, I heard 'Good luck with that' echo throughout the room, knocking the wind out of my sails.

Black women, you know a microaggression when you hear one: because it backhands your spirit and tries to put you in your place. I've been here far too many times, and I know I'm not the only Black woman who's asked herself, 'Am I overreacting? Did that just happen? Or did I make that up in my head?' But as my mother always said, 'Spirit never lies.'

A heatwave began to pass over me. Did anyone else catch that slight? I just launched *Ascension* at AIFW: I should be feeling 20 feet tall; instead, I felt microscopic.

I wished my father's wisdom, 'Don't let them see you sweat', could put out my flames. In essence, this moment wasn't about me. It was about the women who hid their beautiful Black or brown skin from the sun. Who felt pressured to wear Fair & Lovely to be adored and succeed. Who wanted to pursue their wildest dreams but couldn't because they didn't see it personified. Women trying to trace their roots back to where they came from and belong. *Ascension* was bigger than me.

There's nothing you can do in situations like this where your back is up against the wall. On the daily, Black women operate in arenas that remind us speaking up is countered with, 'Don't bite the hand that feeds you.' It's the tiptoeing within the establishment – waiting for the day you've worked hard enough, when they let down their guard and embrace you as 'one of the good ones'. And when that time comes, you pull the rug out from under them and hit them with Formation. You know, 'I've got my foot in the door' strategy: build an empire, become untouchable and pop up at the 2016 Superbowl half-time performance MJ style. Oh, you thought we forgot. It's Black Lives Matter and Wakanda Forever – up in here, up in here. And seal the deal, dropping your own *Lemonade* and *Black Is King* to make sure they heard you loud and clear. There's always a method to the madness: simply put, dance the Dosey Doe until you can do the Electric Slide.

Unfortunately, a lot of us can't get in formation just yet, so we persevere in the meantime. Begrudgingly shrinking ourselves just enough not to lose our dignity, become brainwashed within the system, or get geeked out when we get to rub shoulders with the powerbrokers – as I did earlier, only to come crashing back down to earth.

On the other hand, we can adopt Chelsea Watego's philosophy: fuck hope and fuck strategy.

Sometimes, we have to pull a Bethany Yellowtail when we get in the room. In her interview with James St James for *WOW Presents*, Bethany recalled being invited to a panel discussion where Anna Wintour was in attendance. She shared there was an air of politeness and intimidation among the audience when Anna arrived. But it became clear to Bethany that her Ancestors had sent her on a mission. When the Q&A session came to a close, Bethany took matters into her own hands. She stood up and called for the mic, making it known you ain't about to bypass the only Native person in the room. I will say my piece. On her people's behalf, Bethany posed her question to Anna about accountability regarding diversity and inclusivity in fashion.

Without us even knowing it, we can be placed in rooms for a purpose. We have to be mindful even amid our doubt or measuring our worth against others. It really has nothing to do with us. You may be there to relay a message or learn something. Or remind them, uh excuse me, you're on stolen land. Sovereignty never ceded.

Bay bee, you're not Anne Hathaway; this ain't *The Devil Wears Prada*, so stop glorifying these coteries like they're demi-gods.

My dad used to always tell me, 'Nobody impresses me – concentrate on being impressed with yourself.'

20

Seat at the Table

I left yesterday's troubles behind to embrace the evening of all evenings – the opening night of AIFW. I got off at Town Hall Station and ducked into Woolies Metro for breath mints. Tonight was all about flexin and staying fresh. Stay ready, so you don't have to get ready. A philosophy I live by. I couldn't wait to meet the star-studded guests flocking to witness history.

    A close friend waited inside to escort me backstage. Sydney Town Hall's neo-classical architecture finished with a French empire interior and decadent lighting contrasted a culture that predated the fancy trimmings. Two separate worlds, Indigenous culture and fashion under one roof. When two became one? Or just for one night? None of us was sure. Punters had already placed their bets: Indigenous Fashion Week fly-by-night or here to stay? All bets are off. It was anyone's guess from here. We'd have to let the runway reveal where this fateful night would take Indigenous fashion.

I carefully weaved past the models, flashing them a good luck smile and previewing the collections hanging from the designers' racks. Jolly and pensive faces and a pulsating suspense consumed the hall.

I spotted Medika, the face of *Ascension*.

'Hey, darling, how are you?' I asked her. 'Are you nervous?'

'A little bit.' Medika smiled meekly, slightly fidgeting.

Medika was a Broome girl who deserved to be on catwalks in London, Paris, Milan and New York. She was my muse. I can completely understand when design houses can't seem to let a brand ambassador go – it's their bewitching charm that makes it hard to consider parting ways and introducing a new face.

I hugged Medika and told her I couldn't wait for her to hit the catwalk. Before I left to find my seat, I took some mental notes on designers to watch and what collections were a fashion must.

I got metres down the corridor before I was smacked with the line to the entrance that curved like a python. My god, would it ever stop? The long walk to the back of the line spiked my anxiety. Now *I* was on the runway: every second person glancing over at me as I walked past. God, I hoped what I was wearing was okay. I hate it when you think your outfit is fire in your bedroom mirror, then you catch your reflection in a shop window and the night is ruined.

I asked two ladies how long they'd been waiting in front of me. Thirty minutes. What?! Ummm, Sasha Fierce doesn't do lines or these heels. I hadn't planned on standing in them unless it was time to meet and greet. And the fashion gods agreed because right then, I spotted a familiar face: it belonged to Pauly, one of *Ascension*'s upcoming fashion writers.

'Hey sis, where are you sitting?' he asked.

'Brotha! So good to see you ... I don't know. It just says the front row.'

'No worries, sis. Come with me.'

Yes! I followed Pauly as he walked me back down the corridor to another sista we knew. Pauly kissed me and told me to enjoy the show and that he'd catch up with me afterwards. He kept his eye on the ball when it came to Indigenous fashion.

I was starting to like the Blakfella VIP treatment. Sis went one better and sat me next to a handsome Aboriginal actor. I had two things to look at: the runway and this lubly sing. I casually asked lubly sing what brought him to fashion week.

'My agent said I should come.' He admitted he didn't know what to expect; me neither.

The sudden change in lighting brought the audience to a hush, signalling the show was about to start. The yidaki called out, piercing the air – goosebumps raced up my arms – and we were welcomed to the lands of the Gadigal people of the Eora Nation. Let the show begin.

The ambassador for fashion week, Samantha Harris, glided on stage in Grace Lillian Lee's magnificent Dhari, the ceremonial headdress and the central motif of Torres Strait Islander culture and the Torres Strait Islander flag. Traditionally worn on the head, Grace redesigned it in the shape of a frill-necked lizard to decorate Samantha's neck right down the front of her chest, connecting in a waistband of singular iridescent shells. Black and white cultural motifs coating Samantha's pencil dress fit like a glove. Samantha's hair was slicked back with nothing but sheen, blue eyeliner, rosy cheeks and glistening bee-stung lips.

A delicate emu feather skirt secured by a solid black waistband breezed by, complemented by a rich mustard silk top, draped over the model floating beside her to the rhythm of the feathers. Switching up the beat, Teagan Cowlishaw brought the AARLI funk. The models rocked a vintage cassette necklace and '70s-style headphones paired with a black long-sleeved leotard topped in shredded leather. Teagan's washed-denim razor-edged cuts screamed *Mad Max* and Aboriginal futurism from out of space.

Red and black Island streetwear transported us back down to the earth with dugongs, frangipanis and hibiscus prints that would look great in some breds. Award-winning silk artist Eva Wanganeen's vibrant canary yellow and neon pink silk jackets and shorts made smart casual comfortable like bedwear. Kangaroo and possum skin fur fell off the model's tiny shoulders. Jewelled shell clusters shaped into elegant armour, worn as only Indigenous royalty would.

Various traditional weaving styles hung from earlobes, breastplates protected décolletages, handbags snuggly clutched to the side while Lyn-Al Young's earth, wind and fire silk dresses and leather holsters sashayed one after the other. Emu Designs' (Native Swimwear Australia) playful lolly-striped bikinis sat well with Wild Barra men's swimwear, offering up all the eye candy and telling the average budgie smuggler print to take a hike. His and her swimwear, a match made in heaven.

Desert Designs' soft yellow patterned two-piece cloaked in a black and white cape and umbrella see-through visor armed you for the harsh Australian summer. Retro flower child shifted gears to Mia Brennan's flowy maxi dresses, faux fur headdresses and grungy footwear, so Melbourne. Native flora and fauna and gumnuts delivered the quintessential Australiana. Barefeet, sneakers, stilettos: AIFW served it all.

A fashion show isn't complete without couture. Samantha shimmied in a Letticia Shaw gold sequined goanna cocktail dress for the finale. Samantha's slender frame activated the black goanna's as she swayed.

The verdict was in: Indigenous fashion was here to stay.

Black Cover Girls

Launching a magazine is like the first day of school. Will the teacher like me? Will I make friends? Is my lunch yummy enough to do swapsies? Nothing changes. In the end, we're just big kids trying to fit in.

Becoming editor-in-chief started with a vision board – a snapshot of my target audience and a spreadsheet to plot articles. To get a clearer picture of what was happening for women of colour in the beauty and fashion landscape, I needed to get my hands on the data. The only demographic profiles I could find were from the Australian Bureau of Statistics and some reports published by multicultural marketing agencies. As disheartening as it was that not much research existed on women like me, it became clear why *Ascension* was necessary.

What do you do when your target audience is a mystery? You hit the pavement and interview women from grassroots to affluent communities of colour. The way I consumed publications is the way I approached curating *Ascension*. Until I got a rude awakening – yes, women of colour wanted to see themselves represented frequently and authentically. But they also had pressing issues they wanted to be pushed to the forefront to discuss. Your nude lingerie, hosiery, lipstick and shoes ain't my nude was equally an issue, so was mental health, youth suicide, racial profiling, skin bleaching and sexual consent.

Some of these women hadn't had the spotlight on what was happening in their lives. I vowed to do my best to handle their stories with care. Finding a team willing to abandon a traditional publishing model was another story.

I chose an up-and-coming First Nations model for one of our editions to be our cover girl. From experience, when opportunities are limited for somebody who looks like you, you are conscious in your decision-making when it involves others in the same boat. I mulled over whether it was the correct business decision to choose an unknown talent to be our cover girl. I didn't know what the costs could be from a financial standpoint, but it felt right. We do ourselves a disservice when we believe there is only one measurement for success.

In her 2021 TEDx talk, the then chief marketing officer for Netflix, Bozoma Saint John, asked her audience to ditch the overreliance on data and tap into the creative power of intuition. Bozoma shared how she allowed intuition to place her bet on newly independent artist Beyoncé shortly after Destiny's Child disbanded. Pepsi was seeking talent for a lucrative campaign, and even though the data reflected otherwise, Bozoma trusted her gut and suffice to say her instincts were right. The Pepsi campaigns starring Beyoncé were a huge hit.

The more I learnt about the fashion industry, the more I discovered it loved a tried-and-tested formula: celebrities sell magazines. My decision to shoot a new face was not well received. A list of high-profile Indigenous talent was put forward for consideration. I agreed it would be a no-brainer to launch our cover with a headliner, but I was adamant: a new magazine, a new era.

Remember when they said Black women couldn't sell magazine covers? Quite the opposite: we break records. This long-held myth was debunked when *Vogue Italia* editor-in-chief Franca Sozzani released their All Black special edition July 2008, featuring Liya Kebede, Sessilee Lopez, Jourdan Dunn and Naomi Campbell. Four Black models reclaiming prime real estate, reserved predominately for white models, threw a spanner in the fashion works. The All Black issue was so popular, it forced publishers worldwide into reprint and was labelled a collector's edition when waitlists emerged and copies sold for double the retail price online. We witnessed our success in Australia when Edwina McCann, editor-in-chief of *Vogue Australia*, placed First Nations model and actress Magnolia Maminydjama Maymuru and daughter Djarraran on their September 2021 edition. The cover garnered acclaim for being the most liked cover online in *Vogue Australia* history. Please repeat after me, Black women sell covers. How can you gain further success if you don't shake the table?

I don't know what the conversation was like for Nancy Pilcher when she decided to make Elaine George *Vogue Australia*'s cover girl for their September 1993 edition; how much it meant to Nancy personally. But I knew what it meant for me as a First Nations woman to grab the power back and not wait for the opportunity to be handed to us. Australian publishing, you don't get to dictate what is beautiful. Our beauty, through our eyes, on our terms.

On the set of our cover shoot, I noticed the entire team, even the assistants, checked the monitor to review everyone was playing their positions – making sure hair, make-up, clothes and talent were perfect. Fashion is hierarchical: only the key players – the photographer, stylist, hair and make-up – get the chance to appraise shots via the monitor. So, when the team formed a semi-circle and boxed me out from the preview, I was forced to get on my tippy toes, bob and weave to see how the shoot was coming along. Not one person acknowledged me or moved an inch to allow me to take a look.

I tried not to take it personally. But I couldn't get rid of the churning in my stomach. I knew I wasn't on a power trip – like I'm the editor, move. I just wanted some respect. I eventually heeded the call to boss up and stop acting like a punk. I am the editor; I have every right to be here.

I hovered a good length away from the photographer to see what he was capturing up close. I let about ten frames pass before leaning in when he changed his lens to ask if he would shoot our cover girl per the brief. If looks could kill … like a chastised child, I moved to the back of the bus. When taking a page out of Elaine Welteroth's interning days goes wrong.

In her book *More Than Enough: Claiming Space for Who You Are (No Matter What They Say)*, Welteroth says she worked on a shoot as a production assistant for *Ebony* magazine's August 2008 edition. They were shooting Serena Williams for the cover. Elaine shares how she commits a fashion no-no by suggesting to the head honchos that Serena might look good in a blue swimsuit. Elaine got lucky: her proposal ended up being the bathing suit Serena wore for the cover.

My experience did not turn out triumphantly like Elaine's. I did learn that, when it came to fashion, stay in your lane. I don't care if, traditionally, the editor is not primarily on set, and they leave it up to the fashion editorial team – rules are meant to be broken.

I did have a conversation with the photographer about the cover, but I didn't anticipate it to be about the Angry Black Woman trope. I got the proofs back with two preferred images for the cover – one of those images I hated. Our cover girl had a scowl on her face, and quite frankly, she looked constipated. Fark! How do I begin to explain, graciously, why this image for the cover is not an option? I already had an unpleasant experience on set. I didn't want to stir the pot with controversy.

But you have to ask yourself, 'What is the price I pay for remaining silent?'

I reached for my MacBook and started typing.

Dearest Ben,
As the editor of an Australian first, I am responsible
for representing our women in a way that honours and
celebrates them. In the past, fashion has let down women of
colour, particularly Black women.

Using this image where it appears Sienna is scowling
perpetuates the Angry Black woman trope. Ascension is
about motivating our audience to aspire to be better than
what they are today, embracing everything their heart
desires, and inspiring them to believe in their dreams.

> *This image does not exude our philosophy. I want the world to see the beauty of First Nations women and culture – not through the stereotypes and misconceptions that have oppressed us.*
>
> *We've never had the agency to define ourselves in Australian fashion and beauty – through our voice, our eyes. I want our Elders and communities to feel pride when purchasing* Ascension *for the first time.*
>
> *I want to run with the other image – with Sienna smiling.*
> *I look forward to your response.*
> *Best*
> *Sasha*

Things go awry when Black creatives are not at the helm of the fashion narrative. For example, the US's first female African-American and South Asian Vice President, Kamala Harris, was white-washed, and photographed in a dark suit and a pair of Converse shoes on a horribly mismatched set for *American Vogue* February 2021.

Acclaimed photographer Annie Leibovitz captured the G.O.A.T. – Olympic champion Simone Biles – in poor lighting and unflattering colours, with her muscular back as the feature for the cover. Critics decried it via Twitter, accusing Leibovitz of skipping the editing process entirely. Some sent in their own retouched versions to remedy the mishap.

Harper's Bazaar US dropped the ball too for Megan Thee Stallion. Photographer Collier Schorr did disclose that the shots were in co-collaboration with Meg, and the rapper herself said she wasn't opting for full glam. Glam or no glam, many readers still found the results appallingly lacklustre, yet more proof that Black photographers should be capturing Black people.

For the record, we have our issues on Australian soil too. We're yet to see a First Nations photographer shoot a high-fashion cover; still waiting for our Tyler Mitchell moment: at 23, he captured Beyoncé for *Vogue US* September 2018, the first Black photographer to shoot a cover for the prestigious publication.

A special shout-out to Bobbi Lockyer for shooting her self-portrait cover for *Peppermint* magazine, Autumn 2022. We're getting there.

And I must address this with the utmost respect and speak from my heart. *Vogue Australia*, if you didn't want to honour First Nations beauty for your September 2021 cover, just say that. Of all the images you could have chosen.

In this and cases previously mentioned, it's as if the team saw the brief, said, 'Meehhh, a Black woman [at the height of her career], why bother?' The sheer disrespect. Precisely why I wasn't going to commit the greatest fashion faux pas – publish an unflattering cover featuring a Blak woman. Not today, Satan.

Best believe I got the cover image I asked for. A portrait shot of Sienna smiling brighter than the sun – embracing New Beginnings.

'There are no white women in your magazine? Don't you think that's racist?'

'Ummm, Barbara, when you walk into the newsagent's and turn on the TV – what do you see? Me or you?'

A magazine for women of colour, curated by a Black woman, didn't make me the most popular person at the party. On the contrary, it brought out the trolls and keyboard warriors. It started on social media in a typical manner. I post I love apples and a stranger interjects with, 'So, basically, you're saying you hate oranges. What about poor bananas and grapefruit?' Educate yourself – selfish eye-roll emoji.

Once the word spread about *Ascension*, my public and media appearances were similar, from 0 to 100. The majority of the media I did to promote *Ascension* had white people ringing into radio stations, private messaging or steamrolling me at Q&A panels; giving me a piece of their mind. I had finished an interview with Namila Benson on her show *White Noise* for Triple R Melbourne radio when I was alerted that a caller was on the line. I took the call and held the phone away from my ear from the clanging in the background. A mature-aged white man named Gary told me he was cooking sautéed mushrooms and heard my interview. 'I had to call in.'

Okaaay, Gary, where is this going? I thought.

'You used the term person of colour, right?'

'Yes, I did.'

'I don't know why. Indigenous Elder Connor Smith abhors the term. He says he refuses to use it. Why are you?'

'Respectfully, Gary, Indigenous Elder Smith doesn't speak for me or the rest of the community. I use the term person of colour because that's what I feel comfortable with. Thank you for your call.'

Click. The nerve!

Before I became a culturally confident woman on the path to reclaiming her sovereignty, the questions thrown at me had me stammering as I tried to find the politically correct words to appease tyrants gaslighting me into believing I was racist. Until then, I'd never had this many white people confronting me about something that had nothing to do with them. Unless they genuinely wanted to learn about women of colour or invest in *Ascension*. To cover my ass from further rebuke, I started tap dancing. I was out here using dinner analogies: *Ascension* is like a dinner party, and we have invited specific people to attend. If there's a spare seat, Abbey, by all means, join us. [Cringe.]

I wonder if *Vogue*, *Marie Claire* or *Harper's Bazaar* had to justify who their target audience was to a disgruntled public?

This was all new territory for me: media engagements became a crash course in race and the Australian media. And it was made clear the establishment didn't like a Black woman rocking the boat. I didn't see it this way. All I was doing was minding my Indigenous business Indigenously, on a mission for women of colour, not them.

Lived experience has since taught me that you have to be up for a fight when you decide to bust out of the box they've allocated you.

I am grateful the trolling has been relatively harmless; now I know how to handle it. I find it rather amusing that strangers carve time out of their precious existence to egg my house. I don't delve too much into the opinions of others who I don't love and respect. I did take a swim in the comments section to see how my TEDx talk, 'The (De)colonising of Beauty', was perceived.

It's true we can focus on one bad review for every 10 that are good. In response to my talk, many people thought TEDx had become trash, a woke hivemind. Woe is me again, they said, TED's heading towards a steady decline, pointless.

I shared a childhood story, elements from my culture that I love and my belief that healing is the antidote humanity needs because it leads us to unity. I had no idea it would irk so many people. If words on unity weren't a gesture for peace, then maybe I should have quit while I was ahead? I'm beginning to think the word 'colonisation' triggers people. Hey, why you mad at me? I didn't do it.

I know I'm not for everyone, nor is what I say or do. All that matters is that I know my heart. I knew the purpose of my message when I wrote my TED talk. And it reached the people it was intended for.

When you don't know who you are and what you stand for, you're a sitting duck for people who don't know and love themselves. The quicker we work out who we are – collectively – we can start walking together in a straight line with respect.

I've gotten off lightly in the digital space. My heart goes out to my sistas racially abused, sent rape and death threats for their opinions while walking in their truth.

Although Australia might have moved on, I haven't forgotten how it played out for Yassmin Abdel-Magied.

As I get comfortable with decolonising, I have to check myself constantly: am I operating within the colonial framework or from a culturally competent perspective – is it reactionary or sovereign? Experience has been my teacher.

In the Black community, we are familiar with accepting or declining invitations through one question: who all gon be there?

Once *Ascension* was gaining traction, invitations to events started piling up. To maintain the momentum I'd worked so hard for, I fell into the trap of running around aimlessly, being *seen*, to stay relevant. It was not pragmatic and, in the long run, it led to burnout. But that was not the worst of it.

It's flattering when mainstream media, brands or forums come knocking on your door asking you to *speak* – especially when you've slogged away and finally are getting recognition. So, I got hyped. I accepted an invitation to sit on a panel discussing female genital mutilation/cutting (FGMC) – a forum supporting women's capacity to enact change and find solutions to eliminate the practice that affects 200 million women and girls globally. The questions posed for my panel were: How can we talk about women's bodies and genitalia in ways that empower and educate? What role do media play around language and a more nuanced understanding of 'culture'?

My observations highlighted so many holes in media coverage. It's scary how many media reports lack quality research and are whipped up with hardly any lead time and accuracy. What's the rush when you can change people's lives through meaningful storytelling led by truth-telling and personal accounts? The way people of colour are reported on in the media is horrendous. You only need to look at the track history of the Australian morning show *Sunrise*.

Given that we know this, we must keep the establishments and their foot soldiers accountable. Some media outlets appear to close their eyes and plunge their hand into a bowl with the same names, year in, year out. They are not actively searching for fresh perspectives – other leaders or ambassadors from communities that are already doing the groundwork.

From my research and what I was learning at the forum, some of the challenges were the uncomfortable experiences and feelings of shame endured by survivors and support workers when seeking aid from health practitioners and services within the public system. When the forum began, as stakeholders and allies, our commitment was to listen and support the survivors of FGMC who were also on the panel. And discuss the severe physical, emotional and psychological health risks suffered from the practice but in a culturally empowering way that did not demonise the practice (a long-standing cultural tradition) or the survivors and their communities.

I sat and listened to survivors' personal stories, and the awful treatment they had encountered by Australian institutions still trying to grasp their role on how to address FGMC as a public health crisis.

As the forum went on, the tide began to turn: the white saviour complex had washed in over a few panellists. Some white academics gave the impression they knew better than the women actually living as survivors or within these communities.

I couldn't believe what I was hearing but I tried to fix my sour face. I was a guest and the last person to have an opinion. But I wasn't the only one perturbed by some of the insensitive statements made by the so-called experts. Heavy sighs could be heard from a group of women from the local FGMC NGO. Also fed up by these show-and-tell antics.

Finally, it was my turn to speak. Before I answered the question directed to me, I made an opening statement around what I had learnt, and what I would apply from a media standpoint in order to champion best practice on reporting respectfully about culturally sensitive issues and garnering action rather than condemnation and pity. And I knew I wouldn't be practising what I was preaching if I didn't address the elephant in the room.

Then I launched into how I had noticed the focus to foster change had shifted away from the very women we were there to support, and, instead, had become overridden by extensive data and reports. Not only were we guests, but we were robbing our hosts of their time and resources to 'talk at them' as opposed to listening to them for their knowledge, guidance and pathways for solutions.

Unexpectedly, the sistas started clapping in acknowledgement. Embarrassed: it was the last thing I wanted. All I know is that the mic got passed, and the sistas' voices were centred. I tell you what: I sure did agitate the academics who waited patiently to give me an earful. I took it on the chin. Whatever they said had nothing to do with me; it was all about them being called out for their poor behaviour. Paternalism doesn't like it when you turn on the lights. It makes them scatter like roaches.

I do want to give a shout-out to Khadija Gbla for her human rights advocacy around awareness of FGMC here in Australia. And just being an incredible woman speaking her truth on so many topics that affect women around domestic violence, sexual health, racism and cultural diversity.

That evening gifted me some key takeaways: from those I pulled together a checklist to run through before RSVPing to any future such events:

Am I qualified, and do I have the expertise to participate or speak on this?

Am I doing the work in this space?

Is there somebody else who needs to be in this room apart from me?

What value can I add?

When extended an invitation, it's on you to do your due diligence to make sure you should be there in that room. Please don't rely on the other party – whoever's inviting you – to do it.

And if you make a bad judgement call – which you no doubt will at some stage – learn from it, give yourself grace, dust yourself off and go out there and do better next time.

Sitting on panels or taking up space per se isn't for everyone. But if done mindfully, we can influence change, whether it's the questions we ask behind the scenes or the people and opinions we choose to centre.

We all have a hand in shaping an equitable society; it starts with us.

21

Murray

Majal was a basin of treasures, and we had an impressive collection even Sotheby's would be envious of. Mum and I worked closely with the students from Wangetti College when the calendar hit debutante season. We all squeezed into several motel suites, white ballgown dresses taking up space with all the trimmings: gloves, heels, tiaras, purses and corsages draped the room. The young Indigenous girls, soon to be belles of the ball, laughed and chatted away as the evening got underway.

I had older cousins who'd participated in debutante balls. Historically, this exclusive rite of passage, like many Western traditions, excluded Aboriginal and Torres Strait Islander people until we came along in the 1950s and hijacked the tradition to adopt it as our own while embedding our culture to give it the finishing touch. Even though I missed out on celebrating this ceremony, I played a special role behind the scenes – helping our sistas prepare for their hallmark event, when young girls became young women.

Before any make-up application, Mum prepped each girl's face, making sure their skin was clean and waxed. When Mum started working on the girls from Groote Eylandt, they told Mum they weren't allowed to remove hair from their body – it was against their culture. Mum had never come across this cultural boundary before – we worked with the young ones around stamping out the stigma of being shame and building up their confidence, but this was new territory for Mum. She learnt a meaningful lesson that day. There was more than one framework for beauty.

Mum was taught Western beauty – how to aesthetically present ourselves to society with hardly any input from us. Yet, it was adhered to and widely expected the world over. Mum pocketed her shiny new gem and changed how she consulted her young clients about their beauty. In the past, Mum explained how reshaping one's eyebrows enhanced their natural features – which it did. Mum had no complaints, only happy customers who loved their new look. But now, there was a broader conversation, an infinite spectrum to view and illustrate beauty, thanks to seeing it from a cultural perspective, not as a stock standard template ready to be applied.

I hadn't thought too much about hair in a cultural sense. But hair was a big deal. As a 12-year-old, Mum decided to cut my long hair when I refused to brush out the knots. Beforehand, to pacify me, she told me to find a hairstyle I liked. I grabbed *Dolly* magazine and pointed to Mariah Carey's beach hair. My mum was talented at many things, but cutting hair was not her forte. It was my first lesson on hair texture. Mariah had Type 2C hair. I had Type 3B, which resulted in my curls springing up: my hair looked like a mushroom cap. I cried. Predictably, my schoolmates teased me: 'HAH! You look like Krusty the Clown.'

I hated my 'boy hair' so much, I tied it back with Mum's long silky scarf. I did this to pretend I still had length and to feel pretty again. Mum's promise that it would grow back infuriated me. Fast forward to today and my hair grows like wildfire, but back then it grew as slow as molasses.

My sister suffered the same fate. Dad turned her into what he called an African Queen, cutting her hair with clippers into an Afro. Nearly every photo taken of Ray Ray during her Black Panther days revealed she hated life and everybody in it.

I remember when I caught Ray Ray and our cousins prancing around with skirts on their heads – swaying their new hair back and forth like models from a Schwarzkopf commercial.

Even my baby brother had been bamboozled by Western beauty. One day we found out his baby Afro could hide dirt, pebbles, twigs, foliage – you name it. Mum plunged her hand into his hair down to his scalp. 'Sasha, come feel this boy's head.'

His head felt like the bottom of a creek bed.

'BOY, why aren't you washing your hair?' Mum asked.

'I did?'

'No, you haven't!' Mum barked. 'Are you using shampoo?'

'No!'

'Why not?'

'Shampoo is for girls!'

'Who told you that?'

'Nobody. The ladies on TV use it. It's for girls.'

Mum and I bust out laughing. We couldn't blame him. I mean, there were hardly any Black men in TV ads glorifying shampoo. Just Caucasian men and women with hair that wasn't our texture.

The only cultural connection I had relating to hair was the warnings of Black magic as I reached my teens. Older aunties told us not to leave our hair lying around, especially at other people's houses: wear it in a bun, clean the excess hair from your hairbrush and stash it away safe somewhere; don't throw it in the bin. Same with your toenail clippings: don't leave them lying around either. And don't let people you don't know touch you.

Now it makes me wonder about the hair we leave behind on salon floors. And the estimated $10 billion per year spent on hair extensions, weaves and wigs globally. ('Global Hair Wigs and Extension Market Outlook and Forecast 2018–2023', ResearchAndMarkets.com) Who and where is our hair coming from? What kind of energy does it contain?

Hair is often associated with beauty in the West; our crowning glory. However, in many indigenous cultures, hair is sacred – containing unique symbolisms. Some Aboriginal peoples across Australia cut their hair to signify someone had passed. Some tribes wear Kopi, a mourning cap worn by widows and others close to the person who's departed – depending on their relationship, as a marker of grief. Women cut or shaved their hair off, and a net made from emu sinew covered their head under layers of gypsum (white clay) mixed with water to construct the caps. Kopis weighed up to 2–7 kilograms – carried for weeks up to six months. When the mourning period came to an end, the Kopi was placed on the burial site of the beloved.

I'm glad our people had rituals to honour our sorrow. These days it's so easy to anaesthetise grief through substances, work, hobbies – whatever distractions we can get our hands on. Grief is not something we can run from. It must be addressed; if not today, perhaps years from now – either way, it's waiting for us.

Not only is hair sacred to us, it's functional. Traditionally, not a strand went to waste. It was collected and rolled on women's thighs using a spindle, plaited into strands, as thick as wool, into ball-like yarn. Hair string was also used to make body ornaments: head rings were placed on women's crowns to carry coolamons over long distances, the same with belts to carry game. They also created headbands, toys, bags, jewellery, ceremonial headdresses, instruments and weapons.

A gorgeous depiction of murray (hair) is illustrated by artists Eunice Napanangka Jack, the late Judy Napangardi Watson and Makinti Napanangka in glorious strands of colour raining down the canvas like sun showers.

In my culture, we may not have had hair salons where women came together to bond; instead, we had hair ceremonies, hair Dreamings and women's business.

For so long my relationship with hair has been enmeshed in a political, social and economic debate.

I do hope that one day they stop touching our hair. That the CROWN Act in the US is no longer necessary to protect our hair. That remnants of the Tignon laws, forcing Black women to cover their hair, don't follow us further into the 21st century. And our youth can go to class to learn instead of having to educate faculty on the cultural significance of our natural hair and identity.

I wish for a future where 'nappy hair' and 'good hair' are phased out of our vocabulary – because all hair is good hair if we're looking after it right. Something I wasn't doing because I'd been straightening and bleaching it for 10 years without the proper protections. So, when I joined the natural hair movement, I happily ditched the platinum blonde bales of straw for chocolate swirls. Natural hair, is that you?

Let me introduce you to Rumbie Mutsiwa, the CEO of Rumbie & Co salon, Sydney's wavy, curly, Afro hair specialist. I met Rumbie in 2019 and shortly thereafter entrusted her with chopping off 27 centimetres of my hair. Afterwards, I confessed on Instagram that my long hair was an emblem of beauty and femininity. And how cutting my hair took a lot of courage – because now, there were no more cascading locks to hide my perceived unattractiveness. Embracing healthy hair and the curl gospel was now my priority. Since entrusting Rumbie on my Curly Gurl journey, my curls are poppin – coiling, bouncing in the breeze – hydrated like nothing you've ever seen.

Thanks to Rumbie, it feels glamorous to love the curls God gave me. What people may not realise is Rumbie's passion for curl education also advocates for our under-representation. Apparently, there's a myth floating around in the Australian hair industry that textured to curly hair is rare. Therefore, the requirement to style and care for it is negligible. One of the reasons Rumbie launched an academy and products was to upskill hairdressers in the art of curls and give her clients the service and treatments they deserve.

Rumbie is one of a few Black hair technicians I know fighting for the rare unicorns of hair.

'I can't understand why it's still an issue in 2022. Sis, you've styled Amandla Stenberg, Sabrina Elba and Flex Mami for *Vogue*, and they still don't take Black hair seriously in this country?' I said.

'Ahem, just for the record, Your Honour, sis has also styled Zadie Smith, FKA Twigs, Yemi Alade and Alexis Okeowo. I'm just saying the receipts are all here.'

The fuckery of it all was too much to bear. So we changed the subject: Rumbie now concentrating on far more important matters – my hair.

Is it just me, but who else loves the sound of hairdresser scissors slicing through their tresses?

I think that sound should be nominated for an ASMR award.

'OOOOP! What's going on here … that's real abstract,' I said in excitement.

Rumbie and I examined the sharp triangular cut she had just given me.

'It's giving me Whitney Houston "I'm Your Baby Tonight". Hmmm, I like it! Whitney it is,' I declared.

After Rumbie got me all the way together, I let my fingers skate down my slender neck.

'Ouuuu … neck for days,' I purred.

Sis just made the halter-neck dress my new summer go-to.

Along with the summer hair anthem: Big, Bold and Bubbly.

A colleague I worked with some time ago had a four-year-old daughter. I had just started wearing my hair natural, and Daniel would often bring Aaliyah into the office. She was super cute, and we'd always have a little yarn.

Daniel told me in the elevator on the way to the office, Aaliyah had pulled out her scrunchie and begun ruffling her straight brown hair. When he asked her what she was doing, she pointedly replied, 'I want my hair like Sasha's' – aka big, beautiful and curly. I melted when Daniel shared this precious moment with me.

See, you never know who's watching you. Embrace who you are. When you love your hair, it inspires others to do the same.

Beauty trends come and go – evolving as we do. Some aspects of beauty remain, passed down, becoming a tradition. And some become ghastly trends that haunt us when Facebook Memories remind us pencil-thin eyebrows and glitter eyeshadow was never your friend. I've learnt a lot from Western beauty. After being its Play-Doh for 35 years, I now realise I never had to mould myself into anything I didn't want to be. I could hop off the erratic assembly line of conformity at any time. Beauty is nobody's business but my own. But I am still struggling to pry myself from its clutches. These days I'm just more informed about how the game works.

I used to beat myself up for being duped by beauty. But how do you know you've stumbled across a diamond when it's uncut. To the untrained eye, it just looks like a shabby old rock. But over time, after a lot of pressure, the diamond reveals itself the full lustre of you.

When you've gone through a pandemic the priority on how you look goes out the window. Pandemic beauty became the revolution I didn't know I needed. Okay, the first month was madness. I think we were more focused on washing our hands for 20 seconds and disinfecting every surface within reach, dodging the Rona like we were Catherine Zeta-Jones in *Entrapment* – if only it were that sexy.

Then the cracks started to show. Regrowth started to shine bright like a diamond, batches of muffin tops had us playing patty cake in the street, and acrylic fills were left unattended like two toddlers in the kitchen. Yikes! And Club Thirst Trap went into liquidation.

I don't know how the masses fared, but the extra time I gained gave me a newfound freedom.

Suddenly in lockdown, there was no-one to impress. Nowhere to go: no red carpets, champagne brunches, Bumble dates and island getaways. Just me, myself and I, over and over again.

I secretly prayed the pandemic would become like a chapter from the Bible – when the Israelites wandered in the desert for 40 years. Perhaps after that long, society would have carved out a new definition of beauty. Lip, chin and underarm hair long enough to braid – hang on, we might be onto something.

This is why I've always loved sitting with my Elders. There's a confidence they exude gained from the road less travelled. My feet are like buttress roots when I stand beside them – their self-assuredness becomes mine. I wish everyone could experience how precious that feels, rather than being distracted by the signs of ageing.

I've never been a girly girl who is into make-up, nails, flowery dresses and such. I'm more of a white tee, ripped jeans, Converse Chuck Taylor kind of gal.

Mum's critique of my television appearances and beauty campaigns sometimes stung because I was finding peace with imperfection, but she reminded me the real world doesn't appreciate that.

I'll gladly watch my mother take hours getting ready but eventually wince at how tedious it becomes. There's Coloured People's Time, and then there's my mum Delphine's Time.

I remember my mother came to visit me in Naarm one winter. I lived five minutes from the shopping plaza and suggested we go for a doris. We were in no hurry, so I chilled in the lounge while she got ready. Twenty minutes quickly turned into an hour. Omg, what is she doing? I got up to investigate.

There she was pressed up against the bathroom mirror.

'Muuum, what are you doing?'

'Whaaat?'

'Mum, it's not a beauty contest; we're just going to the shops.'

If doing the most was a person ... that was my mum. And she was head to toe ravishing.

What drives a person to do what they do has always fascinated me. What seeds were planted when they were young and what grew from them?

I can't remember when I noticed Mum's leg and asked her what had happened. She was only 14 when she got into a motorbike accident; she was the passenger on the bike. Mum lucidly remembers having an out-of-body experience. She said she could see the nurses cutting her clothes off her body while on the operating table.

This is why I don't get on motorbikes. Even at eight years old, I declined a spin on a dirt bike. One of the military dads gave the kids in the neighbourhood joy rides up and down the street. I watched from the pavement as he sped past me with my mates on the back. I cheered for them – it was exhilarating to watch. Though, seeing what it did to my mum was enough for me to give it a miss. I didn't want to be held back by a scar and the insecurities that came with it, the ones I knew about and the ones I didn't.

As a child, I'd sometimes forget to tell Mum when I'd invited friends over to play, and she'd scold me when my mates came into the living room and she didn't have time to cover up her leg. One day sticks in my mind: Mum scrambled for a sarong nearby but it was too late: my friend had seen her leg.

My friend turned to me with sad eyes and asked me what happened.

It was different around family – we'd go swimming at the waterhole, and Mum didn't care if the little ones innocently asked, 'Aunty, what happened to your leg?'

Mum would glance down and tell them.

I loved how it didn't stop Mum from playing softball when Dad advised her it was too dangerous. 'What if you get hit by the ball?' he asked.

The only person who got hit by the ball that summer was me. The pitcher threw a death ball at me, hitting me square in my back. In sheer agony, I dropped my bat and cussed her out, 'You fucking whore!'

She cried, and I got ejected from the game.

I think we all have moments where things bother us, and other times it's the furthermost thing from our minds. And some things really matter to us regardless of how much time passes. At 55, Mum underwent an operation on her right foot to correct how she walked. Mum was insecure about how the accident limited her movement, especially her inability to firmly plant her foot on the ground instead of her toes.

Dad asked Mum, 'Why now? Why even bother?'

Although he meant well, it still hit a nerve for Mum.

This is why 'Do what makes you happy' rings true. Nobody holds the weight of insecurity like you do. What a world it would be if we all just minded our business, but then we wouldn't have *The Shade Room*, damn.

Your body is a conversation, a relationship that only involves you. Do what makes you happy, even if others don't understand. All I'm saying is – when it comes to your body – who are you doing it for? You or them?

22

Mundu

I wept for her – my little girl. I'm quite sure she was a girl.

Reign, my spiritual teacher, told me she could feel my little girl around me as she read my cards. She asked if I had lost a child.

I paused for a minute. The question caught me off guard, and I had to think about it – yes. It was so long ago.

'Well, she says if you still want a child, it can happen – if you want it.'

At the time, I didn't pay it much mind. But now Reign's words linger in my thoughts more frequently. I don't feel any guilt. I just wonder if circumstances had been different, could I have made it work – being a mother, that is?

Then I think of him, and how my girl and I would never have had peace. How she would have been raised in trauma; we'd be on the run. Living in torment isn't good for the soul.

That time I filled the bathtub up with water but couldn't

stomach how much it stung when the blade glided against my wrist.

'You can't even get that right,' he said.

Rustling in some old boxes searching for photos, I came across *Djomi Dream Child,* a book my mother illustrated for Burarra storyteller Christopher Fry. I opened it up and ran my fingers across Mum's paintings. If only her art could be animated. I love the magical universes she creates. Turning the book over I read the blurb on the back.

Djomi Dream Child is a story of a little Aboriginal spirit child searching for her parents. With the help of her grandfather, who directs her to an island where she will find them. Hopping into a giant cone shell, she floats to the coast of Maningrida, towards Djomi, the sacred Dreaming waterhole. It is here where all her dreams come true.

I heard a whisper as I read, 'Spirit babies choose you.'

Days later, I was listening to a keynote by Dr Kim TallBear, Professor of the Faculty of Native Studies at the University of Alberta, and author of 'Making Love and Relations Beyond Settler Sexualities', *Making Kin, Not Population* (Prickly Paradigm Press, Chicago, 2018, pp. 145–164).

'The newest baby would be doted on as a newly arrived human who chose our family because that's our understanding about it, that they choose you – they choose to come to your family.'

Dr TallBear's lecture gave me comfort. Nowadays I don't get angry as much – more disappointed in how society can be so ugly; how it tries to control women's bodies. Turns on women, calling us barren. If only they knew about the spirit babies – how they choose you, and you can decide to bring them here or bless your spirit baby to another whose heart is broken because they've lost too many.

Some of us are storytellers, artists, knowledge keepers and medicine people. Our talents are gifted to us by our Ancestors.

When will society learn one size does not fit all?

I'd seen the power of healing hands in the church when the pastor laid his on the congregation, and they caught the Holy Ghost. Watching the Holy Spirit seize an adult as a six-year-old was frightening but after a while I wondered when I'd catch it. I never did; neither did the kids in Sunday school. So, we re-enacted it, forming a ring around the Holy Ghost to contain it if one of us flailed too wildly while speaking in tongues.

If only there were someone around to lay hands on Jr, maybe that might have healed his mundu (spirit). As tumultuous as his last days were, I'm glad his passage to the other side was swift. Although it was eerie still feeling him around.

Before he left Jr made his rounds, visiting close friends. He had checked in on a little boy and his older cousin. Ray Ray and I ran into them the week of the funeral. When they said they'd seen Jr out by the fence, Ray Ray and I immediately asked, 'When was this?'

Jr had already left when they claimed to see him.

The hairs on our necks stood up having to break the news to them.

Their startled faces froze in disbelief. When Jr passed, my uncles smoked out his room, which gave us comfort in the day. But when night fell, I prayed I didn't see his mundu.

Some spirits linger for their own reasons – checking in on us to see if we were okay before they leave. Others have trouble making it to their destination, stuck in the middle of nowhere. Our traditional healers are called upon to help calm the spirit – call it away from chaos and guide it safely to settle where it belongs.

Our people celebrate the circle of life. When one life takes its last breath, another is taking its first. We perform birthing ceremonies to welcome the new spirits to Country by smoking the baby and mother to cleanse, protect and release them from past ancestral trauma. We bless baby, so their spirit remains pure and healthy, and they know where they belong and where they will return. Birthing practices may vary among our women, but it is common for the mother's placenta and/or the umbilical cord to be buried under a tree or a special place on Country. This becomes the child's sanctum for spiritual guidance and direction. Bubs are also bathed and washed in bush medicine – you could say it's our traditional baptism.

I loved listening to an interview with Miliwanga Sandy Wurrben from Banatjarl Strongbala Wimun Grup. She explains the Smokimbal Beibi ceremony, where traditional gubu (leaves) are passed through warm smoke and placed on various parts of the child's body, starting with the jina (feet): to bless them to stay on the right path. The bunggu (knees): so they don't wander from their community and stay out of mischief. Their malas (hands): to discourage them from stealing and partaking in wicked acts. Bina (ears), jili (eyes) and wari (mouth): to hear no evil, speak no evil. Only a clear mind to retain the cultural knowledge and to see the gigorou in themselves and others.

So, it is only natural for our mundu to yearn to biri (return) to where it belongs. Before my grandfather left for the Dreaming, he requested that his ashes be scattered on his Country, where he was birthed – where his life began and where it will continue. There is no need for goodbyes because mundu does not die.

'Mum,' I began one day. 'Do you think we had traditional healers like the Ngangkari?'

'Of course we did.'

I heard a soft voice. Sometimes we don't know we are healers until we are undertaking the work.

'Because we don't know what our mob called it – you think massage could be our healing method?' I asked Mum.

She nodded, her face still stuck in the book she was reading.

'Remember when we'd travel those long winding bends to Wangetti College?'

'Hmmm.'

Back then, Mum knew our young people's hands weren't meant for aggression but that their malas were instruments of peace.

'You just reminded me we gotta call Aunty Nona. She wanted to take us to the healing waters on Grandad's Country.'

'Ahhh, deadly!'

'Did you know there's some on Nana's Country too?'

'True?'

'Yeah. Uncle Henry said if mob were sick, them Old People told them to find a rock in the middle of the creek and sit still and wait for the snakes to come out. You had to let them crawl all over you, and once they left, you could come out the water. After that you'd be cured.'

'What's the healing place called?'

'Yunba.' Water python.

23

First Nations Fashion Is the New Blak

'I Love Fashion, But Fashion Doesn't Love Me Back', read the *Racked* headline. Damn! I mean, where's the lie? Fashion has always been a love–hate relationship for me, but I've remained hopeful, keen to give it another chance. No matter how many times it's let me down. Then something divine comes along, like First Nations Fashion and Design, and you realise why you've never settled before.

First Nations Fashion and Design, you had me at hello. It's the reinstatement of legacy that does it for me. The first design architects: the boomerang, eel traps and gunyahs. The first fashion designs: paperbark dresses, possum and kangaroo skin cloaks, and feather and shell headdresses. The first catwalk, Country, and the first beauties, First Nations women. And what better way for the burgeoning industry we see today, that began over 60,000 years ago, to be led and revived by its First Nations peoples, such as curator Shonae Hobson.

Shonae is the Curator of Indigenous Art at the National Gallery of Victoria and Piinpi: Contemporary Indigenous Fashion Exhibition (Bendigo Art Gallery). As soon as I laid eyes on Piinpi, I fell head over heels in love with Shonae's curatorial fabulousness.

Sidenote: I want to see more sistas like Shonae owning and operating First Nations galleries and museums. More sistas buying Blak Art and selling it directly to Black celebrities like Beyoncé, who purchased a painting by Pintupi artist Yukultji Napangati.

More for us, by us.

What makes Shonae so deadly is her holistic approach when curating Piinpi. A collection with over 60 works, Piinpi is a spellbinding capsule of First Nations fashion excellence, where I, a First Nations woman, find belonging, a reflection of my culture, identity, beauty and femininity in the authenticity of other First Nations women. And the undying connection to our matriarchal lines.

Piinpi voices what First Nations fashion trailblazers have spoken into existence from the beginning – we deserve to be recognised on an international stage. Shonae reassures us:

> *Indigenous fashion is not a 'trend' but an important movement that has put Indigenous voices and artistic expression at the centre of the global fashion agenda. These pioneering artists and makers are carving the future of fashion and design in Australia and leading important conversations about ethical and sustainable practices.*

Touché!

Shonae Hobson isn't the only sista making curatorial waves – cue First Nations Fashion and Design's power couple, Grace Lillian Lee and Teagan Cowlishaw.

Coming full circle since their fashion debut at Australian Indigenous Fashion Week in 2014, Grace and Teagan made history by breaking a 25-year spell at the 2021 Afterpay Australian Fashion Week to deliver the first showcase of Indigenous designers in partnership with IMG. It was launched the day before the 29th anniversary of the historic Mabo decision – opened by the first Welcome to Country at Australian Fashion Week.

The fashion event said to be one to remember was an All Blak affair: the entire team was First Nations. True to form, Grace and Teagan's fashion prowess left a lasting impression. Weaving in a profound cultural and political gesture: the pouring of sand through models' outstretched hands, acknowledging the Wave Hill Walk-Off led by Gurindji activist Vincent Lingiari.

Goosebumps yet? Tears were shed, tissues passed, hugs and kisses all round and a two-minute standing ovation. Brava!

Amid tears, Cowlishaw joyfully stated, 'It's taken us a decade but, we're here, we're here.'

Lee and Cowlishaw passed the baton to Perina Drummond, founder of Jira Models. Drummond started the agency to scout and represent Indigenous talent and provide them with pathways into the Australian fashion industry. Rhys Ripper, Perina's runway co-creator and fashion guru extraordinaire, is doing the same via his Indigenous fashion pathways program, KIN. Along with model and Solid Ochre designer Nathan McGuire's program Mob in Fashion. Both aim to reshape the future of Australian fashion by carving a First Nations imprint into the institution with pillars that sing, 'Always was, always will be, First Nations Fashion and Design.'

When Rhys and Nathan aren't securing mob's future in fashion, they're showing the industry why they have the Midas touch. They've shot a sneaky backyard photoshoot for Dior Beauty Sauvage fragrance, Indigenous fashion collections for *The Guardian* and collaboration for *GQ* magazine.

For *GQ*'s September/October 2020 print edition – and with the blessing of Nathan's father, Wadjuk Elder Morris McGuire – Nathan's face was painted with traditional ochre in his Wadjuk Noongar distinct tribal markings. Rhys infused the colour blue – representative of Nathan's people, as he holds tjun tjuns made by Morris for the editorial.

Together, frame after frame, Rhys and Nathan made art – leaving a calling card to the industry: Indigenous culture and luxury fashion just go together.

The tremendous shift by the Australian fashion industry towards the increase of diversity and inclusion in the last two years is due in part to Black Lives Matter: let's call a spade a spade. As much as it's been an uncomfortable truth for the Black diaspora to admit, we've vacillated between shame and grief from prospering off white guilt and Black death. It's disgusting to put it that way, but it's no fault of our own. And if you're one of the millions of Black people, like me, who have reconciled this rock-and-a-hard-place predicament we've been cornered into, you've concluded it's time to take up space. It's time to seek the reparations we are owed.

Beyond our words, the news, the streets and voices, we are talking to you all the time. Our history, our pain, our pride and our story is all around you. It is in the painting, the weaving, the making. It is in the Country, the grass, the sun, the trees. Open your heart and listen. We have been talking to you forever.

Yatu Widders Hunt,
Founder @ausindigenousfashion

The reparations I envision for First Nations people are the return of profits made by non-Indigenous people from our cultural knowledge and intellectual property. And we can start with the $250 million Indigenous art industry.

I want the cultural freedom to be inspired, access and care for Country to ensure our kin – our partner in creating First Nations fashion – is around forevermore. I want the abundance to move like Fendi – investing €2.5 million into restoring the Trevi Fountain – or Bulgari – €1.5 million for the Spanish Steps.

Can you imagine if the First Nations fashion industry could move like that? Restore our cultural treasures – Country?

But the hard truth is we're too busy trying to Close the Gap while industries and the world profit off us – the people, the land – our culture.

I want more international recognition: luxury fashion collaborations like Jimmy Choo and Peter Farmer's silk satin couture shoes and Hermès' Gloria Petyarre 'Le Rêve de Gloria' scarves. And fewer $2000 Chanel boomerangs, Les Benjamins' misappropriation of traditional symbols and Aboriginal polka-dot face. Fashion collections that feel like sacred rock art was stripped from the cave walls and onto fabric. Next time, Rodarte, credit the artists. Is that too much to ask?

I want more full-circle moments, like the 2021 Cairns Indigenous Art Fashion performance Of Spirit & Story. Fashion runways on Bama Country, that glorious place called Yarrabah where my grandfather was born. Weeping tears of joy because this is my type of fashion; where I belong. No longer the shame little girl who didn't fit into the Western fashion world because her body and features didn't fit their standards. Twenty years on, staring back at young women with eyes, hair, lips, skin, figures like mine when I was their age, modelling in a new fashion era.

I want more Blak curation, creativity, designs and joy. First Nations fashion is the new Blak. If Black curators steer the ship, you get unforgettable moments like Meghan Markle and Prince Harry, the Duchess and Duke's 2018 royal wedding – if that wasn't the Blackest royal wedding in history; Black curation at its finest. Two words: the preacher. All jokes aside.

Black consultation and leadership save us from H&M monkey hoodies, Gucci Blackface disasters and Balenciaga checked shopping bags. Balenciaga, you know damn well that's BIPOC's all-purpose bag. The Ghana Must Go Bag? Have you no shame?! The funny thing about Western fashion is that it steals from us and sells it right back to us at quadruple the price. Gucci Jelly Shoes? Why?

I want more Beyoncé *Black Is King* fashion collaborations.

Nothing can beat the feeling of copping a new piece of First Nations fashion. It's like wearing your favourite outfit but a thousand times better. I shine brighter, and red carpets mean more to me because the Ancestors get to see me show up and show out. Especially sashaying my way to stand on the TEDx red dot wearing my Kirrikin Natures Ant jumpsuit and feeling 10 feet tall.

Wearing, buying and trading Blak is part of the Blakfella ethos: rep culture and carry the mob into spaces – wherever you go.

Sissy Dr Amy Thunig knows what I'm talking about: wearing her Rachael Sarra x Concrete Jellyfish collaboration earrings and Bima Wear top for her TEDx talk. Sporting Sonia Pallett earrings on *The Bachelorette* Season 7 to ask contestant Darvid, do you know whose land you're living on? It's the love we have for our culture and each other. As the first Indigenous and pansexual bachelorette in the franchise's history, Brooke Blurton understood the assignment. Opening the show with a Welcome to Country, wearing Liandra Swim and Made for Olive, sitting down with Tegan Murdock of Ngumpie Weaving to make jewellery, incorporating tradition (women's business) for her date with Holly. To know how special the date was is to know the intimacy, the hands of someone beloved creating jewellery for you from their heart. This is how treasured I feel when my BFF creates custom-made cockatoo feather and echidna quill gemstone earrings for me, adornment from her Country.

The exchange of First Nations fashion gifts is always special to me, like when I received a pair of peach Minaku handwoven earrings for my Because of Her We Can tee. How deadly I feel because 'a sista' made it, and the colour makes my skin and lip gloss pop. It's the pride you feel purchasing your first pair of emu feather earrings from Krystal Hurst (Gillawarra Arts) at the Blak Markets. The joy you feel for Kristy Dickinson (Haus of

Dizzy) – seeing her earrings grace the lobes of Lauryn Hill and Drew Barrymore. Her empowering messages: Stop Adani, Pussy Power, The Future Is Intersectional, Land Back, White Australia Has a Black History and her deadly Faboriginal necklace. Seeing Kristy's bling matched with Keens Curry, You Lubly and Respect the Blak Matriarchy Gammin Threads tees.

It's Teagan Cowlishaw's Deadly Kween hooded jumpsuit and her insistence of embracing Blakfella slang and broken English like Deadly, True Gawwd (True God) and Budju. A reclamation of Blak identity in the absence of our native languages that have been lost.

It's actress Miranda Tapsell's celebration of Blak Beauty in her First Nations romantic comedy *Top End Wedding* but with a Tiwi Island twist; adorned in Lyn-Al Young's designs for her film's premiere. Along with Shareena Clanton, who also wore Young's designs at the 2017 TV Week Logie Awards.

I love how First Nations fashion always comes back to where it all began – our matriarchs. I get sentimental when I think of the Cungelella sisters of Myrrdah paying homage to their aunties, and designers Liandra Gaykamangu and Julie Shaw celebrating Blak women's names – Jedda, Lowanna, Bindi, Marli, Yatu, Alinta, Fallon and Jirra – in their collections.

I was sold the myth that the big smoke is the epicentre of success. Our Elders urged the mob who travelled to the city to pursue their dreams, but to reinvest the skills and knowledge gained back into community.

Now the veil has lifted and the smoke has cleared. I realise success is however you define it. Beauty is how you perceive it, and fashion is a state of mind. Not a formula or a trend. We don't have to leave Country to make it or change who we are. It's everyone else who has to fall in line with us.

First Nations fashion taught me how to love myself, heal and embrace this new cultural renaissance I've waited so long for. I truly hope Western fashion can meet us halfway. They could learn a lot from the First Peoples.

How times have changed, I remember when all I wanted to do was fill my Mariah Carey-style wardrobes with designer clothes. I still do, but this time with an Indigenous fashion altar – my own Piinpi, overflowing with First Nations fashion runway collections.

Cathy Freeman's Nike Swift Suit, the one she won Gold at the 2000 Olympics in – that's going in there too. But it's an aerodynamic suit? I don't care; it's fashion. A comeback waiting to happen. Mark my words!

I grew up lost in the fairy tale of wearing Oscar de la Renta; now, I have Paul McCann's signature ballgowns to make my heart race – the opulence to see Blak Femininity in all its grace.

24

Blak Goddess

The big rains had finally cleared. With the roads now open, Mum and I embarked on our road trip to Ingham. I hadn't seen Mum or Aunty Bella since COVID-19 had locked us away.

We pulled into the sleepy township. Mum pointed to the local bakery and suggested we grab afternoon tea. Since there wasn't any pound cake, I bought apple crumble, my childhood treat.

Aunty Bella's house was past the cemetery. My cousin, Renee, had taken me there one night when I slept over. She and her friends smoked cigarettes while I sat scared shitless, waiting for the walking dead to appear.

I could see Cousin Cassie in the driveway up ahead. When she saw us arrive, the same smile my mother and Aunty Bella shared brightened her face.

Mum and I headed to the patio table where Aunty Bella and Cousin Renee sat, along with a pile of photo albums and shoe boxes. I let Mum and Aunty Bella yarn and began sifting through memories I'd never seen before.

'Aunty Bella, how did you become a beauty queen?' I asked, placing the old photos neatly onto the butterscotch tablecloth. Meanwhile, Mum sliced up the freshly baked apple crumble.

Grabbing her coffee mug, Aunty let out a huge sigh before gathering her thoughts.

'We were at the Victorian Aboriginal Advancement League for an event, and the photographer from the paper came down to capture a story. He asked if he could take my photo and if I had done any modelling. I said no, so he suggested I enter the Gala parade. The League held a fundraiser to help me raise money to enter. And the photographer ended up doing a profile on me after I won.'

Wow! I thought as I recalled Aunty Ruthie's stories of the civil rights movements taking place during her time in the lead-up to the 1967 Referendum – the 'Vote Yes for Aboriginal Rights' campaign. I marvelled at what the atmosphere must have been like. The deadliest Blak minds, advocates and changemakers gathered together fighting for Blakfella rights.

I stared at the black and white photo of Aunty Bella pictured sitting on the drop-top of a '60s convertible, waving as beauty queens do. She looked like an Aboriginal Jackie Onassis to me. She wore a dress with a crisp white bodice and navy spotted skirt that ended just before her knees – her hair tied back with a ribbon. Her cherub cheeks on high beam from her sprightly smile stretched from ear to ear.

I turned the photo over, and on the back of it, written in

Aunty's beautiful cursive writing, was 'Gala Procession Geelong 1968'. Aunty Bella was 15 years old.

'Did you win anything?' I asked, still admiring my aunty, the natural beauty.

'No, but the Advancement League sent me to deportment classes at Elly Lukas Beauty College. I enjoyed that.'

During my work week, I'd walk past the college, not knowing Aunty Bella had been a student, and the college's longstanding history.

'What happened after that? Did you pursue modelling?'

'They said I was too short to be a mannequin model.'

'What's a mannequin model?'

'When you walk down the catwalk. They said I was suitable for catalogues.'

I pulled out another photo from Aunty Bella's shoe box.

'Is this you?' I squealed. Aunty Bella was absolutely divine. She was rocking a bob curled at the base of her neck, wearing a mustard coat and silver gogo boots. Beside her was my mother in a grey coat.

Mum, standing behind me, baulked at the photo. 'I hated that coat. It was so itchy.'

I handed Mum an image of her with her head cocked back, eyes closed in a fit of laughter. I picked up another snap of Aunty Bella teaching Mum how to execute a modelling stance. Another had Mum sitting bored as Aunty Bella showed her how to sit like a lady.

Saving the best for last: there was the natural beauty herself, Aunty Bella, posing in her evening gown the night of her deportment class graduation. Ripples of lace formed a halo around Aunty's neckline, settling neatly into layers met by a single-bow ribbon tied around her tiny waist. The luscious lace fell to her ankles. Aunty Bella wore her hair in a beehive, with singular curl ringlets falling on either side of her youthful face. Her dainty hands clasped an iridescent satin pillow clutch. Satin silk heels upheld the statuesque beauty for all to see.

Aunty Bella was delicate and petite, like the porcelain dolls I collected. If only there was a doll to sell that looked like Aunty Bella. I bet those ones would fly off the shelves. Sadly, they didn't make Blak dolls to treasure when I was growing up.

The last leg of our road trip was Townsville. As I sat down on Uncle Darren's couch, I snickered recalling the time I got nits when I visited him as a kid. I'd sat in his driveway sobbing while Mum tried her best to exterminate the critters crawling in my hair.

Before leaving, I'd called Uncle Darren to let him know I was doing family research, and he diligently had his stash of family photos ready for us.

One of the photos Uncle Darren had set aside was of Aunty Belsie, Aunty Ruthie, Aunty Cissy and Uncle George – with a guitar in his hand – sitting in the living room. The All Australian Blakfella family. I could picture them singing on an evening variety show like *The Jacksons*.

'This was when Uncle George was boxing, right?' I asked.

Uncle Darren nodded.

'Uncle George looks like a Blak Elvis. Gee, he's handsome.'

'Speaking of Elvis, Uncle George sang too. I think he had a couple of records.'

Come to find out, Uncle Darren was right. Uncle George had two rhythm and blues singles in 1959 released by W&G Records Pty Ltd – 'Turn Me Loose' and 'Sea Cruise' – and had penned a few tracks.

And there it was, the famous photo I'd seen circulating online: Uncle George Bracken bruised and sweaty in his silky boxing robe, with his arms around a young Lionel Rose.

'Yeah, Uncle George was Lionel's mentor when he got into boxing,' Uncle Darren said, looking at the picture over my shoulder.

According to my family, Lionel Rose credited Uncle George as his inspiration for taking up the sport.

'I should put on Aunty Cissy's bandstand performance I found on YouTube,' Uncle Darren suggested.

'Gorn den,' I said.

I got goosebumps when Aunty Cissy started singing her medley 'Birds and the Bees' and 'It's Not Unusual'.

'That's Pheeny's face!' I exclaimed, turning to my mother and hugging her. 'Mum, I can see you in Aunty Cissy.' Mum was given the nickname Pheeny by Aunty Alma.

Brian Henderson, the host of *Australian Bandstand*, introduced Aunty Cissy's second medley.

By now, Aunty Belsie was bopping away in her chair. When Aunty Cissy started singing 'Ask Me How Do I Feel', Aunty Belsie started to croon in synch with her.

'Awww, go, Aunty!' we all erupted in laughter.

After watching Aunty Cissy's medleys, Uncle Darren put on the kettle for another round of cuppas. He emerged with a photo of Aunty Belsie and Aunty Ruthie pictured with Aunty Lois Peeler from The Sapphires, all rugged up in winter gear, photographed in what appeared to be snow.

'Too deadly, what that? Destiny's Child?' I joked while the laughter continued.

'Youse mob seen the movie *The Sapphires*? Deadly how Tony Briggs brought his mother's and aunt's story to life.'

Then Aunty Belsie told us about hanging out with the African-American servicemen who came over from the States. They weren't allowed in the pubs because they were Black. So, they danced and drank the night away at the Blakfellas' houses.

'That's how Aunty Kay learnt to fight,' Aunty Belsie proudly announced.

'From who?'

'The servicemen. They knew hand-to-hand combat, so they taught her.'

'Truuuue, Aunty!'

Must've come in handy in those days, I thought. When was a Blak woman not engaged in combat? We've been fighting since well before the Black War in Tasmania.

If I'd been on the front line, Walyer is the type of warrioress I'd have wanted to be. When my best friend Ruby gets fired up, she possesses a Walyer spirit.

'How would you describe me?' I asked Ruby over dinner one night.

'An iron fist in a velvet glove.'

I was surprised that Ruby saw that quality in me; I was glad to be past the pushover phase. I had every faith that had I been living at the height of colonisation, I'd have led like Truganini.

In those times, I wouldn't have had the privilege of gullibility. I imagined the adrenaline coursing through my body before we launched into guerrilla warfare.

It's remarkable how two women led their people in such polar opposite ways: revolt vs diplomacy. Although, in the end, Truganini switched sides and embraced her inner Walyer. Can you imagine if both women had fought alongside each other? What a force to be reckoned with.

If only feminism could do the same. Which leaves me to ask: Blak women, do we need feminism or just our land back?

Patyegarang

The last time I caught a Bangarra performance was *Patyegarang* in 2014, which marked their 25th anniversary. Dancer Jasmin Sheppard, who played Patyegarang, had scenes that I still remember today. Like when Patyegarang undergoes an initiation into womanhood, and the scene showing the attraction when she meets Dawes, played by Thomas Greenfield.

I was enchanted by Sheppard and Greenfield's intimacy and rhythm that belonged only to them. Inviting our eyes and hearts to interpret how much Dawes and Patyegarang meant to each other, no words, no text – just two souls dancing as one.

I had no idea that Patyegarang, at the tender age of 15, was a diplomat and educator, and is considered Australia's first Aboriginal linguist. How Patyegarang's curiosity turned into a friendship with First Fleet Lieutenant William Dawes, which established a cultural exchange. She taught him her language and he returned the gesture. Patyegarang placed her trust in Dawes, which allowed her to translate, settle conflict and pursue peace with the British on behalf of her clan. Through Patyegarang's generosity and Dawe's historical notebooks, their reciprocal relationship ensured the survival of the Gadigal language.

What makes their union saccharine was the tenderness throughout their relationship revealed in Dawes' records:

'Putuwá', to warm one's hand by the fire and then to squeeze gently the fingers of another person.

The fondness and concern.

Dawes: 'Mínyin bial naŋadyími?' (Why don't you sleep?)

Patyegarang: 'Kandúlin.' (Because of the candle.)

The comfort and respect.

'Matarabaun nagaba.' (We shall sleep separately.)

The humour and rile.

When Dawes jokingly suggests Patyegarang might turn white if she keeps washing her skin, she throws down a towel in a huff. 'Tyerabarrbowaryaou,' she retorts (I shall not become white).

Their mutual compassion transcended the political arena. It is believed their close bond pricked Dawes' conscience, resulting in him refusing to participate in punitive actions against her people – in turn, falling out of favour with Governor Phillip and being deported for insubordination. Dawes was dismayed by Phillip's decision; his heart was set on living in the colony.

Patyegarang and Dawes' story can be compared to Romeo and Juliet. I hadn't come across a sentimental story about an Aboriginal woman and a lieutenant, such an unlikely pair. Until Bangarra brought *Patyegarang* to life on stage, I'd never heard a sonnet or read a book about Blak Femininity as revered as Jane Austen's classics *Pride and Prejudice* or *Persuasion*.

Nana Doreen

'I always thought she was such a beautiful woman. She was so refined in her mannerisms and how she carried herself. Everyone I know who knew Mum says that about her. She was just different. You could tell there was something about her, something strong. A lot of people were jealous of her; I used to ask why. Because she was so beautiful, she could hold court, talk to a beggar, and have the same conversation. It was pretty amazing she could do that.

'When I heard you talking, you reminded me of Mum. People would wait on every word she was going to say. I would watch their faces listening to her, thinking, "Wow." That same spirit I saw in our mother, it's come full circle. I cried. It's in our DNA. It might have jumped our generation, but it's still there. I see a lot of Mum in you – the way you carry yourself.

'She would wear lipstick every day. Whenever she'd go down the street, she'd always get her little compact out of her bag. I used to think to myself, "I need to get me a gold compact." She used to wear Pond's cream in the little pink jar. She'd put it on her face before she went to bed or went out. The smell of Pond's cream reminds me of her.

'She'd boil the water in the morning, put a slice of lemon in it and a doily on it. She'd say it was good for the gut. She always ate ginger; she had it growing in the backyard. When Christmas came, she'd make sugar ginger. I'd think it was lollies and bite down into it. I used to think how much of this ginger this ole lady ate.'

25

God Is a Black Woman

'You know everyone comes from a Black woman,' I said. Me and Ruby sat on her verandah with a pot of hot tea to ward off the winter chill.

'What do you mean?' Ruby asked, as she rolled herself a cigarette.

'A Black woman created civilisation.'

'You mean the "Out of Africa" theory?'

'I think so. They call it Mitochondrial Eve – the Black woman's DNA possesses every variation found in all humans.'

'I'm confused. How are we the world's oldest continuous living culture if we came out of Africa?' Frown lines formed across Ruby's forehead.

'I don't know. All I know is I'm a living legend. I've inherited two legacies: Eve's DNA and the oldest ancient culture. You know God is a Black woman.' Pretty chuffed I had the creator's DNA.

'How?' I could see Ruby softening into the prospect of learning more.

'For one, we predate the Bible. Two – Yhi.'

'Yhi?'

'Yhi the deity – the Goddess of Light and Creation,' I said, glad to enlighten Ruby once more.

Yhi: The Goddess of Light and Creation

In the jujaba, a spell of darkness and silence conquered the land. Not a blade of grass sprouted from the dirt or a bristle of leaves waving in the wind. The Earth did not make a sound. Nor did a creature scurry across the rock hills.

The Earth remained still in a frozen slumber. Only Yhi, the Goddess of Light and Creation, could awaken the land, but she was also sleeping. And only the Great Spirit Baiame had the authority to rouse her from it. When it was time, Baiame woke Yhi with a whisper.

From the second Yhi opened her eyes, light fell upon the Earth, and warmth blanketed the cold and gloomy lands. Yhi floated down from the sky to explore, and wherever her feet touched, grass, trees, plants and flowers sprang from beneath them. Seeing the luscious greens, oranges, pinks, purples and blues come to life, Yhi wanted all beings to dance and delight in the paradise she created. Baiame told Yhi to shine her light into the dark caves. It is there she would find spirits to create life. Looking into the crevices, she found evil spirits lurking. They did not welcome Yhi and tried to sing her to death. NO! NO! NO! they cried, but it was too late.

Yhi shone her light until the cave sparkled with ladybugs, grasshoppers and beetles; bees buzzed, hummingbirds and butterflies fluttered about.

The warmth generated from Yhi's light had melted the icy country, and water poured out in abundance, forming waterfalls, streams, rivers, lakes and the sea. As the water flowed, it formed the fishes, snakes and lizards that lay dormant. The creatures came out in copious herds. Admiring her creations, Yhi reassured the animals that although she had to return to the sky she'd visit them each day. She also provided them with the seasons. Summer for regeneration: to partake in harvests. Autumn to shed the old. Winter for purification and rest. Spring to flourish. Yhi told her beloved that their bodies would remain here on Earth when they died, but their spirits would join her.

With that, Yhi returned to the sky. Sorrow befell the animals in her absence as night brought darkness.

It wasn't long until Yhi heard murmurs of discontent from the animals. Some weren't adjusting well to their new bodies. One by one, Yhi listened to their concerns. The lizard felt awkward wriggling on its body to get around, so Yhi gave it legs for freedom of movement. The kangaroo desired a sturdy body, so Yhi granted the roo a strong tail and legs to balance him when he bounded across the plains. The wombat, somewhat of a recluse, wanted a body to wiggle away and hide in shady places. The mopoke had trouble hunting in the night and asked for big bright eyes. When Yhi granted all the animals their gifts, she also sent the Morning Star as a sign of her arrival to soothe the angst of the animals who feared the dark. Realising the Morning Star would be lonely, she brought Bahloo the moon to be the Morning Star's husband.

The Great Spirit Baiame was restless as he saw Yhi's creations: he knew something was missing. Baiame knew his intelligence could not remain solely with him, and he was not confident to entrust it with the creatures that roamed the Earth, so he imparted only a little of it to them. And set off to begin creating. Baiame gathered dust, blood, flesh and cartilage, moulding the atoms and his wisdom into a creature that stood on two legs. A physical manifestation of Baiame. All the creatures came out to see who the new animal was walking alongside them. And it wasn't long until Man felt the pangs of loneliness. He had no-one to share his intellect with, converse with, dote after, and grow with – separate but as one.

Yhi took pity on Man, and while he rested his head to sleep Yhi searched for a single flower, using its long slender stem to form her body. The soft petals for her skin, its bountiful bloom for her bosoms and bottom. The splendid aroma as her womanly scent.

Yhi had outdone herself by designing the most divine creation unlike any other she had before. When Man awoke, he thought his eyes deceived him. In front of him stood a magnificent woman who possessed similar qualities to him. Enamoured by her presence Man did whatever he could to impress, amuse, please and protect her. Woman found Man interesting and was slowly getting used to him. As time went by, the Woman grew fond of the Man.

Yhi and Baiamie watched from the sky as Man and Woman created a family of their own and shared the knowledge they inherited. And creation would continue – thanks to Yhi the Goddess of Light and Creation and the Great Spirit Baiame.

I poured two mugs of chai – for Ruby and me. Now, it was my turn to be quizzed.

'Love versus honour? Are you marrying for love or duty?' Ruby asked.

'Can't I have both?' I joked.

'No, you cannot. It defeats the purpose of the question.' Ruby whacked me with a pillow.

'Love then.'

'Okay, what if I say we're doing it for culture?'

'What do you mean?'

'If we were living like our Ancestors and you were promised to someone – love or honour?'

'Bahahaha ... seriously? Okay, okay, love.' I took a swig of my chai. 'Does that make me selfish? I tried honour before and look how that turned out. Since it's back in the day, call me Oolana.'

'Who's Oolana?' Ruby asked, hugging the pillow to her chest.

Oolana

Oolana was a stunning young woman who was promised to Waroonoo, a wise and respected Elder. Shortly after they were married, a wandering tribe passed through the Babinda Valley. Per their custom, the Yidinji welcomed the visiting tribe to rest at their camp. It didn't take long for Oolana to notice the handsome warrior Dyga from the other tribe. You could say it was love at first sight. The attraction between Dyga and Oolana was so strong the pair agreed to meet secretly. Instantly, they knew their desire for each other could never be, because Oolana was already married to Waroonoo. Knowing the shame and dishonour they'd bring to their families, Dyga and Oolana ran away together. They spent blissful days nestled in the valley, but it didn't take long before their families came looking for them.

The tribesmen spotted the two lovers near the water pool and grabbed Dyga, scorning him for breaking the lore. The Yidinji snatched Oolana, dragging her away, but she managed to wrestle herself free. In her distress, Oolana called for Dyga to follow her as she hurled herself into the still waters. Oolana's calls were in vain. Dyga was hauled away by his people. When Oolana hit the water suddenly, the ground erupted thunderously – unearthing huge boulders high into the air, which came crashing down and became scattered all across the valley.

Oolana's anguished tears turned into violent torrents – her unrelenting sorrow still rushes the once tranquil stream. Oolana still calls out to Dyga her long lost love hoping he will return; her spirit still remains at Babinda Boulders. We warn visitors to be careful and not to swim there because Oolana has been known to lure young men to their death.

'I've had Oolana's grief before,' Ruby said. 'I still wonder if I had chosen to stay with my Waroonoo – would he have been enough? Would Dyga be a distant memory?'

I mulled over Ruby's words.

'Maybe life would have been good, maybe not. I guess you'll never know,' I sympathetically offered.

'So, am I doomed to be heartbroken like Oolana forevermore?' Ruby sarcastically asked.

'Maybe there's another interpretation. Could Oolana's sorrow be a reminder that choosing yourself, in a world that will never accept your decision, is a painful experience?'

'Maybe it's both?'

26

Blak Femininity

Yabu (mother) was dulbun (newly married), and stayed at bulmba (home), caring for her young girls. Me and my jaman (sister) had Yabu all to ourselves, which suited us fine.

Yabu was magic. Passionate and devoted, her love knew no bounds. Her composure chased storms away and protected us like Gumbu (Grandmother), the best way she knew how. Yabu taught us love finds a bulmba in jujaba (creation). Yabu's gigorou brought out the divinity within us.

Yabu, Jaman and I collected flower petals, placed them in the middle of rustic books, pressed flat to preserve their gigorou. We made cards and gifts out of the petals to share with loved ones. Along with potpourri: dried orange peels, cloves, cinnamon sticks, acorns and petals dashed with scented oils. A gorgeous blend scooped up into fetching bags of fine cloth tied with ribbon. Yabu opened our top dresser drawers to place the potpourri bags in there to make our chilanas (undies) smell good.

Yards of fabric stood like soldiers against the wall. I watched Yabu press her foot up and down on the pedal as the needle chewed rapidly through the strips Yabu fed it. Jaman and I decorated each other like Christmas trees with reams of lace. Little House on the Prairie dresses opened like parachutes as we twirled ourselves into dizzy spells. The carpet breaking our fall. Within those four walls, nothing could harm us.

We were poor, but even the poor had a guli dira (sweet tooth). Yabu emerged with vinegar, sugar and butter; no cookbook, no measuring cups. Intently, Jaman and I observed Yabu pouring the ingredients together in a small pot of boiling water. As it boiled, the pungent smell of vinegar singed our nose hairs. Vigorously, Yabu stirred the pot: a sprinkle of more sugar, Yabu's delicate hand became a spinning top. The liquid hastened into a thick honey-tinted glaze.

I never met my Gumbu. Did she teach Yabu this recipe when she was a little girl?

Pointing to the pantry, Yabu told me to fetch the patty cake papers. Carefully, we placed the white pleated skirts on the baking tray. Jumping out of Yabu's way, steam escaped the pot as the golden lava flowed into the patties. Yabu put the tray near the window to cool and set.

Minutes passed; we waited some more.

Keen as mustard, Jaman and I chimed in, 'Is it ready, Yabu?'

'Maya yinda (no, not yet).'

Yabu gave us something to do so we'd stop humbugging her.

When Yabu eventually peeled herself off the seat and made her way to the kitchen, we followed. Smiling, Yabu told us to see if it was ready.

Jaman and I turned to each other to see who would go first. Our little fingers tapped the glass surface; it was hard as a rock. Fascinated, we lit up.

'Yabu, it's hard,' we exclaimed.

'Then, it's ready,' Yabu said.

Greedy, I grabbed two. 'You only need one.'

Yabu was right.

Sitting in the kitchen, we sucked on the treat to make it soft. I bit down on it, convinced I could crack its deceivingly smooth veneer. It bit back. My dira started to ache.

I sucked and licked that toffee for days on end, hardly shifting its composition. Jaman and I placed our treat in a sealed paper bag. And when we arose the next day, we faithfully returned to our treat. Still sweet, still hard, as we left it. Jaman and I tried to tussle our candy into submission, determined we could break it down at will.

It refused. So, we gave in and enjoyed it, as it was.

Our toffee lasted far longer than the other desserts we'd had before. With only a handful of ingredients, it cost next to nothing.

Ask me what Blak Femininity is – it's Blak toffee my Yabu used to make.

'Turn it up!' I screeched as soon as I heard the crazy electric guitar. I shooed the kids from blocking the TV so I could belt out 'Party' without the deadly red shoes.

If I wasn't daydreaming about being Elaine George or Brenda Webb from *Neighbours*, it was Christine Anu. I remember it like it was yesterday. Sissy had a brown figure-hugging dress on, natural hair falling to her shoulders, which alternated from Afro puffs to sleek hair pinned backed and accentuated by a black halter-neck top. God, she was stunning! Apart from Deni Hines from the Rockmelons, there weren't many homegrown Black songstresses on *rage* until Shakaya came on the scene years later. So it was nice to see mob on TV – a sistagal from our way who looked like us.

The way Christine was styled in her 'Party' video reminded me of my mother and Aunty Debbie's style – let's call it urban chic. Think Toni Braxton's debut album cover: tight-fitting white tee, light-wash jeans and a black leather jacket to Selena Quintanilla blinged-out bras and bustiers. The only jewellery their waists ever needed was a rhinestone belt buckle.

I'd watch Aunty Debbie and Mum fuss over outfits in front of the mirror: 'Does this look gammon?'

Aunty Debbie had the exact figure as Christine Anu and she owned bodycon dresses in her closet, which I'd shimmy into when they left to paint the town red. There was a white one with sewn-in bra cups my pancakes couldn't fill. Sucking in my pot belly, I ran my hands down the stretchy material busting into Betty Boop's poses after sliding on a pair of velvet suede heels.

I miss those days because they were my first iterations of Blak Femininity – precious images I pinned to my mood board.

The images have changed now as I have evolved. More comfortable in my skin, my mood board is no longer about aesthetic beauty but gigorou.

Today Blak Femininity is …

'I speak my language, and I practise my cultural essence of me. Don't try and suppress me, and don't call me a problem, I am not the problem.' (The late Rosalie Kunoth-Monks, *Q&A*, ABC TV, 2014)

'I am tired of begging and asking for our humanity. When is it enough? We want to be the author of our own destinies.' (Shareena Clanton, *Q&A*, ABC TV, 2018)

Blak Femininity is …

Lidia Thorpe's Blak fist raised in the air, draped in a possum skin cloak wearing an emu feather necklace, holding a message stick with 441 markings engraved on it. Signifying the First Nations lives lost in police custody as she is inducted as the first Aboriginal Greens Senator for Victoria. Only to return to the Australian parliament to be sworn in, addressing the 'colonising Her Majesty Queen Elizabeth II' in her oath of allegiance.

Blak Femininity is …

The establishment of the Dhadjowa Foundation: fighting for justice despite your loss. Extending love, grace and support to families whose loved ones have died in custody. Standing tall in the midst of it all as your daughters watch and learn the ways of the Blak Matriarch (Apryl Day).

Not letting our past define us and for damn sure not crying over budoo. It's Barkaa's 'Blak Matriarchy' video, where she is painted in ochre, wearing an echidna quill necklace and the colours of Country. Her hair set free, a boondi in her hand in the company of her Blak Matriarchs.

It's Kee'ahn's 'Better Things' and Miiesha's 'Drowning'.

It's the first time I saw Vanessa Turnbull-Roberts at the Sydney Mardi Gras Parade, marching down Oxford Street in her

Aboriginal flag cozzie, thinking, who is that woman? Whenever that woman grabs the mic, you stop and listen.

It's every time Madeleine Madden and Billie Jean Hamlet step in front of a camera. When Madeleine meets the Jackie Gucci 1961 bag reimagined. Mungala's campaign for Estée Lauder's Dream Dusk. It's Charlee Fraser wearing Ngarru Miimi pieces by designer Lillardia Briggs-Houston for *Vogue Australia*. Nakkiah Lui's 'Renaissance Woman' cover for *Harper's Bazaar* October 2021 inaugural edition.

It's Lyn-Al Young's intention of design. Singing and speaking positive words over her creations and how the essence of affirmation feels on your skin.

It's the infectious laughter, bright eyes and dazzling smiles of Miranda Tapsell, Jessica Mauboy and Rärriwuy Hick; how they light up people and places like Yhi. It's the gentle wisdom and integrity I've witnessed in the presence of Marlikka Perdrisat and Magnolia Maminydjama Maymuru. The glow of motherhood they both share and the elegance with which Marlikka discusses the First Law (lore).

It's Bianca Hunt's uncompromising stance – 'I'm a once-in-a-lifetime opportunity' – while Yarning Up with Caroline Kell.

It's Miss NAIDOC, Kimberley and Pilbara Girl and the new generation of Indigenous models taking the Australian fashion industry by storm.

It's our fashion trailblazers – the first models, cover girls, TV presenters, catwalk queens and talent scouts. Aunty Dr Lois Peeler [née Briggs] AM, Sandra King OAM, Cecily Atkinson and the late Elizabeth Geia.

It's the work of my cousin Whitney caring for our Country, Cassie in Aboriginal Health, Aunty Debbie's clinical psychology and counselling in holistic healing, Aunty Coralie's critical pen, Aunty Bella's and cousin Renee's career in Aboriginal Housing, my mother's and sister's work in early intervention and homelessness, diversionary and cell watch programs to prevent Blak deaths in custody. Aunty Dr Pat O'Shane, the first female Aboriginal teacher in Queensland, barrister, and the first Aboriginal person to graduate in law, become a state magistrate and head a government department.

It's Aunty Kym's spirit that gives me permission to be a Carefree Blak Girl every day.

These are the women who made me who I am, who inspired me, who I learn from, lean into for guidance, and admire from afar. Since I can't fit all the Aboriginal and Torres Strait Islander women I admire in this book, I'll have to create more books and chapters to sing their praises.

27

Dear Niecey

Dear Niecey,

This is your Aunty Sassy. Welcome to Womanhood! I am so proud of you. Before you embark on the next leg of your journey I want to share some gems with you, what I've learnt and collected in my travels.

Take your time finding your purpose but don't be too long. Purpose will fill you with unimaginable joy. It's the flint that sparks the fire in your belly. When it fades, let your spirit wanderlust. Allow purpose to find its way back to you.

You don't need to have all the answers. Just keep taking one step forward, one step at a time. If you fall, dust yourself off and try again, again and again. Face your fears; you need to see what you're made of. Forgiveness is for you, not them. Forgive yourself. You are not your past.

Don't look back, and if you need to, do so only for a moment. Leave the past to rest; there's so much waiting for you up ahead. Be in the present; that's why it's called a gift – and so are you. Don't cast your pearls before swine (Matthew 7:6). Protect your magic.

The most honourable thing you can do in this lifetime is to be honest with yourself and others.

All the answers you need, when it concerns you, come from within with a bit of help from your Elders and Ancestors. Listen to your intuition. It's your spiritual compass. It will always point you in the right direction. If you ever lose yourself, know you will find your way home. Just look up into the sky until you see the Seven Sisters: they represent your matriarchs watching and protecting you. You are made of stardust. Pursue your dreams; let them be big, bold and bodacious. Don't put your dreams on the backburner for anyone, not even you.

If you're on the verge of breaking, let every crack show. Let every piece fall to the floor and when you're ready, piece yourself back together again. You are medicine. You are lore. You are magic. You are the alchemist. You are sovereign.

You deserve to be loved deeply, inexplicably, irrevocably (@featherdownsoul). If they don't look at you as magic, disappear. Value does not beg. You will never be too much fire for those meant to dance in your flames (Ara). Don't put all your eggs in one basket. You've got options. Your heart will break, but you will love again, again and again. If it feels too good to be true, then it probably is. Learn everything about love bombing, gaslighting and narcissism.

Use this scripture to vet people and protect your heart:

> Love is patient, love is kind. It does not envy, it does
> not boast, it is not proud. It does not dishonour others,

it is not self-seeking, it is not easily angered, it keeps
no record of wrongs. Love does not delight in evil but
rejoices with the truth.

1 Corinthians 13:4-6

If they can't meet you halfway, then the journey ends there.

The only thing you owe to yourself and others is your fabulous self. Anything less is a crime. You are enough. You are the prize. Be who you want to be unapologetically. Who's better qualified than you? It's okay to change – the seasons do. Never give up your independence. Put *your* oxygen mask on first; you are your number one priority. Learn everything about yourself before you invest in others. What you require from another, make sure you can reciprocate. Check yourself before you wreck yourself. Therapy is your friend.

Travel the world. Dance like no-one is watching you, like when I walked in on you boppin' with your headphones on. Your melanin is vibranium. Stay hydrated; moisturise. Stay juicy, never thirsty. The ashy cannot be trusted. If it doesn't bring you income, inspiration or orgasms, it doesn't belong in your life (Ice T).

Listen to your mind, body, spirit and heart. If your gut turns and you get pins and needles: run. That's your spirit warning you, you in danger, bub. Your body is not a map for lost people to find themselves. Your body is a temple. Where energy goes, energy flows. Energy doesn't lie. Do what is right for you guilt-free. You don't owe anybody your firstborn child; this ain't Rumpelstiltskin. If it's not a *hell yes*, then it's a *hell no*. Don't stay where you are tolerated. Don't rush. Move at your own pace. Fark FOMO: the party ain't going nowhere.

Don't hold court or seek counsel with those you can't trust with your secrets or your life. Don't run with the crowd. Let them report back. Real Gs move in silence. Real Gs let actions speak louder than words. What others think of you is none of your business. Caring about what others think about you robs you of your joy and freedom.

Be a fly on the wall. Observe. Talk less, listen more. Learn from others' mistakes. Get out of your ego – you're not the exception to the rule. Don't give them the benefit of the doubt. If you have to repeat yourself, say goodbye and goodnight. Rejection is protection. What is yours will always find you. Leave an air of mystery about you. It's poor spiritual hygiene for everyone to have access to you. Make them wait; leave them wanting more.

Learn how to play poker and chess. Whip out your poker face, and keep your cards close to your chest. Know when to call someone's bluff and when to fold. Baby girl, you are the Queen in the chess game. Move freely with ease across the board. Don't make an appearance too early on in the game. Remember, you are the Queen, the most powerful piece.

Whatever you want is just a thought away. All you need is faith the size of a mustard seed. Keep your thoughts positive and intentional. Speak it into existence. Write it down. Act as if it's already yours. Life and death are in the power of the tongue (Proverbs 18:21)

Every room you enter, the table you sit down at, the stage you're invited on, you deserve to be there. You don't have imposter syndrome, you have a colonised mind (@dr.rosalesmeza). If they don't open the door or offer you a seat, create your own and better.

The Black Superwoman is a myth. Carefree Black Girl, that's where it's at. Speak up. Say no. Be joyful. Be angry. The Angry Black Woman trope no longer exists. Ask for help. Ask questions – and lots of them. Don't complain; find a solution.

Ask for what you're worth and double it. Don't get mad if they lowball; just make sure they know next time you're not the one. Your time and energy are not free. Have enough money to get up and leave at a moment's notice. Not-for-profit does not exist unless it's for your community and people. Strive to build generational wealth; working for Richard and Eleanor for 20 years ain't cute. Do what you love. The money will find you. Multiple streams of income. No collaboration until you've talked contracts and coins. You define success. You are your source of happiness. Work smarter, not harder. Peace over profits.

Bub, don't tiptoe through life; let them hear every mofo step you take. There's a time to be humble and a time to be Issa Rae accepting the Emerging Entrepreneur Award at the 2019 Women in Film Annual Gala. Watch it – duh, bishes.

They can steal the recipe, but the sauce won't taste the same. You are the blueprint.

'If God be for you, then who can be against you?' (Romans 8:31, quoted by Angela Bassett, 2019 Icon, BLACK GIRLS ROCK® Awards)

Never forget where you come from, where you are going and where you belong. If you happen to forget …

You belong where the rainforest grows tall like skyscrapers, where the red dust stretches for days reaching white sandy beaches. Skylines that kiss the rough to calm sapphire seas. Pristine sanctuaries from north, south, east to west – where untold stories are yet to be discovered. Captivating dawns that rise – promising new beginnings, if you dare to believe. An enchanting place where mindless worries disappear like sunsets.

You are a freshwater and saltwater girl. A young Jirrbal, Wadjanbarra Yidinji, Ankamuthi (Seven River), Badu, Erub (Darnley) and Saibai Island woman. You are royalty – the descendant of sovereign queens. You are a Brackenridge, Sarago and Kendrick.

Playlist

Speeches

Gabrielle Union: acceptance speech, 2013 Fierce and Fearless Award, Essence, Black Women in Hollywood
https://fb.watch/dyp3UxQVBl/

Angela Bassett: acceptance speech, 2019 Icon Award, BLACK GIRLS ROCK!
https://youtu.be/4-Qnwjt7yvY

Issa Rae: acceptance speech, 2019 Emerging Entrepreneur Award, Women in Film
https://youtu.be/Db1dPZ5abn4

Albums

Janet Jackson: *Rhythm Nation 1814*
Lil' Kim: *Hard Core*
Foxy Brown: *Ill Na Na*
Nicki Minaj: *Beam Me Up Scotty* (Mixtape)
Mary J. Blige: *Share My World*
SWV: *Greatest Hits*
TLC: *CrazySexyCool*
Beyoncé: *Lemonade*
Solange: *A Seat at the Table*
Lauryn Hill: *The Miseducation of Lauryn Hill*

Playlist

Sade: *Soldier of Love*
Rihanna: *Anti*
SZA: *Ctrl*
Jhené Aiko: Tiny Desk (Home) Concert

Singles

New Edition: 'Can You Stand the Rain', 'If It Isn't Love'
Soul for Real: 'Every Little Thing I Do', 'Candy Rain'
Michael Jackson: 'The Way You Make Me Feel', 'Remember the Time'
Salt-N-Pepa: 'Push It', 'Whatta Man' ft. En Vogue
En Vogue: 'Free Your Mind'
Whitney Houston: 'I'm Your Baby Tonight', 'I'm Every Woman'
Brandy: 'I Wanna Be Down', 'Full Moon'
Mariah Carey: 'Dreamlover', 'Emotions', 'Honey'
Aaliyah: 'U Got Nerve', 'I Refuse'
Groove Theory: 'Tell Me'
Jill Scott: 'Golden', 'Gettin' in the Way'
India.Arie: 'Video'
Nivea, 'Don't Mess with the Radio', 'Don't Mess with My Man'
Alicia Keys: 'A Woman's Worth', 'In Common'
Toni Braxton: 'You're Makin' Me High'
Destiny's Child: 'So Good', 'Get on the Bus', 'Independent Women Part 1', 'Outro (DC-3) Thank You'
Craig David: 'Rendezvous', '7 Days', 'Rise & Fall' ft. Sting
2Pac: 'Dear Mama', 'Keep Ya Head Up', 'I Ain't Mad at Cha'
The Notorious B.I.G.: 'Hypnotize', 'Juicy'
Dr. Dre: 'Still D.R.E.' ft. Snoop Dogg
Ice Cube: 'You Can Do It'
LL Cool J: 'Around the Way Girl', 'Loungin' ft. Total
DMX: 'Party Up (Up in Here)', [as feature artist] 'Dog & A Fox' (Foxy Brown)
Pharrell: 'Frontin'' ft. Jay-Z, 'Can I Have It Like That' ft. Gwen Stefani
Da Brat: 'Da B Side' ft. The Notorious B.I.G. & JD

Gigorou

UB40: 'Red Red Wine', 'Kingston Town', 'Cherry Oh Baby'

Bob Marley and the Wailers: 'Stir It Up', 'I Shot the Sheriff', 'No Woman, No Cry'

Simply Red: 'If You Don't Know Me by Now'

Minnie Riperton: 'Lovin' You'

Anita Baker: 'Caught Up in the Rapture'

Rockmelons ft. Deni Hines: 'That Word (L.O.V.E.)'

Táta Vega: 'Miss Celie's Blues (Sister)' from *The Color Purple* (song by Quincy Jones)

Barkaa: 'For My Tittas', 'King Brown', 'Blak Matriarchy'

The Last Kinection: 'Are We There Yet?' ft. Simone Stacey, 'Rhythm Is a Dancer'

Shakaya: 'Cinderella', 'Stop Callin' Me'

Christine Anu: 'Party', 'Island Home', 'Coz I'm Free'

Jessica Mauboy: 'Burn', 'Running Back' ft. Flo Rida

Thelma Plum: 'Better in Blak'

Miiesha: 'Drowning', 'Damaged'

Kee'ahn: 'Better Things'

DRMNGNOW: 'Survive' ft. River Boy

Kobie Dee: 'This Life' ft. Bea Moon

Sampa the Great: 'Final Form', 'Black Girl Magik' ft. Nicole Gumbe

Nicki Minaj: 'Barbie Dreams', 'Lookin Ass' [as feature artist]

Maliibu Miitch: 'I Like What I Like', 'The Count'

Kayla Nicole: 'Bundles 2' ft. Flo Milli & Taylor Girlz

Saweetie: 'My Type' ft. City Girls & Jhené Aiko